THE LAST OF THE VALOIS

Vol. II.

The Last of the Valois, *AND ACCESSION OF HENRY OF NAVARRE. BY* CATHERINE CHARLOTTE, LADY JACKSON

IN TWO VOLUMES
VOLUME II.

WILDSIDE PRESS

Large Paper Edition

This edition is limited to one thousand copies, of which this is Number....139...

CONTENTS OF VOL. II.

CHAPTER I.
PAGE

The Results of the Saint-Bartholomew. — Instructions to the Ambassadors. — Abjuration of Henri of Navarre and Prince de Condé. — Catherine Believes that Reform is Trampled out. — Queen Elizabeth's Letter and Catherine's Reply. — "A Consonance" of Views and Feelings. — "The Bayard of the Religion." — The Massacre in Burgundy. — Projected Escape of Alençon, Navarre, and Condé. — The Siege of Sancerre 1

CHAPTER II.

Arrival of the Polish Embassy. — Taking the Oath. — Charles Insists on Anjou's Departure. — Activity of the Huguenots of the South. — Catherine Amazed at Their Demands. — The Duc d'Alençon's Projects. — Catherine's Guard of Halberdiers. — A Second Saint-Bartholomew Meditated. — Attempted Escape of the Princes . 21

CHAPTER III.

Catherine's "Piteous Sorrow." — Montgomery Tortured and Beheaded. — Catherine's Expectations Now Anjou Reigns. — Henri's Flight from Poland. — His Twenty Leagues' Ride. — The Elector's Portrait Gallery. — Acknowledging Savoy's Hospitality. — Montluc Counsels Peace. — Catherine's Illusions Dispelled. — Extravagant Devotional Practices 39

CHAPTER IV.

The Journey from Avignon to Rheims. — The King Casts Off His Mourning. — Arranging the Crown Jewels. — The Bride. — The King's Personal Appearance. — The

vi   CONTENTS

                                                              PAGE
Entry in State into Paris.— Expedients for Raising
Money. — Montbrun a Prisoner.— Condemned to Death.
— Bœsme, the Admiral's Murderer, Hanged in Reprisal.
— Poland Elects Another King.— La Belle Madame de
Suave.— The Seven Months' Truce   57

CHAPTER V.

Escape of Henri of Navarre.— "God be Praised for My
Deliverance!"— Henri Hesitates to Abjure Catholicism.
— Catherine Negotiates while the King is Praying.—
La Paix de Monsieur.— Duc de Guise and the Holy
League.— The Oath under Pain of Eternal Damnation.
— The States General Cannot Agree on the Question
of Unity of Faith, but Agree on Voting the King no
Money.— The Crown Jewels Pledged Again   .   .   . 74

CHAPTER VI.

Chenonceaux, its Parks and Gardens.— A Preoccupied Mind
and Empty Purse. — A Mythological Fête. — Banquet at
Plessis-lez-Tours to the Hero. — The Queen-Mother's
Banquet and Fête.— A Wife's Revenge. — Depravity of
the Court of Henri III.— Cruelties of the Sack of Issoire.
— Peace Signed at Bergerac, in Spite of the Pope.—
A Bold Stroke of Policy 91

CHAPTER VII.

Catherine of Navarre. — Offers of Marriage. — The King's
Piety Lauded by Priests and Monks.— Quarrels and Duels
Amongst the King's Favourites.— Order of the Saint-
Esprit Instituted. — Great Expectations Disappointed. —
Plot of Gregory XIII. and Don John of Austria.— High
Words between the King and His Brother.— The Duke's
Escape ; His Mother Pursues.— Anjou's Visit to Queen
Elizabeth 103

CHAPTER VIII.

Marguerite Conducted to Her Husband.— Henri of Navarre
Declines to Receive Her.— The Venetian Ambassador,
Geronimo Lippomano. — Concessions to the Huguenots;

Marguerite the Pledge of Their Fulfilment. — A Dazzling Display of Crimson, Orange, Purple, and Gold. — A Discourteous and Woman-hating Monarch. — The Lovers' War, and the Conquest of Cahors. — Compelled by the Laws of War. — Maréchal de Biron's Excuses. — The Éclat of Nérac Departed. — Marguerite Depressed in Spirit. — Philip, for the Fourth Time a Widower, Seeks a Fifth Wife 124

CHAPTER IX.

Anjou Elected Ruler of the United Provinces.— The Queen-mother Desires to Fulfil Ruggieri's Prediction. — Embassy to England to Arrange Anjou's Marriage.— Unjust, but Necessary.— Anjou Again at Elizabeth's Feet.— Catherine Claims the Crown of Portugal. — Henri's Arbitrary Proceedings. — Marriages of King's Mignons.— Demands of the Swiss Ambassadors. — The Gregorian Calendar 143

CHAPTER X.

The Duke Thoroughly Defeated.— "Compensatory Works" Excusing All Sins.— The "White Flagellants" of Avignon in Paris.— The King and Queen Set Out on Foot, on a Pilgrimage.— Philip II. Makes Advances to Henri of Navarre. — Marriage Proposed between Catherine of Navarre and James VI. of Scotland.— Marguerite Banished from France.— Marguerite Makes War on Henri. — Death of Duc d'Anjou et de Brabant. — Funeral Processions. — Absence of the Queen-mother . . . 159

CHAPTER XI.

Henri of Navarre Declared Heir to the Throne of France. — Prince of Orange Assassinated. — Spanish and Popish Plots against the Life of Elizabeth. — Henri III. Said to Be Becoming Insane. — The King and the Cardinal De Bourbon. — Gregory XIII. Sends Blessings and Plenary Indulgences to the Leaguers.— Elizabeth Sends the Order of the Garter to Henri III.— The "Demon of the South" Enraged. — The Queen-mother Seeks the Repeal of the Salic Law.— Pacificatory Edicts Revoked.— Treaty with the League 179

CHAPTER XII.

Consternation of the Huguenots. — Priests Sent to Convert Henri of Navarre. — The Thunders of the Vatican. — Sixtus V. Opposed to the League. — A Reply to the Bull of Excommunication. — The Guises Use the Bull to Intimidate the King. — A Mania for "Bilboquet." — "Too Merciful to These Scoundrels." — A Vanished Army. — Elizabeth Joins in the Struggle for Religious Freedom . 200

CHAPTER XIII.

Plots against the Life of Queen Elizabeth. — The Spanish Invasion Deferred. — Henri III. Asks the Consent of Guise to Make Peace with the Huguenots. — Henri Compounds with His Defaulting Treasurers. — The Marriage of the Duc d'Épernon. — Balls and Banquets. — Joyeuse Inclines to the Leaguers. — Revolting Barbarity. — The Catholic Bourbons Join Their Protestant Relatives. — Battle of Coutras. — Great Victory of the Huguenots. — Joyeuse and His Brother Slain. — Gallantry and Romance 216

CHAPTER XIV.

Charles de Bourbon, Comte de Soissons. — Promise of Marriage Exchanged between the Count and Catherine of Navarre. — Count Suspected of Being a Magician. — The King of Navarre's Allies Waylaid and Murdered. — A Governor's "Word of Honour." — Henri III. Capitulates with the German Troops. — A Thanksgiving for Victory. — A Saint of Saints. — Great Events Predicted for 1588. — The Armada. — Death of Prince Henri de Condé 238

CHAPTER XV.

Great Events Predicted by the Astrologers in 1588. — Guise Forbidden to Enter Paris. — The Queen of the League. — The Duke's Entry. — He Visits the Queen-mother. — Rage of Henri III. — King Sends for an Italian to Assassinate Guise. — Guise Feels that He Has Barely Escaped Assassination. — Prepared for Action, but no Orders Given. — Fighting in Paris. — The Day of Barricades. — Terms of Reconciliation. — Threat of Invading

the Louvre and the Tuileries. — Flight of the King from
Paris 252

CHAPTER XVI.

The King and His Ministers Arrive at Chartres. — The
Massacre Countermanded. — Brother Ange and a Scene
of the Passion Play.— Guise Appointed Commandant-
General of the Armies.— The Invincible Armada. — Its
Destruction. — Soissons's Letters of Abolition. — More
Catholic than the Pope. — The Assembling of the States
General at Blois. — The Grande Salle of the Château de
Blois. — The King's Address to the Three Estates. — His
Proposals Rejected or Overruled 273

CHAPTER XVII.

The King's Patience Exhausted. — Arrest and Trial, or a
Coup-de-Main?— Crillon's Reply to the King's Request
that He Would Assassinate the Duc de Guise. — Guise
Warned of the Plot against His Life. — He Refuses to
Give any Heed to It. — Council Assembles at Break of
Day. — A Desperate Struggle with the Forty-five. — The
King and His Dead Enemy. — Death of the Cardinal and
Queen-mother 288

CHAPTER XVIII.

Startling News for the Parisians and People of Orléans. —
Guise's Great Reputation Chiefly Due to the King's
Extreme Weakness of Character. — The Mass of Midnight, of Dawn, of Day. — The Children's Procession. —
"May God Extinguish the Race of Valois!"— Christening of the Duke's Infant Son, François-Pâris.— Henri III.
Seeks the Aid of the Heretic King of Navarre. — Proposing to Assault Paris. — Jacques Clément Sent to the
Royal Camp to Assassinate the King. — Death of the
Last of the Race of Valois 303

CHAPTER XIX.

News of the Death of Henri of Valois Received with Shouts
of Joy. — The Saviour of Paris; the Liberator of the
Church. — The Assassin's Deed Eulogised by the Pope

CONTENTS

in Full Consistory. — Henri IV. Required to Abjure. — He Demands Time for Reflection and Instruction.— The Battle of Arques. — Surprising the Faubourgs. — Sainte-Geneviève Implored to Save Her Good City. — Compliments from the Sultan. — Soissons's Escape from Nantes in a Basket. — Battle of Ivry. — La Belle Antoinette Supplanted 317

CHAPTER XX.

The Blockade of Paris. — Death of the Cardinal-King of the League. — Famine; Suffering and Revolting Horrors of the Siege. — An Appeal to Notre-Dame de Lorette. — Famine-worn Fugitives from Paris. — The Starving People Await Death in the Churches. — Great Joy. — The Besieging Army Decamps. — Death of Sixtus V. — Aid for the Huguenot King from Elizabeth and Protestant Princes. — Death of La Noue and Châtillon . . 335

CHAPTER XXI.

Henri's Latest Conquest. — Soissons Visits Pau in Disguise. Soissons a Prisoner. — Catherine Ordered to Repair to Henri's Court at Saumur. — A New Suitor. — Plessis-Mornay's Sympathy with Catherine. — The Siege of Rouen. — Maréchal de Biron and His Son. — Exploits of the Great Huguenot Hero Lesdiguières. — The States General.—Mayenne's Mishap. — Philip Urges His Daughter's Claims. — Henri Meditates Abjuration.— Gabrielle's Influence. — The Promise of Marriage. — Henri Abjures. 352

CHAPTER XXII.

Henri's Conversion Rejoices the People.— The Truce for Three Months. — Refusal to Prolong It.— Coronation of Henri IV. at Chartres.— The New Crown.— The Sainte-Ampoule and the Holy Oil of Saint-Martin. — Mayenne Appoints a New Governor of Paris.—He Opens the Gates to the King.— The Entry into Paris.—The Foreign Garrison Marches Out.—The King Sends "Le Bon Jour" to Madame de Montpensier. — The King Much Elated; Dines at the Louvre.— Rendering to Cæsar the Things that are Cæsar's 369

CONCLUSION 382

LIST OF ILLUSTRATIONS

VOL. II.

	PAGE
ELIZABETH, QUEEN OF ENGLAND	*Frontispiece*
GABRIEL DE LORGES, COMTE DE MONTGOMERY	42
LOUISE DE LORRAINE	62
FRANÇOIS, DUC D'ANJOU	176
DUCHESSE DE MONTPENSIER	254
PHILIP II. OF SPAIN	278
HENRI III.	316
DUC DE MAYENNE	360

THE
LAST OF THE VALOIS

CHAPTER I.

The Results of the Saint-Bartholomew. — Instructions to the Ambassadors. — Abjuration of Henri of Navarre and Prince de Condé. — Catherine Believes that Reform is Trampled out. — Queen Elizabeth's Letter and Catherine's Reply. — "A Consonance" of Views and Feelings. — "The Bayard of the Religion." — The Massacre in Burgundy. — Projected Escape of Alençon, Navarre, and Condé. — The Siege of Sancerre.

THE results of the Saint-Bartholomew massacre proved widely different from what Catherine de' Medici had expected or intended. Yet for a moment she believed she was fully successful, and that thenceforth affairs of state would glide on smoothy under her guidance in any direction she in her wisdom might choose to give them. For she was accounted wise. The Venetian ambassador, Geronimo Lippomano, who was a favourite at court — Catherine's *ambassadeur chéri* — pronounced her the "wisest of women." In the present crisis she might have been truly called the most audacious. She piqued herself on having accomplished her long-meditated project without becoming dependent on either Rome or Spain, or entering into any engagement with them.

Queen Elizabeth, after considerable hesitation, had signed at Greenwich, on the 22nd of August, the proposed treaty with France, offensive and defensive. The bearer of it did not reach Paris until some days after the 24th, yet in sufficient time to witness the still terrible state of things prevailing in the capital, and to hear the blood-freezing statements of the greater horrors which had preceded it. Assassination and robbery were also far from being stayed in those provinces where the governors had not refused (which to their honour several had done) to obey the murderous orders despatched to them by the queen-mother, in the name and under the signature of the king.

Yet Catherine had resolved to make a desperate effort still to preserve the Protestant alliance. The admiral and five or six of the principal men of the Huguenot party, who, the queen-mother admitted, were thoroughly abhorrent to her, were effectually removed out of her way; the court had also had the indecency, and want of self-respect, to visit Montfaucon, as on a party of pleasure, to insult the mutilated remains of the murdered admiral hanging on a gibbet, and to pass their coarse jokes and jibes upon his headless body. Yet Catherine made light of trifles such as these. She thought it sufficient to inform the German princes and the Queen of England that the king had taken no part in the late events, beyond endeavouring to "suppress a conspiracy, of which Coligny was the head, against his person and the state." It was on the Guises — whom she represented as "having in their thirst for vengeance murdered the admiral when the king desired only his arrest" — that she threw the whole blame; and not of that crime alone, but of all the infamous deeds that followed. "The populace, after the first shedding of blood, proceeded," she said, "from one excess to another in their zeal to exterminate those factious disturbers of the peace of the realm — rage against them being augmented by the fact that they were heretics."

This explanation, the falsehood of which was known to those to whom it was addressed, was considered by Catherine a sufficiently satisfactory excuse to offer the Protestant states of Europe for the cold-blooded slaughter of many thousands of their coreligionists. The ambassadors accredited to those states also received strict instructions to insist on the admiral's pretended conspiracy, and the necessity the king was under to defend his throne and his life.

There was yet the further apparent corroborative circumstance of the absence of religious motive in the cold reception the legate Orsini met with at court, and the difficulty he found in obtaining an audience of the king and queen-mother, whom he came to compliment; expecting to be received by them with open arms. Of part of the "glorious work" he had been a gratified eye-witness; for on his way to Paris he had stopped at Lyons, whose streets were then running with blood, and its rivers filled with gory corpses. Great praises he had bestowed on the murderous zeal of the *bourgeoisie*, and in the name of the Pope had granted them full absolution, and blessed them with his most solemn benediction.

But the queen-mother and her two sons, instead of wearing with pride the gory laurels the legate would have placed upon their brows, shrank, modestly shrank, from giving that *éclat* and finality to their "great victory" which the legate anxiously pressed upon them — the establishment in France of the Inquisition. But Catherine knew that all France would rise in rebellion against any attempt to introduce this infamous tribunal into the kingdom. Terror of the Inquisition has been said to have made more Protestants than all the writings of Calvin.

Orsini, however, soon discovered that Catherine's desire to keep the "glorious deeds of the *grande journée*" in the background arose from her intention still to maintain, if possible, a friendly alliance with the Protestant states. Philip's emissaries, too, failed not to inform him that the "Florentine *intrigante*" was secretly striving to renew the negotiation with the Nassau princes, who yet, in Holland and Zealand, held out against the Spaniards.

The Duc de Guise, in his anger that the responsibility and odium of the sanguinary deed was wholly rejected by the king and queen-mother and laid entirely on him and his family, took his revenge by saving several Protestant gentlemen, whose place of concealment had come to his knowledge, and whom he would otherwise probably have betrayed or slain. He now aided them to escape. Amongst them were two famous Huguenot captains, Crussol d'Acier and Pomponne de Bellièvre, whose escape distressed Catherine greatly, as she imagined that the discouragement the general body of the Huguenots would experience in the loss of their chief men would lead to the gradual dying out of the "new heretical opinions."

The king was also sorely displeased that any men of note should have escaped the meshes of the *filet de mort*. But Charles's murderous fever is said to have soon passed off, and a troubled mind to have succeeded it (D'Aubigné). Yet his violent declaration that "he would tolerate in his kingdom no religion but his own," and the rage he evinced at the opposition he met with from Henri of Navarre and Condé on that subject, scarcely indicated any remorseful feeling for the deed of blood he had participated in and encouraged. So far from it that the prince's resistance to his command to abjure put him into so furious a passion that he vowed he would on the instant take his life. It chanced that he was then without his sword, and, on rushing like a madman from the room to seek one, he encountered the young queen, who "had wept and prayed incessantly during the terrible days of the massacre." On learning Charles's purpose, she strove, vainly for a time, to soothe him. At last, throwing herself on her knees, she implored him not to commit the frightful crime of murdering his cousin, and to her tears and entreaties he, after awhile, yielded.

La mort ou la Messe! the alternative which Charles offered to all those Huguenots who had escaped the general mowing down, if they yet cared to live, was resisted for several weeks by the young Bourbon princes. Their abjuration, however, at last took place. Henri of Navarre needed but little pressure to yield to the exhortations of a Jesuit priest, Maldonato; but Henri of Condé was of firmer principles, and clung with more tenacity to the religion he had been brought up in. But both probably accepted Romanism with the intention of renouncing it as soon as opportunity offered of being useful to "the cause."

Henri of Navarre also abjured for his sister — the poor little orphan Princesse Catherine — still weak and ailing from the copious bleedings inflicted on her, in accordance with the practice of the medical men of that day. She appears to have been lodged in some remote apartment of the Louvre, attended by two or three of her own people; but otherwise, except by her brother, almost forgotten, while the massacre of her own and her mother's friends was taking place around her. Her mother's death had afflicted her greatly. Grief and delicate health, and the little consideration shown her, fortunately saved her from the contaminating influence of the court.

There — notwithstanding the assassinations and robberies still going on in Paris, and which it was found impossible to put a stop to — a large part of each day and night was spent in riotous revelry, feasting, and depravity. This degrading pastime was diligently promoted by the queen-mother in her desire to have the Saint-Bartholomew of Paris and its saddening memories effaced. By such means, also, she thought to divert attention from the atrocities which, in spite of the king's edicts and the queen-mother's letters to governors and military chiefs, continued to desolate many parts of France until near the end of October.

The abjuration of the Bourbon princes was followed by that of many of their partisans. But these were of the timid sort only. The infamous plotters of the 24th had taken their victims so entirely by surprise that very many of the Huguenots, paralysed, as it were, by the sudden shock of the terrible fate that had overtaken them, fell almost unresistingly under the poniards and arquebuses of their murderers, while others saved their lives by promising abjuration. But all who effected their escape from Paris or other towns fled to the cities which the admiral, in his fatal infatuation respecting Charles's sincerity, had given up to the king.

Retaking possession, they closed the gates against the royalists, while silently they reorganised and armed their forces, in preparation for resistance. Calvin's doctrine of passive submission to the powers that be, they had hitherto, in a measure, accepted — "making war under the banner of a prince who led them against a prince who was both his and their persecutor." Their principal men were either dead or in exile; but now the people themselves assembled to consider whether it were not lawful to make war, even against the king, should he abuse his power and become his people's tyrant. They decided emphatically in the affirmative, and, raising up the fallen banner, determined that Reform should be saved.

This was startling news for the queen-mother. She knew that the work of extermination had not been so complete as she had desired. But she fully believed that what had been done, together with the loss of the chiefs of the party, and especially the death of Coligny, had thoroughly disorganised and disheartened the remnant that remained of the Huguenots. Reform could never again, she fancied, rise from the dust into which it had been trampled, to give her further trouble, but with the Reformers themselves would become extinct.

She was also further annoyed at this time at finding that the Protestant princes of Germany were not the dupes of her assurances that Coligny and his staff had conspired to take the king's life, and that the massacre was necessary to frustrate the plan of the conspirators. Everywhere the ambassadors instructed to enforce this version of the events of the Saint-Bartholomew were but coldly listened to. Queen Elizabeth spoke very severely on the subject when she received La Mothe-Fénelon. Yet Catherine thought this a suitable moment for again urging for a favourable reply to the Duc d'Alençon's proposal of marriage.

Elizabeth, however, wrote to Charles IX., on September 23rd, that "she was pleased that what he had done was to punish those who had attempted such serious things against his person, and that it was not on religious grounds. But that she must still regret that his majesty's edicts (of tolerance and pacification) were not put into execution; for in various places many persons were proceeded against without form of judgment or trial, on which account several people from France had had recourse to her; that she had written to her ambassador that if such things still went on, he was to find some pretext for returning to England in order to avoid any affront."*

The queen-mother replied that "they were compelled to order further executions to ensure the firm settlement of their affairs." She also informed her that "princes were not under any obligation of keeping their promises to their subjects; but as regarded the queen personally, she would always be respected and honoured by every one."

The rebellion was rapidly gaining ground. In the few towns in which the Protestants were in a decided majority, as at Sancerre, Nîmes, Montauban, and La Rochelle, the more wealthy citizens, fearing the loss of their property, left the place of their own accord. Nîmes then closed its gates against General Joyeuse. Béarn refused to obey the king's order to reëstablish the Catholic religion and forbid the Protestant form of worship. "Their king" (Henri of Navarre), they said, "being a captive, such an order was evidently extorted from him; they therefore cast it to the winds." But the principal stronghold of Protestantism was La

---

* This letter is taken from the "Report of the Proceedings of the Huguenot Society" (January number, 1887), and is there stated to be published for the first time.

Rochelle, an important city in all respects, and difficult to besiege. The queen-mother hesitated again to take up arms. It was unfavourable to her projects; so that doubts and difficulties as to the course she should pursue perplexed her now no less than before the *"grande journée."*

Catherine's agents in Poland were urging on her and the king the necessity, for the success of their mission, of dealing very leniently with the Huguenots. The Poles, both Catholics and Protestants, at this time — and until the Jesuits obtruded themselves into Poland — were exceedingly tolerant of religious differences, and before proceeding to the election of a king engaged themselves reciprocally never to permit the employment of any violent measures in matters of religion. The efforts of the unscrupulous Bishop of Valence and his colleague, Schomberg, were likely, it appeared, to be successful.

They had flattered the Polish nobility; talked of the " great consonance they had remarked in the gentleness of manners, *humanity of disposition*, high-spiritedness and noble feeling of the Poles, and the traits of character that so eminently distinguished the French noblesse." The "accident" of the Saint-Bartholomew the bishop had accounted for by laying it and its consequences wholly on the shoulders of the Guises, adding that their future king, as he hoped, "was in no manner whatever concerned in it."

Under these circumstances Catherine determined on endeavouring to gain over the Rochellois by promises of liberty of worship and other concessions. But they put no faith in her promises, gave no heed to her proposals, and declared that under no conditions would they open their gates to a royalist army. Charles IX. was then visibly declining in health; his strangely laborious amusements — in which he is said to have sought forgetfulness of his crime — greatly contributing towards hastening his end. He was, however, no less anxious than his mother that his hated brother should not lose his chance of wearing the crown of Poland. It therefore occurred to him to send the Huguenot captain, La Noue, to La Rochelle, charged by the king to persuade the Protestants to lay down their arms and admit within their walls the Grand-Master of Artillery, Maréchal Biron (who was of the "Politique" party), appointed by him governor of the city.

La Noue had for a considerable time held Mons against the Duke of Alva. Famine and sickness had recently compelled him to capitulate, and Alva, contrary to his usual custom, had observed the terms of capitulation. The garrison passed out with the honours of war. Charles immediately sent to the frontier for La Noue, who supposed that he was anxious to put to death those whom Alva had spared. But Charles received him graciously, desiring to make use of him to negotiate between the court and the rebellious Huguenots. The king, of course, promised to reward their obedience by new edicts in their favour, the revival of those lately suppressed, and an amnesty for what had occurred since the 24th of August.

Great was the surprise of the Huguenots to find an agent of Charles IX.—the man who had murdered the admiral, and slain their leaders, their relatives and friends—in the "hero, the Bayard of the Religion." Very sternly they receive him, for "they know him not," they say. "He points to his false arm to remind them that he had lost his own in their service. He strives to convince them of the purity of his intentions, and assures them that he has plainly told the king that, although he would give them pacific counsels, he would not lend himself to promote any act that might prove prejudicial to their interests or their liberties." They then offer him the choice of three courses —"to remain amongst them as a private individual; to take the general command of the nobility and the people; or to pass over to England." He decided to accept the command (D'Aubigné).

While these negotiations were still pending at La Rochelle, other towns repulsed with success the efforts made to subdue them. The small town of Sancerre sustained a siege victoriously—the besiegers being repulsed, when ammunition fell short, by the rapidity and skill with which the peasantry of the district made use of their slings, which henceforth bore the name of the arquebuses of Sancerre.

As the Rochellois would listen to no terms, and rejected the moderate counsels of La Noue — deeming it "impious to enter into any compact with murderers" — Charles, or rather the queen-mother and Anjou, "resolved on making a great effort for the destruction of the last haunt of heresy." For though the Huguenots, and many Catholics who had joined their ranks and accepted their doctrines — from horror of the perfidy of the queen-mother and her sons, and the consequent saturation of the soil of France with blood — were arming in all directions, yet it was at La Rochelle that the final blow, as Catherine knew, must, and would, be struck.

But winter had come upon Catherine and her sons, and "though ready for assassination, they were not prepared for war." Appeals in the king's name were therefore made to the clergy, and to the "good towns" for gifts of money to enable him to sustain this "holy contest." Large sums are said to have been quickly subscribed for this purpose, and forthwith an army was on its way to La Rochelle. The chief command, of course, devolved — to Charles's great irritation — on the lieutenant-general of the kingdom — the Duc d'Anjou. Under him were the Guises, Nevers, De Retz, and others, with Angoulême — who, according to De Thou, nearly succeeded in arranging a second Saint-Bartholomew, for the purpose of pillaging some rich Huguenot jewellers.

The Duc d'Alençon accompanied the commander-in-chief, and nearly the whole of the court, not excepting the King of Navarre and Prince de Condé, who were required to march with the Catholics against the Huguenots as a proof of the sincerity of their conversion. The Montmorencys remained in their provinces, having espoused the Huguenot cause. But even Catherine had her tent, and as many of "the squadron" as could be accommodated enjoyed the excitement of witnessing a siege.

But, alas for the military reputation of the lieutenant-general of the armies of France! no Maréchal Tavannes was there. That able but ferocious general had lately paid the debt of nature. After successfully commanding armies, he had ended his career as an assassin. In no province had more Huguenot blood been shed, after the ever memorable 24th, than in Burgundy, of which Tavannes was the governor and a native. His fanaticism exceeded that of the people, whom he goaded on to frenzy, crying, "Bleed them! bleed them!" "Kill! kill!" until, drunk with blood, they tortured and slaughtered unsparingly.

Other generals there were who had acted with similar ferocity; but in several instances these were afterwards deeply stung by remorse, and died in raving madness, imploring God for pardon they dared not hope to obtain. Not so Tavannes. His career had been speedily cut short, but he was impenitent to the end, and rather gloried in his crime.

The siege of La Rochelle was opened in February; the blockade began a month or two earlier. From the first, the incapacity of the lieutenant-general was evident to all. He thought to make of this siege a party of pleasure, as at Jarnac and Moncontour, where experienced generals gained the victory, while to him was attributed the credit of it. Arrived before La Rochelle, "instead of seeking for the best point of beginning the attack, his first care was to find the most comfortable quarters, and having conveniently established himself at the distance of a league from the trenches, his officers followed his example."

The besieged Huguenots, on the other hand, took every advantage of this distribution of the besieging army, and "defended themselves with ability." Owing to the salt marshes, the ramparts of La Rochelle were accessible only on one side of the town. Four assaults were made on it, which were repulsed with great vigour, and considerable loss to the enemy — each time the Huguenots appearing on the towers singing triumphantly the 68th Psalm as a song of victory. The Duc d'Aumale and many others concerned in the murder of Coligny and in the general massacre were killed or severely wounded in these repulses. The women taking part in the defence crowded the walls and threw showers of stones on the assailants.

It was hoped to reduce these triumphant rebels by famine; but "heaven," as they said, "sent them manna," in the abundance of the shell-fish that year, which the besiegers could not prevent the sea from bringing in to them, though they had closed the port by two forts and a stockade. Proposals of peace were again rejected, the Rochellois refusing to treat without the other Huguenot cities and churches. This the queen-mother would not agree to, and as all hopes of peace were at an end, La Noue was called on to keep his promise and leave the city. La Noue obeyed, and returned to the royal camp — greatly grieved that death had not released him from the painful position he was placed in, between his promise to the king and his duty towards the Rochellois as a Huguenot captain.

Aid had been confidently expected by the Reformers from Queen Elizabeth, but she was then embarrassed by her treaty with France, by the negotiations then under consideration with Spain, and a rising in Scotland of Mary Stuart's partisans. A little ammunition brought by a small flotilla under Montgomery, and very lax measures against the privateers which fitted and revictualled in the English ports, was all she could then do for them.

La Noue, while in Rochelle — knowing how greatly the besiegers outnumbered the besieged — believed that the Huguenots must eventually surrender. But when he witnessed the anarchy and confusion prevailing in the royal camp, the incapacity of both the commander-in-chief and his favourites and youthful lieutenants, the hatred and strife reigning amongst them, and the dissatisfaction of the soldiers, he felt reassured as to the fate of the Reformers.

The Duc d'Alençon openly lamented the death of the admiral, and spoke with abhorrence of the sanguinary deeds that followed it. He and the two Bourbon princes had determined to seize a boat and escape to Montgomery's flotilla, for the purpose of passing over to England and seeking the protection of the queen. La Noue prevented them. It would be of no advantage, he told them, either to themselves or "the cause," but would place Elizabeth in a very embarrassing position.

On the 1st of May the Rochellois planted on the ramparts a May-tree in full bloom — the towers and battlements resounding during the ceremony with the favourite 68th Psalm, "Let God arise," etc., sung with passionate enthusiasm. Four months had passed in useless efforts to subdue these rebels, and the court began to be discouraged. The more so as the army, from its heavy losses, desertion, and disease — apparently cholera morbus — was threatened with annihilation.

Catherine, therefore, resolved on making an effort to come to terms with the Huguenots; proceedings being hastened by the announcement on the 9th that, a few days previously, thirty-five thousand Polish gentlemen, mounted and armed, had assembled on the plain of Warsaw, and proclaimed the Duc d'Anjou King of Poland.

After several conferences with the mayor, Jacques Henri, and other of the principal burgesses — who now, instead of princes and nobles, as formerly, discussed with the ministers of Charles IX. the terms on which they would treat — peace was signed at La Rochelle on the 24th of June. It included the towns of Montauban and Nîmes, full liberty of worship being accorded them, with other favourable concessions. But the treaty appears to have been accepted only to serve some mere temporary purpose.

The isolated town of Sancerre, in Berry, was not for some weeks after included in the treaty. Three-fourths of the inhabitants had then died of starvation or disease, and the survivors were in a state of extreme prostration. The siege of Sancerre is considered "the most tragic episode of the religious wars of France, and has been compared to the siege of Jerusalem in all its horrors. The conviction of its inhabitants that no promises made to them would be kept, but that they would be treated as were the victims of the Saint-Bartholomew, sustained them, as with superhuman force, in their prolonged and heroic resistance."

But the announcement that a grand Polish embassy was on its way to compliment the new king induced Catherine to send immediate orders to the Governor of Berry to capitulate with Sancerre on any terms. On the 14th of August the gates of Sancerre were once more opened. The town was dismantled, but the terms of the capitulation were kept with the people and the refugees. Their courageous ex-governor and their Protestant minister were, however, shortly after waylaid and assassinated by orders emanating from high quarters.

CHAPTER II.

Arrival of the Polish Embassy. — Taking the Oath. — Charles Insists on Anjou's Departure. — Activity of the Huguenots of the South. — Catherine Amazed at their Demands. — The Duc d'Alençon's Projects. — Catherine's Guard of Halberdiers. — A Second Saint-Bartholomew Meditated.—Attempted Escape of the Princes.

THE grand Polish embassy arrived in Paris at a very opportune moment, both for the court and the Parisians generally. It was a welcome distraction after scenes of strife and bloodshed — an amusement with more of novelty and interest in it to attract attention than the usual processions and pageants to which both court and people were accustomed. Catherine's agents had served her well, and vied with each other in supporting the candidature of their prince. They had consented to everything proposed, suggested, or required by the Polish nobility; had denied everything tending to cast the slightest moral blame on their pure-souled hero, or shadow of a slur on his high military reputation. Unhesitatingly they had approved the terms of the oath which it was proposed the new king should take, to maintain the rights and afford equal protection to his Catholic and Protestant subjects.

In the name of the Most Christian King, Montluc had also boldly promised the reëstablishment in their possessions, rank, and honours of all who had been condemned for taking part in the pretended Coligny conspiracy. Also freedom of religious worship, and diligent efforts to discover and punish the massacrers in the late plot. All this, and much more, Catherine's agents had guaranteed to see carried out, leaving to her and her son the disavowal, approval, or modification of as much of it as they pleased. Their business, as the bishop — who preceded the embassy by a few days — told the queen-mother, was to secure a majority of votes, and that they had succeeded in.

Yet the electors were not at first unanimous in voting for a French prince to reign over them. Many preferred the Archduke Ernest, son of the Emperor Maximilian II.* But "when it appeared that the greater number of the Polish nobles would declare for Anjou, the minority gave in their

---

* Catherine had an idea that by "judicious intrigue" the German princes might be brought to place the imperial crown on the head of Charles IX., on the demise of Maximilian; and that his majesty of Poland, aided by his new subjects, might also become the ruler of the Netherlands. Some arrangements were likewise suggested by the queen-mother to her agents for inducing the most influential of the Protestant princes to support the young Duc d'Alençon's pretensions to the hand of Elizabeth of England.

adhesion to the choice of the majority, in order to avert the calamity of an intestine struggle in Poland."

On the 10th of September the embassy made its appearance, and was received by the king, the two queens, the newly elected monarch, and the court, with great pomp and magnificence. The embassy itself formed a grand equestrian spectacle, which excited general admiration. All who composed it were splendidly mounted; the horses richly caparisoned, and having spread-out eagles' wings attached to their head-gear. The semi-Oriental and picturesque costume of the cavaliers, their rich furs, jewelled caps, and waving plumes, were much admired by the people; while their bows, and quivers full of arrows, and the Tartar fashion of showing bare the back part of the head, imparted a singularity to the appearance of these superb cavaliers that greatly increased the interest of the pageant.

It was pleasant, doubtless, to these Polish nobles to be greeted with such intense enthusiasm by the assembled crowds that lined the streets from the Louvre to Notre Dame, where the young duke was to take the oath of King of Poland, and Charles IX. to ratify, also by oath, the conditions agreed to by his envoys with reference to the Polish and French political alliance. Charles, however, omitted the important declaration respecting the Protestants, which Montluc, in his name, had promised. The Polish nuncio did not very earnestly support his "evangelical colleague" on this point, or press the omission on his majesty's notice. But Catherine had been so eager to confirm the assurances already given, that "the Duc d'Anjou was wholly guiltless of any participation in the late 'unfortunate accident,' and the king so highly incensed at the crime committed by the Guises," that the Protestant Polish nobility seem carelessly to have taken it as a matter of course that these greatly maligned royal brothers were neither persecutors nor murderers.

Balls and *fêtes* followed the taking of the oath. But the superiority of the Polish nobles in learning and general attainments, to the vain, boisterous, ignorant, and frivolous young nobility of France, led them to prefer the *réunions* of the *savants* and philosophers to the lascivious entertainments provided by the queen-mother and her court.

Charles IX. had been much gratified on learning the success of his mother's agents in Poland. The Duc d'Anjou, on the contrary, scarcely refrained from reproaching them for their zeal. He regarded his elevation as banishment from all that, to him, made life worth living — voluptuousness and crime. How often the Venetian ambassadors, commenting on the habits and traits of character they remark in Frenchmen of that period, say, "They cannot live out of France." Not that this is attributed to any special love of country, but to a feverish craving for that continual and peculiar kind of excitement which from following the corrupt example of that vortex of depravity, religious fanaticism, and bloodshed — the court of the degenerate Valois — had spread to every class of the community and had become almost a necessity of existence. It was natural, then, that one brought up in the midst of its excesses and steeped in grossest profligacy should shrink from the companionship of men of soberer views and sterner aims in life.

But Charles is impatient. "Is he never to have peace!" as he has exclaimed many times since they brought him word that an assassin had attempted to take the admiral's life. "Will this hated brother never leave him?" Doubtless, he felt that life, if slowly, was yet surely ebbing away. His laborious amusements and occupations — such as blowing a hunting-horn till his eyes almost started from their sockets, forging arms, etc. — were now only occasionally, and for a shorter time, resorted to. Poetry, drawing, and music had taken their place, and apparently he had resigned himself to bear the yoke he had so often longed to shake off — that of the queen-mother — but Anjou's he will not bear. He commands, therefore — and unfortunately is not sparing of profane oaths — that the King of Poland depart forthwith.

His Polish majesty was desirous of passing yet

another winter in the enjoyment of the pleasures of the French Court. He also fancied himself madly in love with the wife of the young Prince de Condé. But Charles was moved neither by his wishes nor his imaginary passionate love for his cousin's wife; nor did the queen-mother now venture to oppose the king, whose rage was extreme, and who even hinted that he would like to send her away also with her well-beloved son (D'Aubigné).

On the 28th of September the King of Poland — unwilling victim of circumstances — set out in sadness for his northern kingdom. Before leaving Paris he pricked his finger, and squeezing out a drop of blood, wrote a line of distracted adieu to the princess. He was accompanied to the frontier of Germany by the two queens and the court. Charles also, anxious to see him well out of France, went part of the way, but was seized on the road by an attack of smallpox. But Catherine did not leave Anjou until their arrival at Lorraine. There she took a tearful farewell of him and the favourite companions he had selected to relieve him from the *ennui* he looked for in the dull Court of Warsaw.

The queen-mother, however, comforted her desponding son, and soothed the anguish of separation by the assurance that his exile would be but of short duration. The infamous Catherine foresaw that the dangerous malady which had attacked the king on his journey was likely to lead to Anjou's accession to the throne sooner even than she had hoped for.

One cannot withhold pity from Charles IX., execrable as were the crimes he was led to perpetrate and to sanction. Already at the age of twenty-three, he was both physically and mentally but a mere wreck of the highly gifted youth to whom France had looked hopefully forward as destined to be one of her greatest kings. But very early the blighting yoke of the Italian *intrigante* was laid on this most promising of her sons. Separating him from all who would have influenced him for good, she surrounded him with plotting and unscrupulous Italians; and determining, in her vain ambition, that France should be governed by her and according to her own methods, she took advantage of Charles's want of will and his highly strung sensitive nature, to make him the instrument for accomplishing her own evil designs and machiavelian purposes.

The Huguenots had been very active while the court was occupied with the Polish election, the arrival of the embassy, and the departure of the newly elected king. There was joy in all classes that France was now fairly free, at least from Anjou; and if there were any measures by which the kingdom could be wrenched from the grasp of Catherine de' Medici, it was agreed on all sides that it would be thoroughly legitimate to employ them. Twenty thousand Protestants were under arms in Languedoc and Guyenne, and the two younger Montmorencys, with other influential leaders of the "Politique" party, had joined them.

On the 24th of August, the first anniversary of the great massacre, representatives from Languedoc and other parts assembled at Nîmes and Montauban, to consider the Treaty of La Rochelle. The concessions then wrung from Catherine were now rejected with contempt, and the audacious project to constitute the party of Reform a republican federation was proposed, adopted, and put into action. Its various regulations were also discussed and agreed to, and the Reformers sent deputies to the king to lay their demands before him. They were principally that he should assign to them two towns in each province; that he should authorise full liberty of worship to the Reformers throughout the kingdom; that he should institute in each province a parliament composed of Reformers; that the sentences passed on the late admiral and other victims for a pretended conspiracy should be annulled, as falsehood and calumny; that the Saint-Bartholomew massacrers should be arrested and punished; and finally, that the Protestants should be declared to have had a sufficient and just cause for taking up arms since the 24th of August, 1572.

Charles was then on his journey with Anjou to the frontier. The deputies overtook him at

Villers-Cotterets. Catherine — for it was to her rather than the king that these demands were first addressed — is said to have been overwhelmed with amazement at their audacity, and to have exclaimed that "if Louis de Condé had been living and had held Paris with seventy thousand infantry and cavalry, he would not have demanded the half of what these people had dared to pretend to." She did not, however, altogether reject their demands, but put off their consideration to a more convenient season; for her attention was then absorbed by her efforts to keep up the saddened spirits of her best loved, who, the nearer he approached his new kingdom, the more piteously he bemoaned his fate. Charles, too, had fallen ill. Dissembling, therefore, her real feelings, Catherine sent the Protestant deputies to Maréchal de Montmorency (Damville), to discuss with him the terms of pacification. Thus "the religion," which but a twelvemonth before she believed to be trampled out, had risen up in that brief space a more formidable foe than ever.

Charles recovered from his attack of smallpox — which appears to have been but a slight one — more rapidly than was expected. But his chances of life were not improved by it. His meagre form and haggard face, his sunken eyes and weary gait, betokened death's near approach. Every intrusion threw him into a fit of passionate anger. He wished only for peace, he cried; but his guilty conscience, while it banished peace, did not wholly restrain him from adding to his crimes.

Owing to the elevation of Anjou, the post of lieutenant-general of the kingdom had become vacant. There were two applicants for it — the Duc de Guise and the king's brother, the Duc d'Alençon. The former, on making his application to the king, received a positive refusal, rendered more emphatic by a torrent of oaths, and threats of personal violence. Assassins, it appears, were always at hand, as one was despatched by Charles after Guise, with orders to kill him, and avenge the murder of the admiral, which, however, he failed to do — probably because he dared not succeed. Towards Alençon Charles IX. had no ill-feeling, and, although this turbulent and ambitious youth of eighteen was, of course, no less incompetent to fill so important a command than his brother of Anjou who had just vacated it, Charles would probably have conferred it on him had not the queen-mother hastened to prevent it.

She knew that, in some sense, it was a matter of life or death to her; that it would lead to her downfall, and, in all probability, a change in the succession — for she was no stranger to the state of feeling then existing in France towards her and her favourite son. Alençon seemed destined to give her much trouble. She detested him, of which he was well aware, and believed that she would not scruple to put him out of her way by poison or poniard.

At all events, she was as anxious to send him out of the country as was Charles to free himself from the presence of Anjou. Therefore, Catherine was secretly promising aid to the Netherlanders, hoping they would receive, if not Anjou, the Duc d'Alençon as their ruler. For the same reason she continued to urge Elizabeth to accept the hand of this interesting youth, whose gallantry did not allow him to offer only his hand, but with it humbly to tender his heart. The King of Poland was also charged to take measures (failing other plans) for ensuring the transfer of his crown to Alençon, when he should be called upon himself to ascend the throne of France.

But the queen-mother returned to Paris to find that, during her short absence, affairs had assumed a far more serious and threatening aspect than before. The movement, too, seemed to be rather political than religious. For pamphlets and passionate appeals to the people daily appeared, many of them of great eloquence, — the Huguenots having far more able pens than their opponents engaged in advocating their cause, upholding their views, and denouncing the authors of the Saint-Bartholomew to the execration of the whole world. That which but recently they had scarcely dared to whisper in the ear in private chambers was now proclaimed, as it were, on the housetops.

The people were reminded that it was the custom of the Gauls and ancient French to elect their rulers, and it was contended that the general assembly of the nation was a power far above that of kings.

Catherine might well tremble for the fate of the future king should the throne of France become elective. It was evident that already she had some fears for her own safety, as her guard of Swiss halberdiers, without whom she had never appeared in public since the *grande journée*, was at this time nearly doubled. She is, however, greatly lauded by her secretary, Davila, for the boldness and ability of her manœuvres in the face of the threatened tempest. She entered at once into negotiations with the Protestants, and in the king's name falsely promised them the speedy convocation of the States General at Compiègne.

Preferring to accomplish her aims by intrigue and deception, rather than by open force, she attempted to gain possession of La Rochelle by treachery. But the plot was discovered, and her emissaries, who had gained admission as pretended deserters from the royalists, were executed by order of the mayor, Jacques Henri, as traitors. The Rochellois had strictly observed the conditions of the Peace of La Rochelle, though rejected by the assembly of Montauban. Finding, however, that no trust could be reposed in the queen-mother, and that the king, languid and apathetic from illness, signed whatever she laid before him, they joined the confederate army in Languedoc and Poitou. La Noue, who, after the peace, had returned to the Reformers, now headed a division of that army, "until a commander of higher rank should declare himself." That commander was the Duc d'Alençon, who, with the King of Navarre, was about to escape. La Noue would then have commanded in his name. Catherine, fearing either his influence or his ability, despatched Maurevert, "the king's assassin" ("*le tueur du roi*"), to Poitou, with orders to find some means of getting poison administered to both La Noue and Maréchal de Montmorency (Damville), who now favoured both Huguenots and "malcontents." Failing to poison them, some means were to be sought for arresting Montmorency for treason. Maurevert, being recognised, became alarmed for his own safety, so failed entirely to accomplish his mission.

Henri of Navarre and Alençon had arranged to escape on Shrove Tuesday. But some misunderstanding, as to the precise day on which they were to be joined in the neighbourhood of Saint-Germain by an officer with a small force from the Huguenot army, caused the failure of the plot — one of Alençon's favourites, thinking the affair was at an end, revealed the whole scheme to the queen-mother. Alençon was summoned to attend her, and acknowledged all. He appears to have had as little stability of purpose as his brothers, or, as with them, his courageous resolves all evaporated in the presence of that much-feared but much-detested mother.

The court made a hasty retreat from Saint-Germain on hearing that Huguenot troops were in its vicinity. Poor Charles was persuaded by his mother that they and the young princes sought his life, and ill though he was, and in a burning fever, she obliged him to enter his litter at two o'clock in the morning, and proceed with all speed to Vincennes. "This is too cruel!" he exclaimed. "They would not have had long to wait for my death."

Notwithstanding the absence of the youthful royal commander-in-chief, the Huguenots of the West took the offensive with great success at Saintonge and Poitou. Catherine opposed them with three *corps d'armée*, in which no command was given to the Duc de Guise. She thought him dangerous, and Charles abhorred him. She was believed to be meditating a second Saint-Bartholomew — if the king should last long enough to take the responsibility of it — in which the princes, the Guises, the Montmorencys, and other leading men should be included.

Henri of Navarre and Alençon, though under strict surveillance at Vincennes, had made another attempt to escape, and were immediately arrested and required by the queen-mother to give an account of their conduct before a commission. On this occasion the Queen of Navarre, though caring very little for Henri, thought fit to identify herself with his position so far as to lend him the assistance of her able pen. Between them they prepared a statement so judiciously expressed and dignified in tone that Catherine, who before had regarded Henri of Navarre as of as little importance as his weak, vain father, was surprised to find that he had qualities which might possibly render him dangerous to her. She therefore began to fear and to hate him.* Fortunately the young king assumed, and as far as was possible in that atmosphere of corruption maintained, an attitude more consistent with the honourable and manly feelings, views, and aims set forth before the commission than he had hitherto done during his enforced residence amongst the riotous and dissolute young nobility of the court.

But Alençon betrayed much boyish pusillanimity, for he was restless rather than energetic, and ambitious without much judgment. He, however, dreaded a similar fate to that inflicted on Don Carlos, — his favourites and confidants having told him that Catherine was consulting the Pope and Philip of Spain on the subject. But she kept the princes in closer captivity than ever. For

* The great merit of this defence is said to belong to Marguerite far more than to Henri.

Condé had contrived to elude the vigilance of the guard appointed by the king to accompany him to Picardy, of which he was titular governor, concerning some affairs of the province. Hastily crossing Champagne, he reached Strasburg in safety, when he wrote to the Reformed churches that he was ready to join them, and to serve and protect "the cause" as his father had done.

Catherine in her perplexity once more meditated murder. She had arrested Maréchals Montmorency (Thoré) and Cossé, and sent them to the Bastille. She also made the king sign letters to the governors of provinces and marshals of France, to inform them that her captives were the principal authors of the conspiracy against his person and the state. So fraught with danger did Marguerite, who knew her mother too well, consider her present mood, that she proposed to favour the escape of Henri or Alençon in the disguise of one of her women. But they were unable to decide which it should be, neither caring to be left behind as a victim to Catherine's vengeance; so both stayed on, hoping for a possible chance of escaping together.

Charles IX. no longer troubled himself with public affairs, or took any part in the queen-mother's schemes, or, indeed, interest in anything. The hand of Death was now raised to strike him. He was troubled with fearful dreams. He fancied he heard sounds of distress, shrieks, and lamentations, mingled with voices appealing for mercy. Once more, in vision, he beholds the dawn of the 24th, and hears the great bell of Saint-Germain-l'Auxerrois. "Hark! Hark!" he cries. "It is the signal for the morrow! Ah! blood, blood! — in the river; in the streets — everywhere blood!" The delirium abating, he would weep bitterly, and in gentler tones whisper, "Spare them! spare them!" and "O my God, spare me! Have pity on me!" Turning to the nurse who sat by his bedside, he said: "Ah, nurse, what evil counsels I have followed! Behold! what murders; what blood has flowed! Lost, lost — I feel it!" The nurse, seeking to soothe him, replied: "Sire, the murders and the bloodshed be on the head of those who urged them on you, and on their evil counsels." "What will become of the country," he exclaimed, "and of me to whom God confided it? Lost! yes, lost — I feel sure of it!"

An interval of calm on the night preceding his death was taken advantage of by the queen-mother to secure his signature to the documents she had prepared for despatch to the governors of provinces, appointing her regent until Henri's arrival from Poland. The regency really belonged of right to the King of Navarre, failing the Duc d'Alençon, who was three years his junior. Though both were actually too young for such an office, yet as royal personages they were of age to fill it. Catherine, however, had artfully inserted in the letters patent that she accepted the regency at the request of the Duc d'Alençon, the King of Navarre, and other princes and peers of France.

On the morning of the 30th of May, 1574, Charles IX. ended his miserable career — pitied if not lamented. His last words were expressive of his satisfaction at leaving no male heir to wear the crown after him.

Though his state of health had long threatened the near approach of death, yet his physicians were of opinion that there were indications of arsenic having been administered to him towards the end. On one alone suspicion lighted. Whether guilty or not, no one doubted that she would shrink from no crime to secure power for herself and serve the supposed interests of her favourite son. Charles seemed to take long to die, and meanwhile rebels were proposing to place Alençon instead of the Polish king on his throne. It was needful therefore to hasten the end.

CHAPTER III.

Catherine's "Piteous Sorrow."— Montgomery Tortured and Beheaded. — Catherine's Expectations Now Anjou Reigns.— Henri's Flight from Poland. — His Twenty Leagues' Ride. — The Elector's Portrait Gallery. — Acknowledging Savoy's Hospitality. — Montluc Counsels Peace. — Catherine's Illusions Dispelled. — Extravagant Devotional Practices.

THOUGH suspicion was strong that Catherine de' Medici had hastened Charles's release from lingering bodily suffering and the terrors of accusing conscience, she yet affected to greatly bewail his death and to grieve over "her piteous sorrow of witnessing the untimely passing away of her children." But consolation remained. She was about to reign conjointly with that perfect prince, in whom, as she then believed, she had prepared for France an able Italian despot of the machiavelian type, who would carry out her views and found political order, as she for years had been striving to do, on the absence of all principle.

"Return without delay," she wrote; and never was summons received with greater joy, or obeyed with more alacrity, so far, at least, as setting out to return; though he lingered by the way in a manner unpleasantly surprising to the queen-mother — the success of whose schemes, then in abeyance, was in some measure jeopardised by it. But the new sovereign of France would seem to have read his mother's despatch no further than the announcement of Charles's death and the command to return to France, as he failed to leave a trustworthy agent in Poland, as she had urged him to do, in order to ensure either the continuance of the sovereignty of Poland to himself or its transfer to his brother Alençon.

Setting aside for awhile the consideration of the Protestant demands, Catherine concluded a two months' truce with the united Huguenots and "Politiques." Expecting the king's arrival before its expiration, Charles's death had changed her plan of resorting to further bloodshed, as regarded Henri of Navarre and the Duc d'Alençon. But she still desired the death of her captives in the Bastille. "Charles IX.," she informed Henri, "was anxious they should receive the treatment they merited." This, of course, was death, but Catherine feared to inflict it, until she had succeeded either in poisoning or arresting the elder Maréchal de Montmorency, who reigned almost as king in Languedoc, and on whose behalf the whole province, Protestants and "Politiques," would have risen in arms to avenge the murder of his younger brothers.

While the truce was being arranged at Poitou, and Catherine was making pacific advances to La

Noue and the Rochellois, the royalist troops were unexpectedly successful against the Huguenots at Saint-Lô. They were commanded by Montgomery, who surrendered under the strange promise that he "should be delivered safe and sound (*remis sain et sauf*) into the king's hands." He was, however, in the absence of the king, delivered over to the tender mercies of the queen-mother. Montgomery had been hitherto a successful as well as able general. He had often thwarted Catherine's plans, and for that reason she is said to have hated him, and to have been overjoyed at having him at last in her power, for he had escaped the Saint-Bartholomew slaughter.

But in Montgomery she affected especially to abhor the assassin of Henri II., though she knew full well that the blow which proved fatal to that monarch at the tournament of 1559, was the result of the accidental shivering of Montgomery's lance. He had unwillingly reëntered the lists; but at the king's reiterated command was compelled to do so. Henri's death was no great sorrow, in any sense, to Catherine de' Medici. It was, on the contrary, emancipation from the impertinence and slights of the king's mistresses and favourites, and the stepping-stone to the attainment of that power she had so longed for, and now for the last fifteen years had, more or less, exercised.

After this lapse of years, Montgomery was sentenced to die for the involuntary act that caused

Henri II.'s death, and which was now termed by Catherine high treason. Before laying his head on the block, Montgomery was cruelly tortured, with the expectation that bodily anguish would draw from him some sort of confession in support of the pretended Coligny conspiracy and the plots imputed to the imprisoned marshals. But all the satanic devices of the demons who tortured him failed to extort the compromising admissions which Catherine wished for. He bore his sufferings with wonderful heroism, and, braving his murderers, uttered no cry expressive of pain or supplication for mercy. His death had not the result she intended. It did not strike terror into the breasts of the young princes, but simply increased their horror of the murderers; nor did it lower the pretensions of the Huguenots, though in Montgomery she had again assassinated one of their ablest and most energetic military commanders.

But all parties in the state were now on the tiptoe of expectation. There was a brief cessation of strife, in the anxious desire to see what the new reign was likely to bring forth. Many conjectures were hazarded as to how this much-favoured prince, whose throne Catherine had carefully prepared for him, and of whose glory she fondly dreamed, would really act, now free to follow his own course in the affairs of the kingdom. Did he actually possess that extraordinary military genius which, so much

Gabriel de Lorges, Comte de Montgomery.
Photo-etching from painting in the Gallery of the
Chateau de Beauregard.

vaunted by the queen-mother and her agents, had chiefly influenced the Poles when offering him the sovereignty of their country? Was he likely to prove a tolerant prince, or, as many believed, influenced by that mother who had trained him to govern France, would he rival the "Demon of the South" himself in his persecuting zeal?

But the prince who left France so unwillingly seems no longer anxious to return. What detains him? "Why tarry the wheels of his chariot?" The Poles are also inquiring what is become of their king. For in the evening of the same day that the death of Charles IX., so impatiently waited for, was announced to him, Henri III. fled from the Castle of Cracow like a thief in the night, taking with him the crown jewels, to the amount of 300,000 gold crowns. He is said to have ridden twenty leagues without stopping in order to gain the Austrian province of Moravia, pursued by a few Polish nobles to the extreme frontier of their country. This was probably to regain possession of the jewels, and not to take back the king.

Both king and people had doubtless had enough of each other during the few months they had dwelt together. The wild, uncultured country had as little attraction for Henri, as the aristocratic haughtiness and independence of spirit displayed by the Polish nobility in their relations with their new sovereign. The puerile occupations or indecent and noisy orgies in which, to the total neglect of the business of state, he and his equally depraved companions indulged, were very much out of harmony with the more severe and manly pursuits of the nobles of his new kingdom. He still kept open the cut or prick in his finger for a supply of blood wherewith to write letters to the Princesse de Condé. His young courtiers followed his example, and with the same crimson fluid addressed their vows of love to their absent mistresses; comparing their compositions before despatching them, and finding amusement in efforts to surpass each other in the extravagance of their expressions of worship and adoration.

Some of the people about him did, it appears, endeavour to prevent his sudden and ignominious flight. They represented to him that it was neither to his interest nor his honour to treat thus disrespectfully the generous people who, setting aside all differences of opinion, had determined to unite and unanimously declare him the chosen sovereign of the nation. They reminded him also of making an effort to secure the Crown of Poland for Alençon. But Henri was intent only on getting out of the country as quickly as possible. When, however, he reached the frontier where a choice of routes was open to him, he chose the most circuitous one for returning to his loved France.

He had a motive for it, certainly. He shrank from taking the route through Central Germany, lest he should meet with a reception from the Protestant princes and French refugees similar to that they had given him when on his journey to Poland, and which, in his extreme mortification, drew from him that recital concerning the massacre of the Saint-Bartholomew, known as "*Le Discours de Henri III.*" The Elector-Palatine took him into his picture-gallery, and showed him a portrait of the admiral, and several others of distinguished men who had perished in the massacre. "These," he said, "are some of the worthiest of men, and the truest Frenchmen I have ever known. Those who put them to death are wretched beings indeed." Henri was cut to the heart; but it was not with remorse, but mortification, that he who usually had abundance of words at command, found no retort to make. His guilty conscience compelled him to hear and be silent.

It was on this account that he determined to reach France by traversing Austria and Italy. He visited first the Emperor Maximilian II., at Vienna. That humane and tolerant prince gave him excellent advice, and especially recommended religious tolerance — the happy results of which he could point to in his own dominions. But it rather grates on one's feelings to find the emperor proposing to Henri III. to marry his daughter, Charles's widow — then mourning in silence and darkness the customary forty days. Both father and daughter, one would have supposed, would have shrunk from a second alliance with the blood-stained race of Valois.

Henri, however, though professing to receive his counsels with very great deference, was not disposed to adopt his matrimonial views. The princess for love of whom he had shed his heart's blood, and whose marriage he proposed to have annulled that he might make her Queen of France, had recently died. Henri mourned her death in black satin doublet and vest, embroidered in white with death's-heads, and bordered with the same. His Venetian hose of black silk were fastened at the knee with a satin band, similarly embroidered. The fronts of his shoes and ends of his shoe-strings had the same decoration, and instead of the diamond he usually wore in front of his velvet cap, a death's-head was substituted (Mathieu). But he did not mourn long, for he remembered that in passing through Lorraine on his way to Poland he had been struck by the beauty — second only, he thought, to that of the deceased princess — of Louise de Vaudemont, the elder daughter of the Comte de Vaudemont, head of a younger branch of the House of Lorraine. Proposals of marriage with a Swedish princess were then under discussion; Philip II. proposed an infanta, and the name of Catherine of Navarre was also mentioned.

But Henri would have none of them. To the last-named princess objection was taken by the queen-mother, who feared that in Catherine the spirit of Jeanne d'Albret survived. Henri of Navarre was decidedly averse to such a match, and the king himself declared that "he would marry no humpbacked dwarf," as some of his companions jestingly had told him that the Huguenot Princesse Catherine was — he, it appears, never having seen her. Besides, he had resolved to marry Louise de Vaudemont, who submitted to her elevation rather than desired it.

Henri passed on from Vienna to Venice, where he was fêted with great magnificence. He was enchanted with the fairy-like attractions of the festivities given in his honour; and immersed in the congenial delights, pleasures, and pomps of "Venice the beautiful," gave no heed to the repeated messages of the queen-mother, urging his immediate return. Luigi Macenigo, famed for his prudence and wisdom, was then Doge of Venice. Excellent were the counsels he gave the young king, while several of the "potent, grave, and reverend seigniors" who composed the senate impressed on their royal guest precepts similar to the emperor's. Venice seems to have changed its tone since it forwarded such flattering compliments to Charles IX. and the queen-mother on the success of the *grande journée*.

After tearing himself from the voluptuous excitement of the life, so congenial to him, that he led at Venice, Henri made another halt on his journey homeward at Ferrara, also at Mantua and

Turin, where again grand pageants awaited him. The homage paid to the young King of France in those cities, and the enjoyment he found in those frequent lively Italian *fêtes* after the gloomy winter he had spent in Cracow and Warsaw, detained him yet two months from "his good people of Paris," and his anxiously expectant mother.

The Duke of Savoy very adroitly took this opportunity of making large presents to the frivolous favourites who accompanied the king, and through them suggesting that the *fêtes* of Turin and the duke's splendid hospitality would be appropriately acknowledged by restoring to Piedmont the fortresses of the frontier — all that then remained to France of her Italian conquests, and termed "the keys of Italy." Henri immediately gratified the duke by offering him those fortresses he so long had vainly coveted. The governor, the Duc de Nevers, though an Italian, would have dissuaded him from such an act of folly. As he could not prevail, he required a formal act of dismissal from the charge confided to him, and the registration by the Parliament of his remonstrances to the king. As he declined also to assist at the evacuation of the fortresses, that useful personage, the Bastard of Angoulême, ready always for any act, from petty pilfering to wholesale robbery, private assassination or public massacre, was called in to complete the act, and hand over the royal gift.

Henri's munificence induced Philibert Emanuel — who doubtless pitied his nephew for the insane liberality by which he profited — to give him some good advice. He strongly recommended, as other princes had done, a peaceful policy, and urged him to receive Maréchal de Montmorency (Damville) again into favour. The marshal had come to Turin to meet the king and to make a last effort at reconciliation — the Duke of Savoy having granted him a safe-conduct for that purpose.

Henri received him in all apparent friendliness, but with the secret intention of arresting him — agents from the queen-mother and her chancellor, Birago, having hastened to Turin to urge the king by no means to let this opportunity of entrapping the marshal escape him. But despite the gift of the fortresses, the duke insisted on his safe-conduct being respected, and Henri dared not greatly press him to be guilty of an act so base as consent to its violation. Damville, being warned of the king's intention, left Turin, returned to Languedoc, and no longer hesitated to sign a pact with the Huguenots, and to raise the Confederate standard.

Catherine appeared to be under the impression, now that the favourite son was king, that nothing he or she determined on could fail. War and destruction alone now dwelt in her thoughts, and Henri had promised her to crush not only the

Huguenots, but the Montmorencys and the Guises. His failure to entrap the marshal was indeed an excessive disappointment. Henri, himself, though caring less about it, thought it time to leave Turin — the *éclat* of his visit being dimmed by the rebuff at its conclusion. On the 5th of September he passed the frontier, where the King of Navarre and the Duc d'Alençon waited to welcome him to his kingdom.

He greeted them pleasantly, and embraced them; asked for some explanation of their rebellious escapades; laughed, and seemed satisfied, when, not caring to complain of the queen-mother, they spoke of the rigour with which they had been treated by Charles. "Well, now you are free," he said; orders already being given to keep a strict watch on their movements. The meeting of Catherine and her son at Bourgoin was no less affecting than their adieux at Lorraine. Proceeding to Lyons, they made their entry into that city together. There an embassy from the Protestant princes awaited him, to intercede in favour of the French Reformers. He would pardon the Huguenots, he told them, if they would lay down their arms and live henceforth as good Catholics. But as for those who obstinately persisted in error, they must leave the kingdom, taking with them whatever movable property they possessed.

Pacific counsels now flowed in from all sides, and from most unexpected quarters. There seemed to be a weariness of this never-ending strife and warfare, and a general longing for peace. But with a military genius at the head of the kingdom, Catherine resolved on a war of extermination. She and Henri were getting together an army of Swiss and Italian infantry and German Catholic cavalry. In distributing the commands a marshal's division was assigned to Montluc, famed for his cruelty no less than his great military ability. But Montluc had grown old, and now looked on all this warfare in a different light than formerly. He declined the command, pleading the many wounds he had received in the course of his long career, some of them now become troublesome.

He, however, ventured to recommend the king to try peaceful measures. The queen-mother thought that the great captain had become a dotard — Blaise de Montluc stigmatising war was indeed something to marvel at. His advice, however, would not be followed. More diligently than her son, Catherine continued to arm and increase her forces. "She cared not," she said, "who thought it right or wrong." The Pope had given permission to levy two millions on the clergy for two years, for the purpose of enabling the king to stamp out this "damnable heresy." It was also generally supposed that the hero of Jarnac and Moncontour would assume in person the chief command of the army destined to strike the great and, as expected, final blow at French Protestantism and its supporters, the "Politiques."

Catherine shared this expectation, which was soon to be disappointed. Henri was ready to proclaim war, but not in person to make it. He was much more occupied with drawing up and establishing new rules of court etiquette, — more after the mode of Spain, and tending to increase the distance between the king and his subjects. His new arrangements greatly displeased the nobility, many of whom left the court rather than submit to such unwise and puerile changes (Mathieu).

The finances of the kingdom, already sufficiently mismanaged, were thrown into inextricable confusion by his interference and withdrawal from the control of the chamber of accounts and superintendent of finance all moneys he chose to have paid directly into his own hands, to pass into those of his dissolute favourites and companions of his vicious pleasures. The part the queen-mother had designed that her favourite son should play, and which he imagined he had successfully assumed, he was utterly incapable of sustaining. She had looked for a hero; but her illusions were as rudely dispelled as were those of his subjects, who, when expecting to see the "soldier king" put on his cuirass, found him donning the sackcloth of the penitent.

The queen-mother had accustomed her children to a theatrical display of superstitious devotion, after finally making up her mind that Catholicism rather than Reform was likely to retain the ascendency in France. This, no doubt, was to atone for an equally public display of contempt for those pious extravagances when, for awhile, Reform seemed destined to triumph. None took so readily to this devotional masquerading as the Duc d'Anjou, who now, as king, began to edify his subjects by extravagant demonstrations of piety and penitential exercises in alternation with gross depravity.

At last, urged by the queen-mother, he bade adieu to the gaieties of Lyons, and with her took the road to Avignon, — zealous Catholics striving to believe that he was really going to take the command of his army. A field-equipage followed the king, which was seized *en route* by Montbrun — the famous leader of the Huguenots of Dauphiny — to whom, that the road might be clear for his journey, the king had sent threatening orders to disarm. But Montbrun tossed them aside with derision, and, thinking that the king's equipage would be more useful to him than following his majesty for mere parade, lay in wait and seized it. Henri vowed that, if ever this audacious rebel should fall into his hands, no quarter should be given him.

Arrived at Avignon, instead of joining his army,

Henri joined a fraternity of Flagellants, who were accustomed to whip their naked backs and shoulders to secure the pardon of their sins. Dressed in a sort of sack, with a hood having two openings for the eyes, they passed through the streets of the papal city of Avignon by night, chanting the mournful *Miserere*, and carrying lighted torches. The whole of the court, following the king's example, joined these fanatics, whose penitential discipline he was induced to take part in — flaying his back and shoulders unmercifully — as expressive of his sense of the loss he had sustained in his cousin's wife being so cruelly taken from him.

The Cardinal de Lorraine, though he had not accustomed himself to perform such uncomfortable acts of devotion, yet thought it not seemly or advantageous to have the appearance of shrinking from giving his personal sanction to the rigorous self-inflicted penance of the sorrowing and pious young king. He forgot that Henri was but twenty-three, while he was forty-eight; that the dangerously heavy night dews of Avignon would be likely to affect him unfavourably, while traversing the streets in a semi-nude condition, his naked feet thrust into sandals, his back and shoulders exposed, and on a cold December night. He repented him sincerely that he had joined in such mummeries when, on the morrow, he could not rise from his bed, and when, as the day advanced, he grew worse instead of better. A few days later (December 26th) he died.

The ultra-Catholic party regretted him. But the Huguenots and "Politiques" regarded him and the queen-mother as the two scourges of the nation. They, therefore, rejoiced that France was freed from one of them.

A fearful storm, whose ravages extended almost over the whole kingdom, occurred on the night of the cardinal's death. The Catholics of Lorraine affected to see in it an indication that God deprived them of this "good, great, and wise prelate," in His anger against the sinful nation. The Huguenots, on the other hand, declared that it was the tumult of assembling demons eager to carry off the wicked cardinal's soul. Hearing that the cardinal was dead, Catherine said publicly at table, "Then there will soon be peace in France." She, however, spoke highly of his abilities and many good qualities, but immediately after, in her private circle, she declared that "there had died that day the very worst man of all mankind." Could they have changed positions, the cardinal, doubtless, would have paid her, as a woman, a similar compliment.*

Henri's ostentatious devotion had not the effect of increasing his popularity. He had sojourned six weeks in Avignon, and during that period Montmorency had taken two towns almost under

* Pierre de l'Estoile — "*Journal de Henri III.*"

his eyes. It was high time, the queen-mother suggested, and Henri concurred in her opinion, that they should proceed on their journey to Rheims, where his coronation and his marriage were both to take place.

CHAPTER IV.

The Journey from Avignon to Rheims. — The King Casts Off His Mourning. — Arranging the Crown Jewels. — The Bride. — The King's Personal Appearance. — The Entry in State into Paris. — Expedients for Raising Money. — Montbrun a Prisoner. — Condemned to Death. — Bœsme, the Admiral's Murderer, Hanged in Reprisal. — Poland Elects Another King. — La Belle Madame de Suave. — The Seven Months' Truce.

IN early February, the king and the queen-mother made their entry into Rheims. Their journey from Avignon had not been wholly free from adventures, which were, however, regarded far more lightly by Henri than by his mother. On their way northward, they passed the camp of Maréchal de Bellegarde, who was besieging the small Huguenot town of Livron. When the inhabitants became aware that their new king was so near them, they saluted him with a volley of shot from the ramparts — they and their women, who with pikes and pistols were aiding the men to resist the besiegers — calling out vehemently as the royal *cortège* passed, "Ha! ha! assassins! massacrers! You'll not stab us in our beds as you did the admiral; there's no easy prey for you here." Henri had also the mortification of knowing that the resistance of this small town was so vigorous and well sustained that De Bellegarde was obliged to raise the siege, and, with the royalist troops, beat a hasty retreat before the eager pursuit of the inhabitants (Pierre de l'Estoile).

A party of malcontents and military men had also agreed to attack the king's carriage at Saint-Marcoul, seize his person, put him in a convent, and place Alençon on the throne,—having with them a sufficient force to overpower the royal escort. But, as it happened with all the schemes of that day, there was a traitor amongst the schemers, who revealed to those who were to be entrapped what was on foot against them. The historian Mathieu says it was considered prudent to hush up this affair, the Duc d'Alençon having made oath that he was no consenting party to it.

The coronation of Henri III. took place on the 13th of February, and on the 15th the marriage ceremony was performed. The see of Rheims being vacant in consequence of the death of the Cardinal de Lorraine, his nephew, the Cardinal de Guise, officiated. The question of precedence, so frequently raised and insisted upon by the ambitious Guises, led, on this occasion, to a violent dispute between the young duke (by the cardinal's death become the head of the house) and the Duc de Montpensier, prince of the blood. The former claimed to take precedence of the latter, not only as an elder peer as his father had done, being a few days his senior, but also as a prince of the blood, which he was not. He, however, insisted on "his rights" in so haughty and insulting a manner, that Montpensier, who would not admit his claim, absented himself from both ceremonies.

Contrary to the usual practice, Henri III. was crowned at night instead of mid-day. His marriage also took place late in the evening, "to the scandal," it is said, "of all serious people," and strict observers of time-honoured usages.* From the inclination the king evinced for devotional exercises, it was supposed by some persons that he had spent the preceding days in prayerful preparation; but when it became known that he had devoted his whole time to arranging his own and his royal bride's toilet, much indignation was expressed by "malcontents" of all classes.

He had cast aside his sombre black satin and death's heads for vest and doublet of blue satin embroidered with seed-pearls. Already he had reduced the size of the trunk-hose, which during the latter part of Charles's reign had swollen into a most uncomfortable and unbecoming garment, stuffed with a quantity of tow, wool, or other material to extend them to their full size — even

---

* François I. was crowned at night, or partially so, and with much speed and little ceremony. The anointing only took place, as the Sainte-Ampoule might not be removed from Saint-Remi to Saint-Denis, where the coronation rites were concluded.

when steel or whalebone was used for their support. His white silk stockings were embroidered with blue silk clocks, and fastened at the knee with satin bands, ornamented with seed-pearls, and having a blue rosette with diamond centre. Similar rosettes were placed on the white satin shoes.

Beginning already to be bald, he usually wore a sort of velvet turban, which he never removed, even at church; the only exception he afterwards made to this general rule was on entering the private council-chamber when the nobility and ministers were assembled.

On the occasion of his coronation, and at his marriage, "the small turban was enlarged and became a toque," with a band of pearls, diamond aigrette, and long white feather. The state mantle was of royal purple velvet, lined with minever, and embroidered with *fleur-de-lys* in gold. Its length and weight were so great that, though borne by ten of the nobility, the assistance of several pages was also required to support it. White Spanish gloves, embroidered in pearls, gold fringed, and fastened with large diamonds as buttons, completed his costume, with the addition of the jewelled orders of Saint-Michel, and the Golden Fleece.

It appears that it was not merely because the king was unable to complete his coronation toilet until the evening that the ceremony was performed so late; but rather that, having spent a long time in personal adornment — for he had certainly done much patching and painting — he thought to do himself more justice, and to appear with more *éclat*, lighted up by the innumerable lamps and wax candles that would at that hour be needed. The assembled princes of the blood, and peers of France, in their robes of state, and plumed hats with diamond clasps, or other brilliant ornament, together with the dresses of the ladies of the court, resplendent with jewels, doubtless made up a very grand show. The old abbey itself, in its gala dress of blue and gold and silver draperies, while shedding lustre on the scene, received some lustre also from it.

The crown of France must surely have been from all time a comfortless, ill-fitting head-dress. For when placed on the head of the monarch who was being crowned, he usually exclaimed, "*Elle me blesse!*" "*Elle me gêne!*" or similar expression of inconvenience. Sometimes it nearly toppled over. It did so on the occasion in question, when Henri, lifting his hand to his head, said aloud, "It hurts me!" This was regarded as foreshadowing evil, and often was this double augury of troublous times referred to during the reign of the vain, indolent, and dissolute Henri III.

On the morrow of his coronation the king was supposed to be resting from the fatigue of the previous evening's ceremony. He was, however, again busy in arranging the crown jewels to be worn by himself and his bride, and trying their effect, either singly or in different combinations. The crown jewels of France were not numerous, and but a few of them of exceptional value. Those which Henri took with him when he décamped so hastily from Poland may have been added to them, temporarily at least, for both king and queen are said to have been "bravely" adorned with jewels. The young queen wore a dress of cloth of silver — over a white satin petticoat, on which fell the tassels of a girdle of pearls and diamonds — with a long sweeping train, and a stomacher of diamonds. The sleeves of silver gauze were looped to the shoulder with pearls and diamonds, and three rows of the same precious gems encircled her throat. A veil of silver gauze covered her shoulders, and fell low at the back. It was fastened by a diamond aigrette, and in her hair, which was frizzed and curled after the new fashion, several fine diamonds were arranged by the king himself.

That the bride was very pretty we have the testimony of Geronimo Lippomano, the Venetian ambassador. "She has lovely eyes," he says, "fair hair, and delicate features. Very graceful also, affable, gentle, and pious, and shows much simplicity of manner. Generally," he continues, " she dresses with elegance, but far from extravagantly; yet on great festivals, to please the king

Louise de Lorraine,
Wife of Henri III.
Photo-etching from an old portrait in the Louvre.

probably, she is covered with jewels, and magnificently attired. Her family is a branch of the House of Lorraine, the most ancient in Christendom, and the most noble. Not on account of the emperors, kings of France, Jerusalem, and Portugal who have issued from it, but because of the great achievements accomplished by its ancestors in Syria, at the conquest of the Holy Land, of which history is full."

The royal bridegroom was no less "bravely" attired than the bride. White satin and silver cloth had taken the place of the coronation blue and gold; and he had reserved for his own adornment an ample share of the jewels. His career of vice was begun at so early an age that already he had a worn and dissipated appearance. Yet his personal advantages were still thought considerable. The Venetian authority, quoted above, describes him as "something above the middle height, but rather thin than well proportioned. His eyes fine, and soft in expression; his forehead broad, and general appearance delicate; his face rather long, and lower lip and chin, as in all Catherine's children, of the Medici type. His bearing is noble and gracious. He is fond of rich dresses, jewels and perfumes; he is almost always shaven, and wears rings, bracelets, and earrings.

"He is a skilful horseman and fencer; but bodily exercises do not greatly amuse or occupy him. He prefers dancing and tennis to hunting;

therefore it is thought that he is more inclined to peace than war. Yet in his brother's reign he acquired much military reputation, and was regarded as a courageous prince, and the enemy of the rebels against God and the Crown of France. But probably this was due to those who then advised and directed him. It was, however, this which induced the barbarous Hungarians" (Poles) "to offer him the crown in preference to all other princes."

Immense sums were expended on the festivities that followed this marriage, which was in no sense a political one, but the result of an amorous caprice. It was sanctioned by the queen-mother, because of the retiring, unassuming character of the young princess; a daughter-in-law likely to exert any influence opposed to hers would never have been permitted by Catherine de' Medici to share the throne of Henri III. On the 27th of February the king, queen, and queen-mother made their solemn entry into Paris with extraordinary pomp and magnificence. Yet distress amongst the people was very great; the salaries of the officials in all departments of the public service were unpaid, and the mercenary troops were clamouring for the arrears due to them, and threatening to disband themselves if money was not speedily forthcoming.

Henri was not received with the enthusiasm he expected and thought he merited. However, to propitiate the people and the "good cities" generally, to whom he was about to apply for a further considerable sum of money, he resumed his devotional exercises. Such good Catholics could not but be touched by the spectacle of their pious young king, who, after spending the carnival in disgraceful rioting and debauchery, edified them by passing the season of Lent in tramping from church to church with the Flagellants, arrayed in the customary sack and capuchon, and carrying a torch in one hand, and a scourge of whipcord in the other. The people mocked, and asked if the king were endeavouring by this unmerciful flaying of his shoulders to make some atonement for his share in the Saint-Bartholomew. But it was suspected that the shoulders were too well padded to suffer much from the flaying.

His penance over, he proceeded to the task of obtaining three millions by way of loan from his already loathing subjects. This sum, with a million levied on the clergy, was soon absorbed by the demands of his favourites, to whom, when money failed, he gave any bishoprics, or other benefices that chanced to fall vacant, to make money of themselves. He had already in this way disposed of the Bishoprics of Amiens and Grenoble to a passing favourite, Berenger du Guast, who sold one for 30,000 *francs*, the other for 40,000. One of the women of the court bought Amiens of him to sell again at a higher price, and realised a substantial sum by the transaction.* The fertile brains of the Italian tax-gatherers, or inventors of new taxes for the king and court, were ever on the rack, devising fresh expedients for exacting money from the people. Taxes already deemed intolerable might yet, it was thought, bear being added to. Or greatly pressed, the crown jewels were placed as security for a loan with some foreign financier.

Even the treasures of the Church were not always respected, and that which to all zealous Catholics must have been held sacred above every other — the so-called "True Cross" — which was kept at the Sainte-Chapelle, was one day found missing. "With the consent of the king and queen-mother, as reported, 'this precious relic' had been sent to Italy, in pledge for a large sum in cash" (L'Estoile). Catherine's unpopularity increased daily — all the misfortunes of the country being attributed to her — and Henri's grew apace with it. New offices, not only useless, but even prejudicial to the state, were being constantly created for sale to the highest bidder; while the increase of the duty on wines, the toll-rates, provisionary custom duty, etc., occasioned serious disturbances in Paris, Bordeaux, Marseilles and other towns.

* Pierre de l'Estoile — "*Journal de Henri III.*" L'Estoile also states that this new favourite, who made a point of opposing Catherine's views, was soon after stabbed in his bed by two masked assassins. By whose orders no one doubted.

Meanwhile war and negotiations for peace were going on simultaneously. The confederates had met with many successes, their demands being now greatly in excess of those presented to Charles IX. in 1573. Henri protested, but no abatement was listened to. He, however, had a revenge which pleased him greatly. The valiant Huguenot captain, Montbrun, who had captured his majesty's field-equipage, was unfortunately wounded in an encounter with royalist troops under the Duc de Guise in Dauphiny, and taken prisoner. It was hoped that Guise would consent to exchange his prisoner for the man (Bœsme) employed by the Guises to kill the admiral, and who was taken prisoner at the same time that Montbrun fell into the hands of the royalists.

Bœsme had been rewarded for the murder which was the signal for the Saint-Bartholomew slaughter, with the hand of a daughter of the Cardinal de Lorraine, and was in high favour with the Guise family. But Henri was not disposed to listen to any proposals of the Duc de Guise, of whose popularity he was excessively jealous, and whom he determined to remove from his command of the royal troops lest his influence with the army and the people should prove dangerous to him. No appeals moved Henri to spare the gallant Montbrun, who was condemned to death for high treason. Bœsme was immediately executed for the murder of the admiral.

About this time the zealous Catholics adopted the appellation of Carcistes, from the name of the Comte de Carces, whom they regarded as their chief, and to mark the distinction also between them and the moderate Catholics or "Politiques" who had joined the Huguenots and taken the name of *rasats*, or close-shaven, the *carcistes* having long beards. Both *carcistes* and *rasats* ravaged the country, and distressed the peasantry for the support of their troops; further misery threatening them from an army of Swiss and German Protestants then marching towards France, headed by the Prince de Condé.

Much mortification also awaited the king. His Polish subjects had invited him more than once to return to Poland, or he would forfeit his crown and another king be elected. He had given little heed to this warning, and took months to consider his answer. At length he sent them word that the affairs of France prevented his return for a time, but that to supply his place he would send them able and trustworthy agents. Again months glided on, and no agents were sent, nor any steps taken to promote the election of Alençon. When, however, he did despatch an envoy his successor was elected, — the Vayvode of Transylvania, Etienne Bathory, for whom also a queen was chosen, — his election being dependent on his consenting to marry the Princess Anne Jagellon, sister of the last king of that distinguished race.

This decisive act of the Poles was an unexpected blow to Henri's self-love. He had thought to keep both crowns, therefore omitted to support his brother's pretensions, which now became a source of much trouble to him. He hated Alençon, who returned the feeling no less cordially. Indeed, hatred of each other seems to have been the one predominant feeling in this hateful family. Being troubled for some days with pains in his ears, Henri attributed them to poison administered by, or at the suggestion of, his brother. Sending for Henri of Navarre, he told him his suspicions, and begged him to kill Alençon, that after his (the king's) death Henri might succeed to his crown. But Henri rejected the proposal with horror (Mathieu).

The warmth of the friendship subsisting between Henri and the Duc d'Alençon had at that moment abated a little, for both were seeking the good graces of the same lady — the beautiful Madame de Suave, one of the belles of the "flying squadron." Yet the rivalship did not move them to jealousy so implacable as to lead to a desire in either to take the life of the other. In the interests of the queen-mother, madame coquetted with both those youths, playing off one against the other, yet striving to keep her hold on both — Catherine seeking to retain them in her power, and, by means of amorous intrigues with the depraved women of her court, to divert their thoughts from escaping and joining the confederate armies.

Miron, the king's first physician, having succeeded in curing Henri's earache, the royal patient no longer sought his brother's life, but contented himself with following up a system of persecution, intended to drive him to acts of rebellion. Alençon, in consequence, took the first opportunity of effecting his escape from the court. The king gave immediate orders to his courtiers to take horse and pursue the fugitive prince with all speed. For both the king and queen-mother were greatly alarmed, knowing that Condé with 15,000 German troops was advancing on France.

But the courtiers showed no sort of alacrity in obeying the king's orders. They even hesitated to obey them at all. The Duc de Montpensier refused pointblank to aid in closing the route to the Loire against the duke. Perceiving that Alençon's pursuers would be more likely to join than to arrest him, Catherine herself determined to pursue her son. He had reached Chambord ere she overtook him with her proposals of peace. He would not listen to them. Her first act, he said, must be to liberate the marshals, De Montmorency and Cossé, whom she had imprisoned now nearly twelve months.

Nothing more unpleasant to her could have been proposed. Ever since the death of the old constable, Anne, she had steadily clung to her resolve to work the downfall of the House of Montmorency. A report was spread at the time she left Paris that De Montmorency (Damville) had been slain in battle. Overjoyed at this news, she had earnestly impressed on Henri that the opportunity now offered of privately strangling the captive marshals must not be neglected.

The marshals were deprived of their usual attendants. The king's physician, Miron, spread a report that they were threatened with quinsy, and the court assassins were waiting but the signal to do the deed of blood. But the Comte de Sauvré, Master of the Robes, who apparently had some influence with the king, persuaded him to defer, at least for a time, giving the final orders for their death. As Henri III. was utterly wanting in decision of character, whether for good or for evil, he was immediately plunged into a state of hesitation, unable to make up his mind to do, or not to do, his mother's bidding.

During this period of irresolution, Damville's death was contradicted, and Catherine, in a great fright, lest the deed should be already done, sent off a messenger with orders to ride with all speed night and day to prevent, if possible, the fatal effects of the quinsy.* Following closely on the heels of this messenger comes another. Alençon has not yielded to his mother, but compels her to yield to him. " Peace is imperative, or the king

* Mathieu — " *Histoire de France.*"

is lost," Catherine writes to Henri III. "The doors of the Bastille must be opened."

"The two marshals are free," is the reply the messenger carries back. But none the less does Alençon join the confederates on the confines of Touraine and Poitou (L'Estoile). The defeat of the vanguard of the Genevese army, about 5,000 men, under Montmorency (De Thou), by the Duc de Guise, with a force of 15,000, encountered by the confederates while crossing Champagne, had not the effect of bringing them to terms — Montmorency being able to make good his retreat, and to effect a junction with Alençon.*

Nothing daunted by fatigue or by the inclemency of the weather, but braving all hardships and even the indisposition resulting from them, Catherine followed her son from post to post, — her eagerness to negotiate rendering him more exacting. In her despair Catherine took the strange step of seeking the mediation of the two men whom she had so long and so unjustly imprisoned, and who only through the intervention of a friend were rescued from the cruel death to which she had condemned them. In the interests of peace they did not refuse her. But zealous

---

* It was in this engagement that the Duc de Guise received the wound in the right cheek from an arquebuse, that took off also part of his ear, from which the surname of "Le Balafré," formerly applied to his father, was henceforth given to him, though his wound was a far less serious one.

Huguenots put little faith in the professions of the Duc d'Alençon, while Catholics, no less than Huguenots, entirely distrusted Catherine, even to the king himself.

After many long conferences, a seven months' truce only was agreed to by Catherine in the king's name, — he assenting to it for the purpose of deceiving the princes, but without any intention of observing its conditions. The Prince de Condé, who on the signing of the truce had stayed the march of his army, finding that the king failed to execute his part of the pact, at once crossed the Rhine, and entered France with his German cavalry, — Queen Elizabeth having advanced the money to pay them and their commander, Jean Casimer. The escape of the King of Navarre at this time rendered the state of affairs more perplexing.

CHAPTER V.

Escape of Henri of Navarre.—"God be Praised for My Deliverance!"—Henri Hesitates to Abjure Catholicism.—Catherine Negotiates while the King is Praying.—La Paix de Monsieur.—Duc de Guise and the Holy League.—The Oath under Pain of Eternal Damnation.—The States General Cannot Agree on the Question of Unity of Faith, but Agree on Voting the King no Money.—The Crown Jewels Pledged Again.

IT was indeed high time that Henri of Navarre should be rescued from the enervating seductions of the dissolute Court of France. He was then twenty-two years of age, and, when required, after a former attempt to escape from Vincennes, to give an account of his conduct, he had shown himself wanting neither in manliness nor high principle. Yet, unfortunately, he had since relapsed into an apparently contented state of voluptuous indolence. No longer he appeared to yearn, as at first, for liberty. His just resentment, too, at his enforced absence from his paternal domains, erewhile so strongly expressed, was now, if not wholly obliterated, yet very sensibly diminished.

Sometimes, however, conscience did awaken in him a sense of his deep abasement, and Alençon's escape would naturally revive the desire to shake off his fetters and be free. He was not very closely guarded. For Catherine, though she had momentarily believed that the spirit and firmness of Jeanne d'Albret were to some extent inherited by him, had since changed her opinion. His amorous intrigues with the belles of the "squadron," and the lure she held out to him of succeeding to the post of lieutenant-general of the kingdom, were all-sufficient, she fancied, to hold him a fast-bound prisoner. This apparent insensibility to the welfare of "the cause" had the further effect of greatly alienating the Huguenots, who no longer looked to him as a leader, esteeming him weak and vain, and as little to be relied on as his father had proved to be. The young nobles of the court treated him as a good-natured, jovial companion, but laughed at him in his absence, Catherine joining in mocking at his credulity in putting faith in her promises. He was even the jest of the frivolous and vicious Henri III., who "for his own and his *mignons*' amusement kept a strict account of his sister Marguerite's scandalous intrigues, often comparing their number with those attributed to Henri, and declaring it difficult to determine on which side the balance lay."

Informed of this by Catherine's *dames d'honneur*, with whom Henri III. was no favourite, "the Béarnais" (the sobriquet they had given the King of Navarre) began seriously to reflect on his disgraceful position. Two or three of the gentlemen of his suite, who three years before accompanied him to Paris, and fortunately had escaped the massacre, still remained with him, hoping eventually to effect his rescue. Occupying the same, or an adjoining apartment, they noticed his unusual restlessness. Sometimes he murmured his mother's name, or repeated in a low tone verses of the psalms especially in favour with the Huguenots.

Agrippa d'Aubigné — the historian and poet — was one of those friends whose attachment to Henri kept them prisoners also at the Court of France. Hearing him one night repeat a portion of the 88th Psalm, "Sire," he said, "the Spirit of God truly then still dwells within you." He then urged him to endeavour at all risks to free himself from the degrading bondage he was held in. Very readily Henri consented, and a day was named for putting a plan of escape into execution. Henri, it appears, was allowed to hunt in the forest of Senlis, though more narrowly watched than he fancied.

The preparations for flight were not yet completed when Henri, returning one evening from Senlis, perceived D'Aubigné and two or three of his companions coming towards him at full gallop. "Sire, we are betrayed!" exclaimed D'Aubigné. "The king knows all; the road to death and shame is that of Paris; that of life and glory everywhere else." "Then let us at once depart," replied Navarre. Putting spurs to their horses, they rode swiftly through the forest, and at daybreak arrived at Poissy, where they crossed the Seine. Thence on the following day they reached Alençon and Saumur, passing the Loire at the latter place.

Considering that he had now made good his escape, Henri heaved a sigh of relief, and raising his eyes towards heaven, exclaimed: "God be praised for my deliverance! My mother's mysterious death," he continued, "occurred in Paris; there the admiral and all my best friends were murdered, and, but for God's protection, there was no intention of offering better treatment to me. Never, never, unless I am dragged thither, will I ever return." *

However, but for the unexpected suddenness of his departure, and the excitement of so hurried an escape, Henri of Navarre would probably yet have lingered long at the Court of Catherine de' Medici, and, like his father, have fallen a victim to the seductive lures of the wily, unprincipled Florentine. For his ardour seemed to desert him, when the necessity of eluding pursuit had ceased. He hesitated, also, to abjure the Romish faith which was thrust upon him at the time of the massacre. This seemed strangely suspicious to his Huguenot

* Pierre de l'Estoile — "*Journal de Henri III.*"

friends, and in their eyes contrasted very unfavourably with the religious zeal of the Prince de Condé. But his chief motive appears to have been to conciliate some of the moderate Catholic nobles who promised him their support. Several French writers attribute it to the doubts he entertained respecting both religions, and it must be confessed that if he was far from being a good Catholic, he was also a very lax Calvinist — indifferent to both faiths probably, except from political necessity.

Three months had elapsed when he resumed his profession of Protestantism, and attended as sponsor the baptism of the child of one of his Huguenot friends. But meanwhile the Duc d'Alençon, at the head of 30,000 men, was advancing in Gâtinais — Condé with the German auxiliaries having effected a junction with him, in spite of the efforts of the royalist troops under the Duc de Mayenne (younger brother of the Duc de Guise) to prevent it. Henri of Navarre had also begun to make war in Anjou and Le Maine, on a more limited scale, but with some success.

The aspect of affairs was threatening to royalty. But Henri III., leaving his mother to negotiate with the rebels and come to terms with them if she could, employed himself in the performance of his *neuvaines*, or nine days' acts of devotion, in the various churches of Paris. Usually he was accompanied by the young queen, who, being very devout herself, regarded her pious husband as almost a saint. "Afterwards," says L'Estoile — that indefatigable chronicler of the acts of Henri III. — "they drove in their coach through the streets of, Paris, or in the neighbourhood of the convents in the vicinity of the city, in search of small pet dogs, which the king carried away, to the great annoyance of the ladies to whom they belonged.

The great projects which Catherine had formed and proposed to carry out, aided by the martial prowess of this warrior king, had vanished into empty air. To the Montmorencys, who were to have been crushed, root and branch, she was compelled to make the most ample *amende honorable*, and to be indebted to their forbearance for an escort to the camp to treat for peace, while the king, not caring to be troubled with such matters, was engaged in puerile and effeminate amusements — painting, patching, and perfuming, and inventing new fashions. To the Guises, who were to have been wholly driven from any share in the government, and from every post, military or otherwise, of any importance — to be replaced, like the Montmorencys, by Italians — she was obliged to confide the chief commands in the army, and to depend on them to give some check to the troops of her rebel son and the confederate Huguenots and "Politiques," who, elated by their success, were exorbitant in their demands to an extent hitherto unparalleled.

Never before had such conditions been imposed on the crown. They were regarded as overwhelming and debasing to royalty, annoying and oppressive to the "pure Catholic party." Liberty of public worship was conceded to the Reformers throughout the kingdom, at any hour and at any place, except two leagues around Paris, and wherever the court were in residence. The marriages of priests and monks were to be declared legitimate; chambers, half Protestant, half Catholic, to be created, to judge any causes affecting the interests of the Protestants and "united Catholics;" the restitution of the confiscated property to the widows and children of the slaughtered victims of the 24th of August, 1572, and following days; the abolition of processions, and destruction of monuments founded in commemoration of the assassination of the first Prince de Condé and of the Saint-Bartholomew massacre.

These and many other conditions were agreed to, respecting reduction of taxes, the payment of 3,600,000 crowns to Jean Casimer for arrears of pay to the German cavalry; the triple increase of the Duc d'Alençon's appanage, by which he henceforth became Duc d'Anjou, and received an extra pension of 100,000 gold crowns. Also the restoration of the charges and offices in the government inherited by the King of Navarre and the Prince de Condé, together with the declaration that they and the Duc d'Alençon in the course they had taken had acted only in the service, and for the interests of the king.

In the name of Henri III., as authorised by him, this peace — known as the "Peace of Monsieur," it being chiefly on Alençon's account that it was concluded — was signed at Loches by the queen-mother towards the end of April. She was of opinion that it was necessary in the then state of affairs to submit to such a peace, and to concede everything that was asked, but with the full intention of observing none of its conditions save those concerning Alençon. By means of liberal concessions to him, she hoped to induce the duke to separate himself from the Protestants, while the full reconciliation she meditated with the Montmorencys, whom so lately she sought to assassinate, would detach them and the "Politiques" also, she supposed, from their alliance. The Huguenots, thus isolated, she still believed she could exterminate; the Guises for a time being tolerated, to assist, under Alençon, in that meritorious work.

Henri III., like his mother, was the very incarnation of falsehood and dissimulation. He assented generally to her views respecting this peace. But jealousy of Henri of Guise was one of his strongest feelings, and wholly to extirpate the heretics would, he thought, remove a wholesome check on the young duke's ambition. To a certain extent, then, heresy and heretics were to be tolerated in the land. Guise was to have the command of troops to oppose them, and thus be diverted from more dangerous occupation; but beyond that, the king's aim being to abase that family, no post of trust was to be given him.

But the Catholic party were not aware that the queen-mother had entered into engagements with the full purpose of breaking them as soon as the temporary difficulty she was in was removed. Nor did they seek to know what were either her or the contemptible king's secret motives for placing heretics on a political, social, and religious level with the "sons of the true Church." They looked at the fact only, and the more they considered it the greater became their indignation. Expressions of anger and contempt were heard on all sides against the king and his mother. In Paris especially, where they had urged on the people to commit the great crimes and sanguinary horrors of the 24th of August, which they now so basely disowned any complicity in, the Protestants and "Politiques," no less than Catholics, denounced their conduct in this respect as dastardly in the extreme. On the other hand, the privileges accorded them were considered by the Protestants as within their rights as Frenchmen rather than beyond them; while the Parliament, the clergy, and the people were as strongly opposed to them as the Catholic noblesse had declared themselves to be.*

The general exasperation of the Catholic party and the king's degraded position were promptly turned to advantage by the Duc de Guise. Under his influence the "pure Catholics" separated themselves from the royalist army, and, emboldened by the continued and excessive opprobrium cast on Henri and Catherine, attempted the formation of the league projected by his late uncle, the Cardinal de Lorraine. Faction was everywhere rife, and none possessed in a higher degree the qualities suited to the chief of a successful faction than Henri of Guise.

The influence of the House of Guise was supposed to be weakened by the death of the cardinal, the chief schemer and plotter of the family. This, however, was erroneous. The young duke was now twenty-four, and reputed one of the handsomest — if not actually the handsomest — man in France. "He is taller than the king," says the Venetian, Lippomano, "and more finely proportioned. His countenance is majestic, his eyes are lively and sparkling, his hair light and curly, his beard of similar colour. He displays admirable grace in all bodily exercises; as a fencer he has few equals. He is princely in his liberality; but

---

* The clergy of Notre-Dame refused to chant the customary Te Deum on the signing of peace, and the populace prevented the lighting of the bonfire in front of the Hôtel de Ville.

is said to spend more than he possesses. He is not satisfied with the manner in which affairs are conducted, for he is of that race of Catholics who have done so much for the faith."

The ambassador might have added that his ambition was excessive, and that on the ruins of the kingdom whose ill government he so deplored, his aim was to raise the throne of the self-asserted descendant of Charlemagne — Henri, Duke of Guise. He needed not the counsels of his uncle to guide him, as he possessed all the cardinal's political talent with the energy and audacity which were wanting in him. He had less military genius than his father, but more shrewdness, with a graciousness of manner and persuasive kind of oratory highly seductive to the people. The first proposal of the "Sainte Union," or Holy League, was made in Paris.* Papers were privately distributed amongst the most zealous of the Catholic *bourgeoisie*, containing the project of an association for the defence of religion, the king, and the liberty of the state.

It was first solemnly signed at Peronne, and soon after almost throughout Picardy. Other provinces then joined the League. The Pope hastened to give it his authorisation, and Philip II. his protection, aiding it both with men and money. "The members or associates of the League were

---

* The plan of the League, as drawn up by the cardinal in 1568, is amongst the MSS. of the Bibliothèque Nationale.

held bound to attack any and every one, without exception, who should attempt to oppose the 'Sainte Union.' Any member wishing to retire from it should be pursued, even unto death. The associates should swear strictly to obey the chief who might be elected to preside over them. Whoever should refuse to enter the association should be treated as an enemy and pursued as such. The oath was taken under pain of eternal damnation."

Thus was founded the famous Holy League. Subsidising committees were formed in almost every town in the kingdom, though Paris was the chief seat of its operations. More briefly described, the threefold object of the Leaguers was "to exterminate the Huguenots, confine the king in a monastery, and place Guise on his throne."

The King of Navarre and the Prince de Condé, on attempting to take possession of the Governor-Generalships of Guyenne and Picardy, secured to them by the secret articles of the Treaty of Loches, met with the greatest resistance from the inhabitants of those extreme Catholic provinces. Their complaints to the king being unheeded, they appeared in arms before several towns, and obtained possession of them without bloodshed, the inhabitants at once yielding.

The King of Navarre now demanded his sister, the Princesse Catherine, whose liberty was promised by the Peace of Loches. She was accordingly sent to Parthenay, where she was met by her brother, who conducted her to La Rochelle, and thence, after solemnly resuming her profession of Protestantism, to the Château of Nérac. His wife was refused him. But as it does not appear that he demanded her, her retention at the Court of France was probably rather a relief than a grief to him. Meanwhile, that part of the treaty concerning the Duc d'Alençon — become, in virtue of it, Duc d'Anjou — was being carried out with great ostentation. Favours and caresses were lavished upon him, and Catherine had appeared to be deeply moved when tenderly embracing those two dear sons, who so hated each other and whose reconciliation she had effected. He was installed with extraordinary pomp in the chief cities of his new appanage, Bourges and Tours, and his household established on a scale equalling the king's in numbers and magnificence. This was to induce him to forsake the allies by whose aid he had succeeded in the object of his ambition.

But the king — pressed on the one hand by the Protestants, who demanded more liberty than it was considered right to grant them, and on the other by the Leaguers, who desired to deprive him of his own freedom of action — thought to achieve a great stroke of policy by declaring himself the head of the League; rendering its conditions even more stringent than they already were, as regarded the maintenance of the "true Faith;" and at the same time preventing Guise from directing the association. He and his mother also proposed to bring all their influence to bear on the deputies of the States General about to assemble at Blois; their aim being to obtain from them the rejection of the treaty in conformity with whose stipulations they were themselves actually convoked, and thus adroitly to get rid of that embarrassing contract without the odium of refusing to fulfil its conditions.

The discussions of the states had been limited by the treaty to political questions, but were artfully turned to the frequent consideration of the advisability of maintaining but one religion in the state. Opinions differed concerning the method of securing this uniformity in matters of conscience. *La Messe ou la mort* pleased the fanatics of the three states; milder measures those of a more Christian spirit. But when, on the 1st of March, after several meetings, the king finally dismissed the deputies, the question remained undecided.

What the king had especially desired was that the states should vote him 300,000 gold crowns; ostensibly to enable him to secure by force the unity of religious faith in France, but really to squander on his worthless favourites, and in the licentious diversions he and his mother were so fond of indulging in. But Henri was disappointed. The states would give him nothing.

Hostilities were immediately renewed on all

sides, the terms of the treaty being generally disregarded. "Such a kingdom," says a French writer, "could only be governed by much iron and gold;" and Henri III. with great difficulty obtained either. His new taxes were resisted. The new offices he created none would buy. The army, receiving no pay, ravaged the country, pillaged the peasantry. There was also famine in the land, and a contagious epidemic increased the general distress. Henri could scarcely be said to reign; for in spite of him the Catholic League and the Protestant Confederation made war on each other. Once more the crown jewels were pledged; this time to Jean Casimer, who threatened to advance on France if the arrears due to his cavalry were not paid. The jewels not sufficing for the whole amount, the Duke of Lorraine became guarantee for the balance — 3,000,000 *francs*.

The King of Navarre was carrying on war with some success in Guyenne. The Prince de Condé had retired to La Rochelle — the indiscipline of his army and want of money to pay the arrears compelling him temporarily to leave Brouage. The League in consequence advanced a sufficient sum to the king to put on foot two small *corps d'armée*. The command of one was given to the new Duc d'Anjou, who proved himself a worthy Valois by marching against his friends, the confederates, now that their alliance had served his purpose. He had also become an advocate of "unity of religion." The command of the second corps was given to the young Duc de Mayenne.

This young gentleman — of whom the Venetian ambassador says, that "in form, feature, and manners no handsomer prince could be found in the world " — was so self-confident that on setting out with his troops he sent word to the king that he would on the morrow occupy Brouage and forward him the details of his entry by his major-domo. But neither on the morrow nor for several succeeding days did the major-domo make his appearance. Many conjectures were hazarded, and the Huguenots charged with spreading a report that Brouage neither was nor could be taken, that the duke had been put to flight, and with difficulty saved himself on board the fleet. At last the major-domo arrived, but with an account by no means so triumphant as the young general had led the king and queen-mother to expect. Brouage, though valorously defended, had finally capitulated, but on its own terms, which were forwarded as the basis of a new peace.

Maréchal de Montmorency had been prevailed on by Catherine to follow the example of the new Duc d'Anjou, and turn his arms against his recent allies. The towns he had placed in their hands refused to join in his defection. The command he had held was transferred to his brother, Maréchal Thoré, who had made profession of Calvinism at Geneva. With him was associated his nephew, Châtillon, the late admiral's eldest son.

But the great event of this short campaign was Anjou's siege of La Charité-sur-Loire, which capitulated after a short resistance. A terrible scene of carnage would have thus ensued, it appears, but for the interference of the Duc de Guise — second in command — who was courting popularity, and prevented Anjou from yielding to the clamorous demands of the brutal soldiers, eager for murder and pillage. The terms of the capitulation were therefore strictly observed.

This successful siege was exalted by the king, the queen-mother, and the court, into a great victory. Had Anjou conquered a whole province, his prowess could not have been more loudly proclaimed, or the trumpet of fame have blown a fiercer blast in his honour. He hastened his return to the court to revel in the glory of his triumph, and receive the laurel-wreath awaiting him at two grand *fêtes* of unusual splendour and even more than usual licentiousness. The first to be given by the king at Plessis-lez-Tours; the second by the queen-mother at Chenonceaux.

CHAPTER VI.

Chenonceaux, its Parks and Gardens.— A Preoccupied Mind and Empty Purse. — A Mythological Fête. — Banquet at Plessis-lez-Tours to the Hero.— The Queen-Mother's Banquet and Fête. — A Wife's Revenge. — Depravity of the Court of Henri III.— Cruelties of the Sack of Issoire.— Peace Signed at Bergerac, in Spite of the Pope.— A Bold Stroke of Policy.

THE most charming of all the royal residences of the sixteenth century, perhaps not excepting even Fontainebleau (in the time of the last Valois neglected and falling to ruin), was the picturesque château — one might almost say villa — of Chenonceaux. Unlike the royal châteaux generally, there was nothing of the monastery, state prison, or feudal fortress in its architectural aspect. It was then a veritable *maison de plaisance*, rising Venus-like from the midst of the limpid waters of the River Cher, which glided through a smiling valley of the province of Touraine. It was connected with the river's banks by an elegant bridge on either side, of five arches.

Catherine, as before mentioned, had long coveted Chenonceaux, and from the time it passed into her hands, at the death of Henri II., in exchange for the gloomy fortress of Chaumont, she had added a grand gallery to the château, and greatly embellished the extensive gardens, according to the taste of the period. It was at Chenonceaux that Catherine de' Medici proposed to fitly celebrate the Duc d'Anjou and Touraine's great feat of arms by a splendid *fête*, or "triumph," as such festivities then were named.

Preceding it by some days, an entertainment in the young hero's honour was to be given by the citizens of Tours, to be followed by a royal banquet. But Catherine had a double object in view. Besides fêting the younger son on his taking possession of his appanage, and on the military success he had achieved, she was desirous of raising the spirits of the elder one. Henri III. had lately shown symptoms of a sombre preoccupation of mind very unusual with him — occasioned by the unsatisfactory result, as he considered it, of the conferences of the States General, in refusing to vote him the large sums of money he then needed for his own and his favourites' use. The menacing increase of the popularity of the Duc de Guise, of whose projects against his dynasty and against his crown revelations of undoubted authenticity had reached him, added greatly to his perplexity.*

"The League, too, 'the Holy League' — what embarrassment that project of the Guises seemed likely to end in! He would find some means of

---

* A copy of this project of the League was sent to Henri III. by Saint-Goard, ambassador at the Court of Spain.

freeing himself from it. He would put an end to the association, after he had made use of it for awhile to weaken and perplex the Huguenots and oblige them to accept conditions of peace very different from those of 'the Peace of Monsieur.'" The next peace, in opposition to it, should be the King's Peace — for the concessions wrung from him by his ambitious brother, with arms in his hands, and supported by heretics, seemed to Henri no cause for great rejoicing.

However, money would be forthcoming from some quarter. Those Italian financiers who followed Catherine to France, and now farmed the royal revenue, were accustomed to make advances to royalty when the treasury was empty — as it usually was. It was not usual, however, to pay the so-called loans. "The farmers" paid themselves from any surplus of revenue they might consider, after their own claims were satisfied, due to the king. From that source the queen-mother — who was an adept in arranging these private fiscal transactions — supplied the monarch's wants. Troublesome concerns of state were at once forgotten, and under the cheering influence of a full purse, so soon again to be empty, the king banished gloomy thoughts and returned with fresh zest to his dissolute pleasures.

On the 15th of May the new Duc de Touraine made his entry into Tours, "wearing a dress of sky blue and silver brocade, bordered with pearls and precious stones." A triumphal arch was erected at the entrance of the city, the façade representing an altar surmounted by a statue of Concord, which many persons were heard to say should have been Discord, as the statue had borrowed the features of Catherine de' Medici. But to make it clear to all whom it was intended to represent, a stork and a pelican — emblems of maternal tenderness — were placed at Concord's feet, with the motto, *Æquus Amor* — an allusion to the equal love the queen was supposed to bear towards her two sons. The king and his brother, as Castor and Pollux, stood at the sides of the altar, carrying in their hands blunt-edged swords (*épées émoussées*).

The *fête*, given by the city of Tours, was entirely of a mythological character. There were nymphs, naïades, and Olympian divinities, who presented the duke with verses, extolling his many virtues, and comparing him to Mars himself. Ceres came down, it appears, expressly from Olympus, bearing the arms of Sicily to implore the victorious general to deliver her from captivity — the House of Valois thus declaring that its former pretensions to that kingdom were not abandoned.

In the evening of that day Henri III. received his brother at Plessis-lez-Tours, the sombre château of Louis XI. The entertainment there offered to the duke and his conquering companions-in-arms was "one of those Asiatic orgies fully justifying the appellations of Herod and Sardanapalus, given by the leaguers to the King of France." The ladies of the court, "the most beautiful and the most virtuous," took upon themselves the duties of the service of the banquet. They wore male attire, and guests and attendants were all clad in green silk, which, to the amount of 60,000 *francs*, was furnished for that occasion by the silk merchants of Paris (L'Estoile).

On the following Sunday the queen-mother invited the court to repair to Chenonceaux to share in the festivities she had prepared in honour of the victorious general. In the picturesque beauty of scene, and the splendour of the preparations, this *fête* far surpassed the preceding ones, and eclipsed, it is said, in its immodesty and sensuality even the orgies of Plessis-lez-Tours. Henri III. was dressed, as was his habit, in a style which, excepting the trunk-hose, was more feminine than masculine — lips and cheeks rouged, earrings, bracelets, and a necklace of pearls. His favourites were similarly attired, and painted and perfumed like their master; their hair curled, and over it a small velvet cap, such as women had lately taken to wear. "To look at their heads," says L'Estoile, "rising immediately out of their wide, stiffly starched ruffs, one is reminded of John the Baptist's head in a dish."

Opposite the king sat the Duc d'Anjou, also surrounded by his favourites, who omitted no occasion of braving those of the king's suite. Bussy d'Amboise, the duke's first gentleman, whom he had already made Governor of Anjou and Abbot of Bourgueil, affected a very cavalier air, for the purpose of contrast with the effeminate manners of his adversaries. On the occasion in question he was well dressed, but simply and plainly. Standing behind him, however, were six of his pages in cloth of gold, which gave him the opportunity of remarking, while he looked steadily at the king's gentlemen, that the time had cóme to give up all these gay dresses and finery to his rascals or serving-men.

The three queens, Catherine, Marguerite, and Louise, were present at this banquet and *fête*. Louise de Vaudemont was regarded as remarkably devout; but devotion at the Court of the Valois was not rigidly unsociable, and confessors readily came to terms with their penitents. As at Plessis, the ladies of the "flying squadron" waited on the gentlemen at the queen-mother's banquet, some of them in male attire, others with very little attire of any kind. The wife of the marshal, Duc de Retz, acting as *grande maîtresse*, had the general superintendence of the *fête*. The beautiful Madame de Suave—afterwards Marquise de Noirmoutiers—who had fascinated both the King of Navarre and the Duc d'Anjou, and privately flirted a little with the Duc de Guise, played the part of *maîtresse d'hôtel*. Amongst other court beauties was the celebrated Madame de Châteauneuf, who waited on Catherine's princely and noble guests. She had been Henri's mistress until he fell so desperately in love with the Princesse de Condé. Very lately she had married, for love, a Florentine named Antinoli, one of Catherine's *protégés*. A few days after this *fête*, having discovered that her husband was intriguing with one of the queen's suite, she unhesitatingly stabbed him and laid him dead at her feet.

The beautiful park of Chenonceaux was brilliantly illuminated on the evening of the *fête*, and a ball was given in the recently completed grand gallery of the château. Catherine had sent to Italy for choice marbles for its decoration, also for pictures, for painting was then at a low ebb in France. One or two sculptors of note yet remained; but art generally had suffered from continual intestine warfare, and the struggle for religious freedom.* At the end of the gallery was a small but elegant theatre, where some Ital-

* The celebrated sculptor, Jean Goujon, mysteriously disappeared at the time of the Saint-Bartholomew massacre. He had adopted the "new opinions," and is supposed to have been butchered by some jealous inferior artist, while engaged in working on the bas-reliefs of the Louvre. Many eminent men of various professions or distinguished for learning — the philosopher Ramus, for instance — were slain from revenge and similar base motives on that dreadful day of bloodshed.

ian comedians played a farce, with which the queen-mother's *fête* concluded.

"The king," says L'Estoile, "had sent to Venice for this troupe, called 'les Gelosi,' to amuse him during the weary time that the States General held their discussions at Blois. On their journey thither they were taken prisoners by a detachment of the confederate army, who compelled the king to ransom them. Their repertoire was not, it seems, a very edifying one, though well suited, apparently, to amuse a court abandoned to an unparalleled course of depravity. Licentiousness was unbounded; decency was outraged with unblushing effrontery; duels and murders were of daily occurrence; all favours and dignities were bestowed on the king's favourites. Money would buy his clemency; fear often extorted it."

"Nothing in our history," writes a French historian,[*] "offers the slightest analogy with the Court of Henri III. To find any similar union of debauchery and ferocity, of folly and sanguinary levity, we must go back to the most depraved epochs of ancient Rome. On the surface of this chaos of impurity floated a taste for art and literature. Henri III. greatly honoured Ronsard, and heaped many favours on the poet Desportes — the latter an agreeable writer, but less brilliant, and either wiser or more timid, than

[*] M. Henri Martin.

Ronsard. Henri encouraged the arts after the manner of his mother — provided they lent themselves to his vices — another trait of resemblance with the Court of the Cæsars. Nero also was an artist!"

That which gave a peculiar character to the Court of Henri III. was, on one part, the association of bigotry with the most hideous libertinism; on the other, a remaining trace of the chivalric spirit — vitiated, corrupted, yet bold and adventurous even to madness. The younger courtiers played with death with a sort of frenzy — making it a point of honour to defy the same dangers for women steeped in depravity, audacious, voluptuous, but sparklingly witty, as the knights of old braved for their chaste lady-loves."*

* Catherine revived at these *fêtes* the Courts of Love (Cours d'Amour), which had been held throughout France from the twelfth to the sixteenth century. They were at once the schools and the tribunals where prizes were decreed to the best poets and the most faithful lovers; where problems of gallantry were solved; where proceedings were instituted and individuals condemned. There the ladies officiated as judges, and from them there was no appeal. In spite of the ridicule attaching to such an institution, vanity and fashion made these tribunals — over which princesses sometimes presided, and in which husbands were not permitted to complain of the indifference of their wives — much sought after, and even feared. The Comtesse de Champagne, daughter of Thibaud, Duc de Champagne, decided in her tribunal that "In love, all is favour; in marriage, all is necessity; consequently love cannot exist between married people." The Queen Eléonore, wife of Louis VII., to whom an appeal was made against so startling a decision, replied, " Ah, Heaven for-

The *fêtes* of Chenonceaux having come to an end, the Duc d'Anjou set out to rejoin his army, which during his absence had laid siege to Issoire. This town made but a poor defence, and surrendered when called upon, at discretion. The army thereupon fully compensated itself for the loss of the sack of La-Charité — pillaging and burning the town, insulting the women, and inflicting horrible cruelties on the inhabitants generally, finally putting them all to the sword — sparing not even the poor children.

Further success at Tonnay-Charente and Rochefort attended the Catholic army under Mayenne, commanding the second *corps d'armée* — both those young generals being guided by officers of experience. Union and good order appear to have existed no longer among the confederates. The nobles were not on good terms with the *bourgeoisie*, and great indiscipline reigned amongst the soldiers. To this was attributed Mayenne's successful siege of Brouage — the second maritime city possessed by the Huguenots. Two of the larger vessels of the Rochellois fleet, in endeavouring to revictual Brouage, were taken by the united Bordelais and Breton squadron. The King of Navarre, who was

bid that I should be so audacious as to dispute the decisions of the Comtesse de Champagne." As this countess was afterwards queen, and Eléonore was divorced, there may have been some jealousy existing between these ladies. Eléonore in 1154 became Queen of England, having married, six weeks after her divorce, young Henry Plantagenet, Henry II. Her dowry was Poitou and Aquitaine.

carrying on a sort of guerilla warfare in Guyenne, was unable to aid his party in sufficient force to prevent the fall of Brouage, whose inhabitants, dissatisfied with the surrender, attempted further resistance.

War at this time was renewed in different parts of the kingdom, and proposals of peace carried on simultaneously with it. Henri desired peace that he might less interruptedly give up his time to his pleasures and his devotions. The Pope, Philip II., and the Guises used every secret influence in their power to prevent it. They desired the work of extermination to go on. Gregory XIII. even tempted the king with the offer of 900,000 *livres* as a contribution towards its expenses. But Catherine's voice was also for peace, and neither Anjou's, nor Mayenne's partial successes, nor the Pope's offer, dazzled her.

Maréchal de Biron was despatched by Henri III. to the King of Navarre offering favourable conditions, which being accepted by the latter, who on his side showed great moderation in his demands, preliminaries were concluded, and peace signed at Bergerac, on the 27th of September. The confederate army, under Thoré de Montmorency and Châtillon, had just succeeded, in spite of opposition, in revictualling Montpellier, preparatory to standing a siege against royalist troops, commanded by their former general, Damville de Montmorency. Already were they drawn up under the city walls, when, on the 2nd of October, La Noue arrived *en courrier* from Bergerac, to inform the combatants on both sides that peace was concluded between the King of France and the King of Navarre.

This peace, being established on a sufficiently reasonable basis, moderate Catholics and Protestants were fain to be content with, though not fully granting all the confederate demands. At all events, as a truce only, it was welcome to the people, from their utter weariness of this never-ending warfare and its attendant evils. In opposition to the peace of the preceding year, "*La Paix de Monsieur*," the king called this peace "*La Paix du Roi.*"

He piqued himself also on having effectually thwarted the views of "the Lorrainers — those *soi-disant* descendants of Charlemagne" — by so bold a stroke of policy as including the Holy League itself in the decree which dissolved the Huguenot Confederation and annulled all leagues, associations, and fraternities whatsoever. This, with the failure of the League to find acceptance at the States of Blois, postponed for a time the realisation of the plans of the Guise faction.

"Thus, breathing-time was given to each party while preparing for further hostilities;" and as all desired repose after so much fatigue and anxiety, the court returned to Paris, the king henceforth rarely absenting himself from his capital.

CHAPTER VII.

Catherine of Navarre. — Offers of Marriage. — The King's Piety Lauded by Priests and Monks.— Quarrels and Duels Amongst the King's Favourites.— Order of the Saint-Esprit Instituted. — Great Expectations Disappointed. — Plot of Gregory XIII. and Don John of Austria.— High Words between the King and His Brother.— The Duke's Escape; His Mother Pursues.—Anjou's Visit to Queen Elizabeth.

IN default of a queen, who was amusing herself elsewhere, the little Court of Nérac was presided over by the Princesse Catherine of Navarre. Henri had no sooner obtained his own and his sister's liberty than he strove to fulfil his mother's dying injunctions, as expressed in her testament, prepared in the presence of Admiral de Coligny and the Cardinal de Bourbon. In it she exhorted him "to take his sister Catherine under his protection, to be her guardian and defender, and, after God, to serve her as a father; to treat her with gentleness and goodness; to have her brought up at Béarn, and to appoint only ladies of the same religion to attend her and to be her companions until she was of an age to marry a Protestant prince of her own rank."

All this to the best of his ability he had done. He also confided to his sister, during his frequent absence from Nérac, the government of his small kingdom, assisted of course by experienced advisers, for Catherine was but seventeen. Her natural gaiety, in which she greatly resembled her brother, had received a severe shock from the sad events of the last few years. The death of her mother, to whom she was deeply attached, her separation from her brother and the murder of many of her friends during the frightful Saint-Bartholomew massacre, had a great effect on the young princess.

She fell into a state of profound melancholy, which all the care and maternal attentions of the Duchesse de Tignonville — her mother's friend, who had accompanied her to Paris and now remained with the orphan daughter — long failed to banish. But time and a joyous temperament, and especially her return to her home, produced happy results. The young Huguenot princess had at least regained cheerfulness, and is said to have very skilfully succeeded in restraining the pretensions and gallantries of the more youthful and ardent members of the court; also in feigning not to perceive, what she lamented but was unable to prevent, her brother's numerous amours.

The Court of the Princess of Navarre sometimes removed to Pau, and though it was strictly Calvinistic, and possessed neither the brilliancy nor the vices of the Court of France, yet it was not, on the whole, a dull court. We hear of Sully — or rather Maximilian de Béthune, Baron de Rosny — then a youth of sixteen or seventeen, being instructed by Catherine herself in the steps and figures of a ballet she had arranged to give, and desired that he should take part in it.* High also in her favour at that time was the Vicomte de Turenne; there was even a question of their marriage. But Henri did not approve, and Catherine's feeling towards him appears to have been that of friendship rather than love.†

Du Plessis-Mornay, too, was very assiduous in his attentions to Catherine. He was a rigid Calvinist of very serious manners, and his aim was to confirm the princess in her Protestant profession. He was greatly attached to the King of Navarre, but his relations with Catherine were strictly religious. His "*Méditations sur l'Evangile*" was written for her use, and was dedicated to her.

The Duc d'Anjou, though he had not renounced the hope of sharing the English throne with Eliz-

---

* Rosny, at twelve years of age, was near falling a victim to the massacre of Saint-Bartholomew. A Roman Catholic *livre d'heures* he had in his possession saved him. The principal of the College of Burgundy afterwards concealed him for several days until the massacre ended in Paris (A. de Beauchamp).

† Until 1572 Turenne had been a Catholic; but horror of a religion that could sanction and approve the sanguinary deeds of the Saint-Bartholomew massacre led him to renounce the Roman faith and embrace Protestantism (L'Estoile).

abeth, yet privately sent Maréchal de Biron to Nérac to ask the hand of the Princesse Catherine. Both she and her brother declined the honour, on the ground of difference of religion. But had it been otherwise, as the queen-mother was opposed to the alliance, she would doubtless have prevented it. For to her it was merely a choice between the middle-aged heretic queen of a powerful kingdom, and a young heretic princess with a few estates in Gascony. Whatever the son might have done, had his proposal been favourably received, Catherine de' Medici certainly would not have hesitated in deciding for the former.

Henri III. was too much occupied with his devotions to give heed at that time either to Anjou's matrimonial views, or to his ambitious aims respecting the Netherlands. His public processions, his pilgrimages, his gifts to the Church, his foundation of new convents, and general participation in all ecclesiastical mummeries, while they excited the anger and contempt of all who were not fanatics, gained him the loudly expressed praises of certain priests and monks. The head of the newly established and severely ascetic Order of reformed Bernardine monks "declared the king to be so much attached to the crucifix that it was no longer himself, but Christ who dwelt within him." A mystery and a miracle that should have edified the faithful. He had also in his favour the further testimony of his Jesuit confessor, the famous Edmond Auger — one of the most violent and sanguinary of his Order — that "France for long years past had not been blessed with a ruler so pious as Henri III."

This ought surely to have closely bound in brotherhood those ardent defenders of the Holy Catholic Church — the House of Guise — and the devout monarch who sat on the throne of France. But an inextinguishable hatred alone subsisted between them. In Henri, terror of their great influence was allied with hate; and the desire of opposing some obstacle to their designs was regarded as one of his chief motives for instituting at this time the famous military Order of the Saint-Esprit. It was also considered in some degree as a tribute of respect to the memory of three of his favourites who had recently been slain in a duel.

This duel, an instance of the many that were constantly taking place amongst Henri's courtiers, had for its cause one of the dissolute intrigues of the court, called love affairs, in which the name of Queen Marguerite was mentioned. The quarrel arose in the court of the Louvre, between the Marquis de Caylus, Livarrot, and Maugiron, Henri's three favourites, and Riberac, Schomberg, and the young Comte d'Antragues — the creatures, or favourites, of the Guises. It led to a meeting at five the next morning — 27th of April — in the horse market, near the Bastille Saint-Antoine, there to settle their quarrel at the point of the sword. They fought so desperately that Maugiron and Schomberg soon lay dead on the Place. Riberac died the next morning, and Livarrot, after being six weeks ill from a severe wound in the head, recovered only to die soon after in another duel. Caylus received nineteen wounds, and died after languishing five weeks. Antragues escaped with a few scratches.

The king during Caylus's illness scarcely stirred from his bedside. He promised him 100,000 gold crowns if he recovered, besides a fee of 100,000 *livres* to the surgeon. This, however, did not save him. Throughout his illness, while sighing heavily, he was constantly exclaiming with all the force and regret he was able, "*Ah! mon roy! mon roy!*" without (says L'Estoile) ever mentioning his aged mother, or uttering the name of God. The king had the greatest regard for Caylus and Maugiron. He embraced them when dead; had their heads shaven, and preserved their flowing locks. He took the earrings from Caylus's ears; having formerly given them to him and placed them in his ears himself.

Their bodies were laid on beds of state, as though they were royal personages. The whole court attended their funeral, and Henri erected two splendid monuments to their memory in the Church of Saint-Paul, where the ancient royal Houses of France, and those of the chief nobility, had for two or three centuries usually buried their dead. The celebrated sculptor, Germain Pilon, was employed to execute these monuments, to which, shortly after, a third was added, to the memory of Saint-Mesgrin, another favourite, who, one evening on leaving the Louvre, was assassinated by three men, masked, who were lying in wait for him at the corner of the Rue Saint-Honoré. Henri dared not order an inquiry into the affair, or command the arrest of the assassins, for it was well known to him that the Duc de Guise had deprived him of this favourite on discovering that Saint-Mesgrin was intriguing with his duchess. The king had therefore to content himself with spending the public money on his funeral, which was of almost royal splendour.*

On New Year's Day, 1578, vespers having been said on the previous evening, the king solemnised with great magnificence, in the Church of the Augustines at Paris, the foundation of his new Order of the Saint-Esprit. Henri gave as a reason for placing this military Order under the invocation of the Holy Ghost, that it was in memory of his having been elevated to two thrones — those of France and Poland — on the day of Pentecost. His object in instituting it was to

* The three tombs, which were remarkable as works of art, were destroyed by the people in 1588, a few days before the day of the barricades, in the excess of their rage against the king, and their enthusiasm for the Duc de Guise.

maintain, he said, the Catholic religion, and to reinstate nobility in its due dignity and splendour.

On the two following days, after hearing mass, the king entertained the new chevaliers at dinner, in the refectory of the same church, afterwards holding a council of the Order. The chevaliers were twenty-seven in number, to be increased as occasion served to a hundred. They wore black velvet caps; trunk-hose and doublet of cloth of silver; shoes, and sword-scabbard of white velvet. The grand mantle was of black velvet, embroidered with *fleur-de-lys* in gold — tongues of fire being intermixed — the king's monogram also appearing, embroidered in silver thread. The mantle was lined with orange-coloured satin. Over it, instead of a hood, was worn a small mantelet embroidered to correspond with the mantle.

The grand collar of the Order was interlaced with *fleur-de-lys*, tongues of fire, and the king's monogram. A gold cross, elaborately chiselled and enamelled, and having in the centre a silver dove, was suspended to the collar by a blue riband. The members were called Knights-Commanders of the Holy Ghost. They were sworn to defend the Catholic religion, the King of France, and his domains. The king's intention was to present each chevalier with 800 crowns in the form of a commanderie on certain benefices of the kingdom; to provide for his knights, in fact, at the expense of the clergy, by disposing of Church lands to the extent of 200,000 gold crowns.

But the Pope, who had not forgiven Henri his concessions to the Protestants in the Treaty of Bergerac, disapproved; declaring that he could not in conscience consent to it. He also desired the nuncio to decline attending the ceremony of the king's installation as grand-master. Besides the chevaliers, there were present but six bishops, two ambassadors — Venetian and Scotch — the reigning queen, and two or three princesses, all resplendent with jewels. The institution of the new Order by a less unpopular ruler would not have been unwelcome to the royalist nobility, — the Order of Saint-Michel having become so common that no person of any rank cared to possess it. The collar of that Order was called "*le collier à toutes bêtes.*"*

The king appears to have conferred the Order judiciously in his first promotion — the knights being either men of high rank, able diplomatists, or military officers of merit. In a second promotion he included the Duc de Guise, — the statutes of the Order strictly imposing on the knights certain engagements, of which Henri thought to take advantage and turn against Guise when occasion should arise. He had, indeed, looked for great results from the creation of this new Order; but disappointment followed. It was not sought after,

* Pierre de l'Estoile — "*Journal de Henri III.*"

and but few valued it more than the Saint-Michel. Stability to his throne was not to be gained by such means, any more than his pious amusement of masquerading about Paris in a penitent's sack could secure the respect of the people.

Whilst Henri was fruitlessly engaged with his vain precautions against the Guises, his ambitious brother of Anjou, since the great increase of his appanage — almost a kingdom within a kingdom — had also become an object of his fear and hatred, though in a somewhat less degree than the "Lorrainers." The tyranny and sanguinary deeds of the Spaniards in the Netherlands, equalling in atrocity the horrors of the Saint-Bartholomew massacre, had occasioned the separation of the seven northern provinces and the signing of a new compact amongst themselves, called the "Union of Utrecht." The Duc d'Anjou aspired to the sovereignty of these provinces, at the same time continuing secretly to press his suit on Elizabeth.

His sister Marguerite returned to Paris about this time from the baths of Spa, where she feigned to have been for her health. But during her residence there she concluded the treaty between the Duc d'Anjou, the Comte Lalaing, and other Flemish nobles, without raising any suspicion in Don John, whom she dined with at Namur, of the real object of her journey. Don John (the natural son of Charles V. of Spain) had also his views on

England and her queen, but differing greatly from those of the restless Anjou.

In concert with the Pope and with the sanction of his half-brother, Philip II., Don John proposed to foment a rising of the Anglo-Scotch Catholics; to release Mary Stuart from captivity; to marry her; to dethrone Elizabeth and put Mary in her place — he, of course, sharing the throne with her. The Prince of Orange revealed this plot to the queen. Naturally she was incensed against Don John. She immediately signed a defensive treaty with the States General of the Netherlands; undertook to pay the troops Jean Casimer was then levying, and to send besides a strong detachment from England. Don John's death at Namur, a few months later, put an end to his and the Pope's vain scheme against Elizabeth.

The Duc d'Anjou was very anxious at this moment to enter Flanders, but with a sufficiently numerous force to contend effectively with the Spaniards. His sister, well informed of the state of things in the Netherlands, pressed him to carry out this enterprise. But the king would not aid his brother's designs, though he did not forbid them. He thought that he had already made him too powerful. Still Marguerite secretly urged Anjou to persist, and even more emphatically than before.

One of those frequent quarrels between the king's and the duke's favourites, the latter — incited usually by Bussy d'Amboise — jeering and laughing at the effeminacy of the former, produced at this time high words between Henri III. and the Duc d'Anjou. The duke determined to leave the court that night for his own city of Angers, and no persuasion could induce him to remain. He resisted the entreaties of both the queen-mother and the Queen of France, who, leaving the ballroom where the marriage festivities of one of the king's favourites were being celebrated with great magnificence, earnestly prayed him to stay; pointing out the unpleasant consequences that would ensue from his sudden departure. But "Monsieur" was too highly incensed to yield. He desired, also, to assert his independence; "he was no longer to be detained at court against his will at the good pleasure of his brother." The ladies left him in despair.

The king himself then resolved to seek the duke, and condescend to entreat when, as he said, he might well command. When the king entered, "Monsieur" was drawing on his travelling boots, his horses and equipage being then in waiting for him. "For his own sake, his own interests as heir to the throne, Henri implored his brother to avoid an open rupture. If it should not prove an offence to honourable men, it would certainly embolden evil-doers and strengthen the pretensions of the rebels." With an affectation of brotherly solicitude, Henri eloquently argued with the obstinate prince, for it appears that he had eminently the gift of eloquence, though he employed it for no good purpose. However, it failed to make Anjou give up his project.

The king then, in a great passion, rising from his chair, said: "As you are determined to go, go then—if you can!"

He then called the captain of his archers, and ordered him to prevent any attempt of "Monsieur" to leave his room. The duke's favourites were then arrested and sent to the Bastille. Bussy d'Amboise was said to have left the city, but was found in the duke's cabinet hidden between the mattress and paillasse of the bed. The king's declared resolve to punish all who had taken any part in this quarrel occasioned great alarm. Many of the duke's attendants, expecting either the block or the gibbet, disguised themselves and sought refuge in the Venetian ambassador's hôtel.*

Early on the morrow the Queen of Navarre visited her captive brother. She advised him to bend to circumstances, and to dissemble his purpose of leaving. The advice was at once adopted; he asked to see the king, and expressed his regret at what had occurred. The brothers embraced each other; the queen-mother, with a display of

* The Venetian ambassador at that time was Geronimo Lippomano, who being greatly in favour at court, and on terms of greater intimacy with the king than was the case with ambassadors generally, his intercession was probably entreated. It is from his report and L'Estoile's "Journal" that the above account is chiefly taken.

tender emotion, embraced her sons, and all concerned in this silly affair were pardoned, the king and the duke eventually promising that harmony should henceforth subsist between them. Peace being made, and all angry feeling in appearance subsided, the court — it being carnival time — resumed its *fêtes* and dances.

On Shrove Tuesday, the 14th of February, another marriage, that of Henri's favourite, Epinay, with Mademoiselle de Brissac, was celebrated with great pomp at the Louvre by the expressed command of the king. The bride was wealthy, but is said to have been deformed, humpbacked and ugly, and what, according to the scandal and gossip of the court, was deemed worse, she employed every artifice to appear otherwise, which, certainly, was scarcely blamable. The quatrain upon her by one of the court rhymers was:

> "Brissac aime tant l'artifice,
> Tant du dedans que du dehors,
> Qu' ôtez lui le faux et le vice,
> Vous lui ôtez l'âme et le corps."

This marriage, as was usual at the marriages of the king's favourites, was accompanied by lavish gifts of lands, money, jewels, and titles to the bridegroom. It was disapproved apparently by the queen-mother and her daughter, who, to avoid attending the ceremony, went in the morning for a ramble with "Monsieur" in the wood of Vincennes. Marguerite probably knew, though the queen-mother was not aware of it, that he intended to escape that night. The brothers seemed to be on the best of terms, and concord — as Lippomano observes when moralising on the event — firmly established between them. "But," he continues, "the imprudence of founding any hopes on the secret intentions of man too soon became apparent."

About seven o'clock in the evening the duke, pretexting that he had promised to sup with the abbot, repaired to the Abbey of Sainte-Geneviève. At a certain part of the abbey, prepared for the purpose by the abbot, who was in his confidence, he let himself down by a cord into the moat, Bussy d'Amboise and others following. Horses awaited them, and with all speed they departed for Angers. Having allowed a few hours to elapse that the duke might be well on his way, the abbot late at night went to the Louvre to inform the king of his brother's departure. He had been tied in his chair, he said, while the duke and his companions made good their escape, or he would have brought the intelligence earlier.

Henri flew into a terrible rage — one of those frenzied fits of anger to which, like François I., he was occasionally subject. The queen-mother, more calm, listened quietly to the abbot's report, of which, probably, she was not the dupe. Early on the morrow, 15th of February, she set out in pursuit of this troublesome son, whose ambition, instead, as she had thought, of being satisfied, seemed rather to have grown with the increase of his possessions. On the 20th of March she returned from Angers, by no means pleased with the reception she had met with. She expected the duke to ride out, escorted by the gentlemen of his suite, to receive her; a courier having been despatched to announce her arrival. Bussy d'Amboise and La Châtre, another of Anjou's gentlemen, alone, at three leagues from the château, awaited her.

"Where was 'Monsieur'?" she inquired.

"He was indisposed."

"Perhaps they were detaining him a prisoner?"

They smiled, but replied, "He was unable to walk, and had sent them to conduct her to the château."

She, however, declined to accompany them, saying she "preferred to lodge in a place of safety." She therefore remained some days, awaiting the duke at a residence in the vicinity. But as he came not, she determined — well accompanied — to venture to the château.* But what was her indignation when, instead of the great gates being

---

* It had been predicted a few months back that a "great queen" was to die in the course of the year; but whether "naturally or otherwise," as it was customary to say at that period, the astrologers had refrained from mentioning. Cather-

thrown wide open to receive her, she was invited to pass through the wicket. "Such an affront," she declared, "had never before been offered her;" and "Monsieur" was not there to receive her. Presently, however, he made his appearance carried in an armchair by two of his servants, and pretending to have broken his leg.

The interview was most unsatisfactory to the queen-mother. She could not turn Anjou from his purpose of making war on Flanders. And his bandaged leg, to which he pointed, excused him from escorting her, as she expected, a league or two on her return to Paris. Thus he escaped her further importunity. But he had already written to the king that his enterprise was in no way directed against him or the state. Yet while professing to have renounced all connection with the Huguenots, he was then in communication with La Noue and other Huguenot captains, and secretely employing them to levy troops for his expedition to Flanders.

With about 7,000 volunteers, Protestant and Catholic, he crossed the frontier on the 10th of July, "this small army of Frenchmen on its march across France causing more havoc and devastation

---

ine was in a terrible fright lest she should be the "great queen" referred to. Hence her precautions, and her unwillingness to enter her son's château. Even there some plot might be organised against her life. And who would regret her? None. There would rather be rejoicings.

than that of a barbarous enemy — killing, pillaging, destroying." The duke announced himself as " having taken up arms for the defence of an oppressed people, being authorised to embrace their cause by the ancient rights of France on Flanders." In the following month the States General concluded an alliance with him, and declared him " Defender of the liberties of the Netherlands." But there were more "defenders of the oppressed" in the field than the Duc d'Anjou — the Queen of England, the Prince of Orange, the Prince Jean Casimer, the Archduke Mathias, all with their armies, but all with different views and interests. Nor did Catholics and Protestants act together with the unanimity that had been looked for from their common hatred of the Spaniards. This was very favourable for the latter, who, had discord not prevailed amongst their opponents, might have been effectually overthrown.

Two small towns were taken by Anjou, who, weary of waiting for a brilliant victory by the combined forces, and having too small a troop to attempt conquest on his own account, returned to France in January, hoping to induce the king to aid him with the means of getting together a larger body of men, horse and foot. He, however, did not return to the court immediately. Thinking it right that his arrival should be as unexpected as his departure, he and his suite at two o'clock one morning in March clamoured for entrance at the gates of the Louvre, rousing the king and the whole of his household from their slumbers. There was some momentary alarm, but Henri received his brother cordially. He attempted to dissuade him from further military adventures, and spoke disparagingly of the English marriage, but did not positively refuse the aid he sought.

Four days later, "Monsieur" was on his way to Angers. After sojourning there a month or so, he suddenly decided on taking a step from which he expected results as great as those he was still flattered with in the Netherlands. Accompanied only by M. de Chauvillon and a *valet de chambre*, the Duc d'Anjou set out for England, without a word of notice to his brother, to ask the hand of Queen Elizabeth in person. His servants even thought he had returned to Flanders. But wind and weather detaining him seven days at Boulogne for a favourable opportunity of crossing the Channel, his destination became known. Yet this was considered but a pretext to cover his views on that country. He, however, continued his journey to London, and took up his quarters with the French ambassador. Afterwards he was invited to the Palace of Greenwich as the queen's guest, Elizabeth receiving him very graciously on his journey two miles from the city.

Personally unattractive, being, like his mother, very short and inclined to corpulence, and his face — whatever it may have been as a youth — so terribly scarred and seamed by the ravages of the smallpox, that not a trace of good looks was left in it, he yet was so lively, so full of youthful spirits, that Elizabeth appeared to be pleased with him. A few vague words were all that passed with reference to the marriage; but presents of considerable value are said to have been exchanged. "It was further said (Lippomano) that the queen every morning, with her own fair hand, brought the prince a cup of bouillon, and that he had appeared before her in a doublet of flesh-coloured silk, that she might see that he was not humpbacked, as had been reported."

"But political matters formed the chief subject of their conversation. The prudent Elizabeth held out the bait of marriage, only to sustain her suitor's professed hatred of Spain." However, "Monsieur" was satisfied with the result of his visit, and buoyant with hope he recrossed the Channel. The matrimonial negotiation, notwithstanding, rather languished after Anjou's visit. "Various untrue rumors," says the ambassador, "were afloat respecting it, owing to the precipitation, or rather volatility, of the French, who report things as done before doing them, and sometimes do them before having even thought of them."

Anjou, it appears, had made some promise to his brother, after his return, to reside at the court for a time. "And he kept his word," Lippomano tells us, "showing that the devil is less black than he is painted." The king also seems to have been astonished that his brother should have kept his word, as he gave him in acknowledgment of it 800,000 *francs*.

CHAPTER VIII.

Marguerite Conducted to Her Husband. — Henri of Navarre Declines to Receive Her. — The Venetian Ambassador, Geronimo Lippomano. — Concessions to the Huguenots; Marguerite the Pledge of Their Fulfilment. — A Dazzling Display of Crimson, Orange, Purple, and Gold. — A Discourteous and Woman-hating Monarch. — The Lover's War, and the Conquest of Cahors. — Compelled by the Laws of War. — Maréchal de Biron's Excuses.— The Éclat of Nérac Departed. — Marguerite Depressed in Spirit. — Philip, for the Fourth Time a Widower, Seeks a Fifth Wife.

WHILE war with all its accompanying horrors was still raging in the Netherlands, peace was scarcely maintained in France. The Catholic provinces were menacingly energetic in resisting the exactions to which the king resorted to support his own prodigal expenditure, and to satisfy the avarice of his favourites. He fancied, and justly it appears, that this opposition was prompted by the Guises. Becoming alarmed, and fearing the revival of the spirit of the League, he lavished pecuniary and other favours on them, and consented to many measures imposing restraints on himself, regarding the disposal of the benefices of the Church, pardoning assassins, etc., which measures, it was ironically said, might possibly continue in force for full three days.

The queen-mother, to quiet the Protestant chiefs and maintain the internal peace of the kingdom, thought she could not do better while Anjou was paying his court to Elizabeth than conduct the Queen of Navarre to her husband, and urge on the Prince de Condé the desirableness of his taking a second wife, at the same time offering him the hand of the young queen's sister, Marguerite de Vaudemont. The prince, however, pleaded that "want of money and a suitable escort prevented him from kissing the queen's hands, as he otherwise would have greatly desired to do." This reply seems to have been also intended to express regret at his inability to marry the lady, whose fortune, as doubtless he knew, was extremely small.

But the King of Navarre, who had not seen Marguerite since he made his escape from Vincennes, three years before — or remained inconsolable during that period — positively refused to receive her. Before he did so, they must be married, he said, according to the Protestant rites. Other difficulties were also suggested respecting the cities assigned as her dowry, of which he had not been put in possession. Maréchal de Biron, who was then at Nérac discussing a rearrangement of some stipulations of the last treaty, was deputed by the queen-mother to settle this question also.

Meanwhile, still carrying out her programme, she and Marguerite, with a certain number of the "flying squadron" (always an indispensable part of her retinue), passed through several of the provinces with a view of discovering the designs of the leaders, both of the religious and political factions. What was the cause, she desired to know, of the prevalent discontent and general agitation? Yet she must have been well prepared to hear that, in whatever else Catholics and Protestants disagreed, they were at least united in the opinion that "to support any longer the intolerable burden of taxation the king imposed on his subjects, would be to submit to tyranny of which France had never yet known the like."

After passing the winter in the South, she returned to Nérac, a second interview having been agreed to by the King of Navarre, who — according to Lippomano — rode out to meet her with an escort of five hundred gentlemen. Entering into the views of Henri III., she spoke mournfully to her son-in-law of the projects of the "Guisards," and entreated him not to persist in his heresy, lest the Catholic states should declare him deprived of his right of inheritance to the crown, a matter, she said, of the greater importance to him, considering the king's and "Monsieur's" bad state of health, and the pretensions of the Duc de Guise to lineal descent from Charlemagne.*

As he did not yield to her arguments, she secretly strove to sow discord and treachery amongst his followers, and, by her usual means, to seduce his friends and corrupt his servants. But while awaiting the desired results of these efforts, she made further concessions to the Reformers, in secret articles — lest the Catholics should oppose or resent them — and as a pledge of their fulfilment she delivered the unwilling Marguerite to her no less unwilling husband. He still was indisposed to receive her; but was at length prevailed on by the advice of friends to give her, at least in appearance, an honourable and affectionate welcome.

While the queen-mother and Maréchal de Biron were engaged with their diplomatic mission to the King of Navarre, Henri III., with a numerous train of courtiers and favourites, and accompanied by the Venetian ambassador, retired to Fontainebleau. The château, says the ambassador, was then falling to ruin; the gardens neglected; the lake filled with mud. Yet its fine position, and what yet remained of the works of art of the time

* One of the queen-mother's astrologers had lately predicted that the death of both the king and his brother would shortly occur. Catherine placed faith in this prediction, and, accordingly, was taking measures for ensuring for herself some remnant of power either with the Guises or the Bourbons — she cared not which.

of François I., made it still one of the most favoured, if not the finest, of the royal residences.

Henri III. was not fond of building. His lavish gifts to his favourites; the expenses of the wars, and his own and his mother's prodigality, exhausted every source of revenue, and swallowed up the immense sums exacted from his people. His favourites, however, built for themselves. Thus, what the king threw away, they employed in erecting hôtels in Paris, and châteaux in the environs and the provinces. When the court returned to the Louvre, the favourite ambassador took leave of the king, and he departed for Venice. He was generally spoken of by the king, the queen-mother, and the court, as "*l'ambassadeur chéri;*" the favour shown him being intended to express the king's gratitude for the splendid reception he had met with on leaving Poland from the Doge and Senate of Venice.

He mentions in his report to the Senate that "the king and princes, though extremely frank and familiar amongst themselves and their court, yet hold very little intercourse with the ambassadors, except on grand state occasions, or in political negotiation." But Lippomano appears to have been a man of pleasing manners as well as a shrewd diplomatist. He was invited by king and queen to all their jousts, grand hunts, tournaments, and *fêtes*, public and private, as no other Venetian ambassador had been. When he was ill, the king ordered prayers to be said for him in various churches. But he was a bigoted Catholic, and approved of the Bartholomew massacre. Coligny, he said, was "the cause of all the troubles of France — his death and the manner of it on that ever-memorable 24th of August being nothing more than he merited."

On taking leave of the king, his majesty created his favourite ambassador a chevalier of the new Order of the Saint-Esprit. Twice he declined the proffered honour. But the king said: "I pray you, M. l'Ambassadeur, to do me the favour of being my chevalier and brother, as a slight return for the love I bear you, receiving my sword as a pledge of it." This was an unusual honour. He also presented him with a remarkably fine diamond, of the size of a hazel-nut, mounted in gold. A beautiful small Turkish dog, of which the king was very fond, completed his presents. The king took the little dog in his arms, kissed him, and offering him to Lippomano said: "I beg of you to accept him for my sake."*

* This ambassador, in his report to the Doge and Senate of Venice, mentions the state of Paris at this time. He speaks with surprise at its populousness, and says "the departure of the court, though so numerous, seems to make no difference whatever in that respect. Foreigners are there in crowds," he continues, " Scotch, English, Italian, Spanish, Portuguese, and others. Such a *pêle-mêle*, such a confusion; but less in their diversity than their numbers. Therefore are there so many hostelries, inns, and taverns, also chambers to let; so many vintners and butchers ; so many boats with the produce of the gardens that sometimes they

After an absence of some months the queen-mother with her troop returned to Paris, rejoicing, by anticipation, in the dissensions which the presence of Marguerite would, she foresaw, occasion at the Navarrese Court. On the queen's departure Henri and his sister transferred their household to Pau, whither Marguerite, who had clung to the hope of leaving with her mother, soon followed. Between the intriguing Catholic Queen of Navarre and the simple pure-minded Calvinist Princesse Catherine, there could of course be little sympathy. Differences soon arose, religion being the pretext.

Catherine was said to be as intolerant as Jeanne d'Albret herself, and to have forbidden the exercise of the Catholic religion in Béarn; which was, of course, not more deserving of condemnation than forbidding the Protestant worship in cities where Catholic governors ruled. Exception, however, was made in Marguerite's favour, and mass was said on Sundays in her apartment; but during its celebration the drawbridge of the château was raised. This appears to have given offence to the princess's ladies, who were all strict Protestants,

quite cover the Seine; so many *rôtisseries*, where cooked meats may be had; and so many pastry-cooks, who indeed fill half the city — wonderful to see! Everything is there, and in great abundance. Dearer, certainly, than elsewhere, except meat. Houses, in absence of owners, let furnished, by day or by month. But in less than two hours you may furnish a house thoroughly and magnificently — everything, whether for the richest or those of more moderate means."

no less than to those attendant on the queen, who were equally zealous Catholics, and to have occasioned disputes amongst the servants of both religions.

Henri was therefore unwillingly compelled to interfere, in order to restore harmony. He was raising an army, and — taking advantage of the peace, or, rather, a short suspension of hostilities — was striving to bring it to a better state of efficiency than was possible with the mercenary troops which both he and others were wont to rely on. This, with his numerous amours — always a serious part of the business of his life — fully occupied him. His first act was to remove his small court from Pau to Nérac. Pau was a dreary abode — the castle an old feudal fortress with its moats, drawbridges, dungeon, keep, and five towers; while Nérac, which was Jeanne d'Albret's favourite residence, had its gardens, pleasant promenades, and cheerful rooms; more in the style of the *maisons de plaisance*, which Diane de Poitiers and Catherine de' Medici had built for themselves and brought into favour.

The change appears to have had a beneficial effect, as Marguerite remained there for two or three years, on very good terms with her sister-in-law and her husband — Henri requiring of his consort only toleration of his gallantries and outward decorum in the conduct of her own. A small chapel was built for her, amidst groves and shrubberies, and there Marguerite heard mass, while Catherine attended the Protestant worship in the château. The little Court of Nérac became celebrated for the charm and elegance of its society, and under Marguerite's direction the abode of the noble-minded yet severe Calvinist queen assumed an air of festivity and youth.

Before the windows of the principal *salon* there stretched a well-tended parterre of choice flowers, pleasing the eyes with their many-coloured blossoms, and filling the air with their fragrance; while away in the distance, winding amongst the prairies, the river's mazy course might be traced by the lines and groups of that beautiful shrub, the rose-laurel, which flourished and bloomed luxuriantly along its banks. The princesses occupied their mornings with music and poetry, and in studying or reading Latin, in which Marguerite was a proficient. Sometimes they took long walks and planned improvements in the grounds of the château. In the evenings the court assembled for flirtation and conversation; and at stated times for balls.

Marguerite had a rather numerous retinue of ladies, chiefly young and fair, but too generally indiscreet. In their society many of the younger Huguenot gentlemen threw aside that austerity of manner believed to be inseparable from the Calvinistic profession. Their king, in fact, set them the example. But the elder, or the more seriously disposed, often expressed disapprobation of the levity more than gaiety prevailing at Marguerite's receptions, while the Huguenot ladies attendant on Catherine of Navarre deemed it prudent to be frequently absent, and of course their princess also. The revels at the Court of Nérac, unfortunately, too often proved that the religious Reform had not yet greatly reformed either the morals or the manners of the time.

Marguerite, in her memoirs, says: "Time sped away so pleasantly at Nérac in *fêtes*, conversation, and innocent amusements, that having with me Madame la Princesse de Navarre, my sister, I envied not the more brilliant festivities of the Court of France." Yet she was diligently occupied with political as well as amorous intrigues, and the Vicomte de Turenne was the favoured confidant of her projects. She also kept up a correspondence with the Duc d'Anjou, and secretly employed her influence with the Calvinist nobility to induce them to follow the duke to Flanders.

So well did she succeed, that she was able to assure him of the support of a considerable number of Huguenot gentlemen and their followers. She also endeavoured to further his views with reference to his marriage with Elizabeth, by urging on the negotiation, and seeking, through Huguenot influence, to have the great advantage that would ensue from the match to the queen and to England pressed upon Elizabeth. To carry out her scheme, Marguerite was accustomed to repair daily to an old isolated house, near Le Mas d'Agenais, to discuss, as was alleged, her political schemes with Turenne. The court maintained a discreet silence with reference to these interviews, but without accepting the political motive assigned for them.

Marguerite had with her the splendid litter in which she made her journey to Flanders, and of which she has given a description in her memoirs. In this unwieldy but sumptuously decorated and luxuriously furnished vehicle Marguerite took frequent excursions in the neighbourhood of the château, always attended by M. de Turenne, whose exclusive privilege it was to converse with her as he rode beside her at the door of the litter. The ladies of honour followed the queen on mules or in litters, while the twenty-five gentlemen of the House of De la Tour d'Auvergne, wearing casaques of orange-coloured velvet embroidered in gold and silver, escorted her and the viscount at a respectful distance.

When this brilliant *cortège* was first seen crossing the fields at Agenais, the simple country people, who had never before beheld so dazzling a display of crimson, orange, purple, and gold, were positively alarmed at its splendour. Two beneficent fairies, Urgèle and Mélusine, were believed by them to have taken the district of Agenais under their protection. Much talk there had been at times of the deeds of this fantastic pair; but mortal eye had never beheld them.

A bright thought now occurred to one or two of these intelligent peasantry. "Perhaps this pompous procession was a freak of the fairies, who, in mortal shape and size, had come to visit them." It was a daring suggestion, and its effect was to thin the number of spectators. But the bolder spirits, who laughed derisively and remained on the field, were rewarded by the information that the glittering show was but their new queen's retinue of ladies and gentlemen exploring with her the more distant surroundings of her château. It, however, surprised them. Queen Jeanne d'Albret — to them the greatest of all queens — they had often seen, but never had she dazzled them by her finery. Her virtues, her wisdom, and her many trials had secured their love and sympathy; while her dignified yet courteous manners commanded their due respect. These feelings were now transferred to her daughter, whom they seem to have regarded as their sovereign rather than the frequently absent Henri. It remained for Marguerite to make known to those simple people the follies and vices of a queen, forming quite a different picture from that of the wisdom and virtues they had revered in Jeanne.

However, life at Nérac sped on merrily for a time, Marguerite and Turenne conspiring together in concert with the Duc d'Anjou in the most friendly manner. But Henri III., being informed of his sister's intrigues and of her intimacy with Turenne, against whom he was exceedingly wroth for his desertion with his followers from the Catholic to the Huguenot party, determined to put an end to the harmony existing at the Court of Nérac. He wrote to the King of Navarre, telling him that his wife was unfaithful to him, and was intriguing with the Vicomte de Turenne, the recent convert to Protestantism.

Henri was by no means jealous of Turenne, but several of the young nobility were. He, however, could not do otherwise than show the king's letter of accusation to Marguerite and her lover, though he was well assured that no solicitude for his honour had prompted his brother-in-law to inform him of his wife's infidelity. Both the accused vehemently protested their innocence, casting the calumny on the king's malevolence. "His intention," they said, "was to set Navarre at variance with his best friends." Having driven one devoted partisan from him, he would find some means of disgracing and alienating others. "His accusation," said Turenne, "is probably put forth as a specious pretext for withholding the delivery of Cahors and other cities of his sister's dowry. Why not take them? and by force if needful."

This idea put the whole court into high spirits. Languor seems to have been stealing over them, and a little excitement was welcomed. The King of Navarre yielded to their views. It furnished him with a brilliant opportunity both of adding to his territory and augmenting his power. The ladies of the court joined their entreaties to those of the queen, and urged their lovers to take the field with Henri of Navarre against that most discourteous monarch and woman-hater, the King of France. The Duc d'Anjou, in furtherance of his own views in the Netherlands, secretly encouraged this rising in arms against his brother, expecting that he would seek his mediation, and pay him for it in the manner he desired.

The chiefs of the party, weary of inactivity — so accustomed had they become to the excitement of war — were fully prepared for a new campaign. All being thus agreed on the necessity for war, the King of Navarre gave to each of the principal captains the half of a gold crown, with the injunction to hold himself ready for the day on which he should receive the corresponding half.

On the 15th of April, Henri was prepared to send to the Huguenot chiefs the signal agreed on. Meanwhile the Prince de Condé had resorted to arms on his own account, to recover possession of some part of the province of Picardy, of which he was nominally governor. He had taken La Fère without bloodshed, was fortifying it, and Henri III. was negotiating with him, when, unexpectedly, the King of Navarre opened his campaign. He was far from fortunate at the outset. His army was smaller than he had expected it to be, many Protestant towns refusing to join in a war originating in a scandalous intrigue of gallantry. On account of its origin, it was called "*La Guerre des Amoureux*," or the "Lovers' War."

Plessis-Mornay, referring to it, says: "It would be greatly embarrassing to give any sort of dignity to the events that led to this war were it desired to do so." It, however, led to the taking of the strongly fortified city of Cahors. Henri had with him but about 4,000 men, dispirited by successful resistance where they had looked for easy conquest. Their leaders, too, were dissatisfied, as was Henri himself, at having, in a spirit of levity, joined in a causeless war. But what was thoughtlessly begun, he resolved to pursue in a spirit of heroism, and by some striking act to raise the courage of his partisans.

Henri III., with the hope of inducing the Huguenot soldiers and captains to abandon their leader, published a decree in favour of those of "the religion" who should refrain from joining the "rebels." They, however, did not desert him, but obeyed with alacrity when he called on them to follow him to Cahors. The city was well garrisoned, and the inhabitants armed. But the newly invented petards, which Henri on this occasion first made use of, soon opened the gates. The *corps de garde* was forced, and the king and his

Huguenots rushed in sword in hand. A frightful combat ensued, lasting continuously for five days and five nights with varying success, as reinforcements were continually arriving both for besieged and besiegers.

Henri, during this terrible conflict, gave proofs of the most daring valour; but more as a brave and dashing soldier than a prudent general. Many times he was implored by his lieutenants to order a retreat, his armour being bruised and battered in many places; his feet cut, torn, and bleeding, and scarcely able to support him. But his invariable answer was, "He would be carried out a dead man, or march out a conqueror" (D'Aubigné). At last the governor, General Vezins, being severely wounded, evacuated the city, all who were able following him. This victory was the foundation of Henri of Navarre's great renown as a warrior. Otherwise, it was little to his advantage, and but slightly influenced the general result of the campaign.

Marguerite and Catherine remained at Nérac during this siege, and Henri III., as though to show them that he was not quite so discourteous as the ladies of his sister's court had represented him, ordered that the city of Nérac should be considered neutral, on condition that the King of Navarre did not enter it while hostilities continued. But Navarre, then deeply enamoured of Mademoiselle de Montmorency-Fosseuse, could not refrain from stealthily leaving his army one night to pay a furtive visit to this lady, to quiet her fears for his safety.

This breach of the engagement being made known to Maréchal de Biron, he at once attacked Nérac. The queen and the princess, with the ladies of their suite, informed probably that this feint of an assault was not likely to prove very murderous, valiantly went out on the towers of the château to look at the enemy's army and see the skirmish under the city walls. Maréchal de Biron having directed a few cannon-shot against them and broken a few windows, deemed his honour satisfied, and sending his "excuses to the ladies for what the laws of war had compelled him to do," withdrew his troops.

Probably he would have amused them a little longer had he not met with an accident and broken his thigh, and thus was compelled to send his excuses somewhat earlier than he otherwise would have done. This puerile war was ended by a treaty signed at the Château of Fleix, in Perigord, November 27th — the Duc d'Anjou mediator, but the queen-mother, with her usual *cortège*, being present. The treaty was more favourable to the Huguenots than that of Nérac. It also put the King of Navarre into possession of his wife's dowry.

Turenne now thought it time to leave Nérac. Accompanied by the Huguenot captain, La Noue, and several of the younger nobility, he purposed joining the Duc d'Anjou's expedition to Flanders. With the departure of these gentlemen, departed the *éclat* of Nérac, which so weighed on Marguerite, and depressed her spirits, that she judged it advisable to leave the now dull Court of Navarre and return to the exciting gaieties of the Louvre. Catherine also changed her residence, her presence being necessary at Pau. Having completed her twentieth year, Henri of Navarre had named her gouvernante and lieutenante-général of Béarn, where she was regarded as Henri's sole heir, and during his absence the rightful sovereign.

It seems evident that Henri's reputation as a valorous soldier must have been considerably increased by his daring and persistent efforts to achieve victory at Cahors. Otherwise, it was scarcely from Philip II. of Spain that especial envoys would have been sent to the heretic prince with offers likely to flatter his ambition and dazzle his sister's imagination. For the fourth time, this cruel monster had become a widower, and to the youthful and gentle Catherine of Navarre he proposed the honour of becoming his fifth wife, urging his pretensions with much assiduity. He offered to obtain a divorce from Marguerite, and to give Henri in her place the infanta, Clara Eugenia.

Philip had threatened Henri III. with war, and Henri had hastened to assure him that he had no part in his brother's aims on the Netherlands. But this did not satisfy him, neither did the queen-mother's intrigues with all parties. He would have had Henri of Navarre join him in making war on France, and he relied for his consent on the troubles and embarrassments in which the League was about to plunge him. Doubtless he would have stipulated for the renunciation of heresy.

But when, through Henri's minister, Du Plessis-Mornay, both brother and sister declined the flattering offers made them on the ground of difference of religion, Henri adding that he could not take up arms against a country it was his duty to protect, the Spanish envoys could scarcely give credit to the rejection of their sovereign's offers by the king and princess. "Surely," they exclaimed, "they know not what they are doing." Philip is said to have kept in reserve some time, at a village in Upper Navarre, 800,000 ducats, believing that Henri would yet be glad to accept his offers.

CHAPTER IX.

Anjou Elected Ruler of the United Provinces. — The Queen-mother Desires to Fulfil Ruggieri's Prediction. — Embassy to England to Arrange Anjou's Marriage. — Unjust, but Necessary. — Anjou Again at Elizabeth's Feet. — Catherine Claims the Crown of Portugal. — Henri's Arbitrary Proceedings. — Marriages of King's Mignons. — Demands of the Swiss Ambassadors. — The Gregorian Calendar.

SCARCELY was the Peace of Fleix concluded when the Duc d'Anjou was gratified by the intelligence that the "Union of Utrecht," in accordance with the eventual promise made to him in 1578, had elected him sovereign of the United Provinces. The deposition of Philip was proclaimed at Antwerp by the States General, in the name of the "Law of Nature," which they declared "authorised subjects to depose their prince if he oppressed them, instead of governing according to Equity and Reason." "Subjects," said they, "are not created by God for the use of the prince, or to obey him in whatever he may please to command, be it just or unjust, or to serve him as slaves. But the prince is established for his subjects, in order that he may govern them in accordance with Equity and Reason, as enjoined by the Law of Nature."

The deposition of Philip II. by the Netherlanders — "the first blow then aimed at the monarchical principle" — caused immense sensation throughout Europe. Notwithstanding the great provocation the Netherlanders had received in the unspeakable horrors inflicted on them "in the name of God and the Church," many of them trembled at their own temerity. "One of the deputies of Frise, when the pen was put into his hand to sign the act of Philip's deposition, was seized with such extreme terror and nervous agitation that he died in attempting to put his signature to it."

The Duc d'Anjou's compact with the United Provinces was signed at Plessis-lez-Tours towards the end of September. His power was limited by many safeguards and restrictions, which made his position rather that of the head of a republic than a sovereign ruler. Again Philip II. remonstrated with Henri III. and threatened him with war, and again the latter disavowed any participation in his brother's proceedings, and declared himself powerless to suppress them. He, however, issued an edict prohibiting the levying of troops, yet did not trouble himself to have it carried into effect.

The queen-mother was anxious to fulfil Ruggieri's prediction that all her sons would reign.

She would, therefore, have had Henri aid his brother's enterprise. But it was merely to gratify her own *amour-propre* — the Duc d'Anjou, of all her children, being the one she liked least. She is, indeed, believed to have had affection for none of them but the contemptible Henri III., and in him, who was to have been the realisation of Machiavelli's model prince, how deeply was she disappointed!

She, however, prevailed on Henri to further Anjou's views on the English throne, in case that of the Netherlands should escape him. For the States General had not yet proclaimed him their sovereign, and Philip's great captain, Alessandro Farnese, Prince of Parma, was on the alert to take advantage of every opportunity of bringing back the revolted provinces to their allegiance to Spain. A numerous embassy, bearing presents from the king and queen-mother, was therefore despatched to England to arrange the terms of the marriage of Elizabeth and the Duc d'Anjou. A magnificent reception awaited the ambassadors, and a most gracious welcome from the queen. Some brilliant *fêtes* in honour of the event also took place, in anticipation of more brilliant ones to come.

Two years before, preliminary articles had been agreed on between the queen and the duke, and on these the contract of marriage was now based. On the 11th of June all was arranged — certain explanations alone excepted, that were to be reciprocally given before the marriage was celebrated. It had occurred to Elizabeth to introduce this restriction at the end of the contract; but little heed was given to it by the French negotiators. A sum of 600,000 *livres* is said to have been sent by the king for the expenses of the queen's journey to Paris.

Much gratified with the successful result of their mission, the ambassadors took leave of her majesty. Their report gave great satisfaction to the duke, who fully believed that he would henceforth share with Elizabeth the throne of England. And no less was he sure that the independent sovereignty of the United Provinces was his. The army he had been leisurely raising in different parts of France had now assembled to the number of 14,000 or 15,000 men, with whom were joined the flower of the Protestant nobility and many Catholic gentlemen. Full of spirits, hope, and gaiety, the duke and his army began their march, and crossed the frontier of the Netherlands at the end of August, leaving behind them sad traces of their passage through France. The imperial city of Cambray was entered in triumph; the blockade having been raised by the Prince of Parma, whose forces were far inferior in number to those of the Duc d'Anjou.

Henri III. was by no means willing that his brother's ambition of becoming a powerful sovereign should be fully gratified. Yet he was glad that Philip of Spain should be kept in check by that brother's exploits in the Netherlands, rather than that his own diversions and devotions should be interrupted or set aside for that purpose. He therefore the more readily yielded to his mother's suggestions that it was advisable secretly to furnish Anjou with a considerable subsidy, which she was disposed to some extent to add to. This unlooked-for assistance probably inspirited the jovial duke on his departure almost as much as the promise of Elizabeth's hand.

But like a true Valois, after marching into Cambray — with which his brilliant exploits of arms began and ended — he set about squandering his money, which he speedily accomplished with a recklessness worthy of Henri himself. Nothing was left for the pay of the army. Pillage was therefore resorted to, though Cambray had placed itself under his protection. He was also alarmed in his pecuniary distress by the intelligence forwarded to him by the queen-mother, that his bride-elect had suggested to Henri III. that, "previous to the ceremony of her marriage, the king should enter into a treaty with her, offensive and defensive, against Philip II. of Spain."

To Henri III., who could never make up his mind to act decisively in any matters concerning the affairs of the kingdom, this was the most embarrassing of proposals. He was not prepared for anything so energetic. By every means that the tortured fancy of his Italian financiers could devise he was then extracting money from the pockets of his people. The Italian chancellor, Birago, acknowledged that these "exactions were for the most part unjust; but as the king's coffers were empty they must be considered necessary."

Anjou, uneasy concerning the apparently new obstacle to his marriage, determined to disband the greater part of his army; to leave the rest in Cambray and pass over to England, once more to plead his suit at Elizabeth's feet, and learn his fate from her own lips. As usual, he was well received; treated quite as a lover — his presence appearing to smooth away all obstacles and to brighten pleasantly the path before him. Elizabeth on the 22nd of November placed a ring on Anjou's finger as a token of their betrothal. A messenger was instantly despatched to Antwerp and Brussels to inform the duke's friends of this event of happy augury, which was celebrated by illuminations and bonfires. But the course of Anjou's love still ran far otherwise than smoothly. The Fates seemed to have set their faces against this union; Elizabeth's Puritan subjects certainly had. Zealous French Catholics also exclaimed vehemently that it was "ruinous to the faith." Elizabeth, therefore, bowed before the tempest, and withdrew her promise to Anjou. She impressed on the disconsolate prince — whom, probably, she never had intended to marry — that her grief was great as his; but that "reason imposed on her affections the course she then pursued." Anjou did not, however, immediately take leave of the queen. He lingered at the English Court yet two or three months, and appeared to be regaining the ground he had lost. It was, however, suspected by some persons that the queen still encouraged his hopes, and kept him dangling beside her merely to prevent him from establishing himself in Flanders.

At last Anjou by a desperate effort tore himself from the influence of her wiles. Elizabeth had him conducted with the greatest respect to Flushing and Antwerp by the English admiral and the Earl of Leicester. Also, she still allowed him to hope, and lent or gave him £30,000, doubtless a welcome loan or gift to the spendthrift prince, who was proclaimed on the 19th of February Duc de Brabant. Much magnificence was displayed on the occasion. The ceremony was imposing and the rejoicing great.

Catherine de' Medici, while her son was pursuing his plans in England and the Netherlands, had been claiming a throne for herself — that of Portugal, which, on the death of Cardinal Dom Henrique, had become vacant owing to the failure of legitimate heirs. The cardinal had been appointed regent by his nephew, the famous Dom Sebastião, during his absence from his kingdom while combating the Moors in Africa. He was believed to have died in battle in 1578, at the age of twenty-four. But for many years his return was expected by the people, who thought him only imprisoned.

In 1580 Dom Henrique also died, when many claimants for the vacant throne put forward their pretensions. The chief of them was Philip of Spain, and amongst others was Catherine de' Medici, who claimed to be descended from a son of Dom Affonso III. and his repudiated wife, the Condessa Mathilda. Affonso reigned in Portugal from 1235 to 1279. Catherine, however, could not prove that the son from whom she claimed descent ever existed.

Henri III. was as little inclined to encourage his mother's ambitious views as his brother's. But she contrived to equip two small fleets on her own account and to send them to the Azores. In an attempt to take possession of San-Miguel, her friend and countryman, Strozzi, who commanded the first expedition, was killed, his vessel captured, and all on board put to a cruel death.

The second venture was no less unfortunate in attempting to take the island of Terceira. The Spanish admiral, Santa-Cruz, compelled the troops the queen-mother had sent to evacuate the islands, and put them to death or imprisoned them as violators of the peace existing between France and Spain.

Philip's claim was not quite so vague as Catherine's; but it was disallowed by the Portuguese. The prize, however, fell to him; for Philip sent an army under the ferocious Duke of Alva to take the country by force. The Azores and other possessions went with it, and soon all opposition was rigorously put down, and Portugal united to Spain. Her prosperity declined from that time. It was the then wealthy kingdom of Portugal that furnished him with the means of fitting out his armada for the conquest of England, and gave him the splendid and spacious Bay of Lisbon to prepare it in and to receive back its shattered remains.

Whilst these events were occurring, the plague had made sad ravages in France, and especially in Paris. Earthquake shocks had been felt there, and Calais and Boulogne are said to have been also much affected by them. Many persons thought that these calamities expressed the displeasure of Heaven at the course of folly and depravity pursued by the king. During the past autumn he had selected from his troop of favourites the two who then stood highest in his good graces — Joyeuse and La Valette — with the intention, as he said, of so "elevating them in rank and wealth that neither the shafts of envy nor the changes and chances of fortune should be able to injure or destroy them."

To accomplish this laudable purpose, it was necessary that he should lay on his subjects a more crushing burden of taxation than even he had hitherto attempted to do. The check to his prodigality, which but a short time since he had met with in the opposition of the Catholic provinces to his exactions, had passed quietly away on his promise to abstain from levying further contributions on them for purposes other than the needs of the state. Instead of adhering to those conditions, he was emboldened to try the experiment a second time. A few more promises of greater economy for the future would, he fancied, again produce the supplies he demanded.

He began by doubling the amount of the ordinary taxes for a period of six years. He then held a "bed of justice" to order the publication of nine or ten "bursal edicts," creating new offices for sale, and fresh taxes on the people. The greater part of the presidents and magistrates present at this council informed Birago — the king's Italian councillor — that these edicts could not, and ought not, to pass. Birago was then commanded by Henri to take no notice of that, but to proceed to publish them at once.

The first President of the Assembly, De Thou, then rose, and said aloud: "According to the law of the king, which is his absolute power, these edicts might pass; but according to the law of the kingdom, which is reason and equity, they cannot be published." Notwithstanding these remonstrances, Birago — who was the king's chancellor, not Chancellor of France — published them immediately by the king's commands.*

This was but a small part of his arbitrary proceedings for obtaining money for his favourites. Twice he forcibly took possession of the funds set apart for the payment of the Rentes of the Hôtel de Ville; obtained large sums from the clergy; taxed many articles in ordinary use that hitherto had been free; considerably increased the *gabelle*, or salt-tax; and compelled every family to take a certain quantity of salt, whether needed or not. He seemed, too, to take a malicious pleasure in these acts, and in knowing that he annoyed and irritated the people.

It is surprising that they should have tolerated this tyrannical *débauché* so long on the throne. Already he had elevated his two chief favourites to ducal rank — the vicomte became Duc de Joyeuse, and La Valette, Duc d'Épernon — with precedence of all other peers of France, except only those of the blood, or of sovereign houses. He had found wives for them also, the queen's two sisters, youthful princesses of the royal House of Lorraine.† Joyeuse was betrothed on the 18th of September, in the queen's apartment, to Marguerite de Vaude-

---

* Pierre de l'Estoile — "*Journal de Henri III.*"

† He at first thought of Catherine of Navarre as a suitable bride for D'Épernon. But the proposal was rejected with indignation by Du Plessis-Mornay on behalf of Henri of Navarre and his sister.

mont, and their marriage was solemnised on the 24th at Saint-Germain-l'Auxerrois. "The bride was conducted to the church by the king, followed by the queen, princesses and ladies; all so sumptuously attired that none remembered having ever seen *toilettes* of such magnificence.

"The king and the bridegroom were dressed alike, their doublets and vests being so covered with embroidery and precious stones, that it was impossible to calculate their value. The making up alone cost 10,000 crowns. Seventeen *fêtes* were given by the king and the nobility related to the newly married pair — each in his turn, by order of his majesty. At each of these *fêtes* an entirely new dress was worn, the greater part being composed of gold and silver cloth, enriched with guipure, gold and silver embroidery, and precious stones of great price.

"It was reported that the expense incurred by the king alone, including tournaments, masquerades, music, presents, and new liveries for the household, would exceed 1,200,000 gold crowns. The ballet — called "*ballet comique de la reine*" — was arranged, but not composed, by Ronsard and Baïf, who each received 2,000 crowns for his part in it. The bride's portion not exceeding 20,000 crowns, the king undertook to pay Joyeuse 400,000 crowns, besides buying him the estate of Limoux for 160,000 crowns."

When the chancellor placed before the king in

council the amount of the enormous sums he had lavished on his favourite, he replied to the mild remonstrances made to him on that occasion: "I will be prudent and economical when I have married my three children," meaning La Valette and another favourite, D'Argues, — these two yet remaining to be advantageously married, and with the same prodigality suitably provided for.*

Of the seventeen marriage festivals, that given by the Cardinal de Bourbon was intended to be the most magnificent as well as strikingly novel. An aquatic procession was arranged to take place on the Seine, and a grand and superb "bacq," in the form of a triumphal car, was constructed to convey the king, the queen, princes, and princesses in solemn pomp down the river, passing the Louvre to the Pré-aux-Clercs. This grand car was to be put in motion by means of small boats disguised as sea-horses, led by tritons and accompanied by sirens, while whales and other marine animals — twenty-four in number — sported before them.

Inside the horses a band of musicians was to be concealed, with trumpets, clarions, violins, and hautbois. Outside there was to be a grand display of fireworks. But alas! this wonderful machine, intended to astonish the king and the royal party as well as to please them, refused to leave its moorings. Nothing would persuade it to get under way. The king, with admirable patience, waited

* Pierre de l'Estoile — "*Journal de Henri III.*"

two or three hours with the hope of embarking, but all in vain.

The shades of evening were coming on, and his majesty, getting both weary and angry, instead of stepping into his triumphal car, got into his coach, saying, as he drove off, to those who had been for hours striving with might and main to get the refractory car afloat, that he perceived *"que c'étaient des bêtes qui commandaient à d'autres bêtes."*

From the riverside he drove to the cardinal's residence at the Abbey of Saint-Germain, in whose grounds other wonders were prepared — an artificial garden of fruits and flowers — "just like May and June," says the chroniqueur. Yet it was in fact chill October, the sunny atmosphere of those months being represented by the light of some hundreds of wax candles veiled with gauze. Thus did these marriage *fêtes* proceed; each succeeding one, we are told, "being *plus belle et pompeuse* than its predecessor."

D'Épernon's intended bride was too young for her marriage to take place at the same time as her elder sister's. But, lest there should be any jealousy between his favourites, the king paid the marriage portion of the younger princess, 400,000 gold crowns, on the same day that Joyeuse received Marguerite's; conferring also on D'Épernon places and pensions of equal value to the revenue of the estate he had bought for Joyeuse.

The Swiss ambassadors, deputed by the Cantons

to demand payment of the money due to them for troops furnished to the state, on being told that his majesty was then without funds, replied that was impossible, and that his coffers must, on the contrary, be overflowing. "Has not the king," they said, "been spending for the last four or five months sums incalculable on the marriage *fêtes* of M. de Joyeuse, simply a poor gentleman, until the king honoured him with the title of duke and his majesty's *mignon*? If he scruples not to spend so lavishly on such trifling matters, he must surely have in reserve larger sums still to provide for the important affairs of his kingdom." They thought that "if he had not, he must be considered very indiscreet or very badly counselled."

This language Henri III. regarded as little less than high treason, and, doubtless, had he dared to treat these outspoken ambassadors as he often treated his own subjects for no greater offence, he would have decapitated or hanged them on the Place de Grève. But not ambassadors alone were urging their claims on the king; the holders of small official posts and necessitous pensioners were daily sending in petitions praying his majesty to order some portion of the arrears of their salary or pension to be paid to them; whilst remonstrances against the excessive taxation that so grievously oppressed the people were pouring in daily in large numbers.

But Henri cared for none of these things so

long as they did not interfere with his amusements or his devotions. Around him might be heard the angry mutterings of an impending storm, but he slumbered on, heeding them not.

At the close of the year the reformed calendar of Gregory XIII. was adopted in France. The edict ordering that it should be conformed to — counting the 5th of October for the 15th, and in consequence cutting off ten days from the year — was published in November, on the day following the death of the president, Christopher de Thou. He had hitherto prevented its adoption, refusing to regard it from a scientific point of view, and looking at it only as a usurpation of authority by the Church in a matter purely secular. He was not alone in his strenuous opposition to it; the resolutions of many Protestant states were for a long time influenced by a similar prejudice. It was, however, registered without opposition by the Parliament of Paris after De Thou's death.

CHAPTER X.

The Duke Thoroughly Defeated.— "Compensatory Works" Excusing All Sins.— The "White Flagellants" of Avignon in Paris.— The King and Queen Set Out on Foot, on a Pilgrimage.— Philip II. Makes Advances to Henri of Navarre.— Marriage Proposed between Catherine of Navarre and James VI. of Scotland.— Marguerite Banished from France.— Marguerite Makes War on Henri.— Death of Duc d'Anjou et de Brabant.— Funeral Processions.— Absence of the Queen-Mother.

IT soon became evident that the Duc de Brabant was utterly incapable of fulfilling the duties of his position in which the Netherlanders had placed him. He had accepted that of the head of a free state; but his desire was for absolute power, which most unwisely he attempted to usurp by force and treachery. Maréchal de Biron and the young Duc de Montpensier had been sent to him with a detachment of troops, and the duke determined, though earnestly dissuaded by the marshal, to employ this force in making war on his subjects.

He would listen to no advice, for, besides the irritation he felt at the restraints imposed on his authority, he was exceedingly jealous of the Prince of Orange. With the eight or nine thousand men

— Swiss and French — now at his disposal he thought he could perfectly carry out his plan of a surprise and military occupation of Bruges, Antwerp, and other cities of the Union. At Dunkirk and one or two of the smaller towns he succeeded; but at Ostend and Bruges a serious check awaited him.

At Antwerp he was thoroughly defeated, after having surprised one of the gates of the city, killed the guard, and effected an entrance. The people, becoming aware of what had happened, sounded the tocsin, rose *en masse*, retook the gate and closed it. All who had entered the city were either killed or made prisoners. Some few attempted to escape by jumping from the ramparts into the moat, and several of them were drowned. The duke, who had left the city to await the result of his enterprise, imagining that these fugitives were the inhabitants pursued by his soldiers, and that victory was his, laughed and joked and enjoyed the sight amazingly.

But they proved to be his own troops, and on them, and those who were with him outside, the cannon of the ramparts was now directed. He was compelled to beat a hasty retreat, with some peril to himself and the remnant of his army, the country being inundated by the opening of the sluices. The duke fled from the scene of his disgrace and failure, and, stung by chagrin and shame, retired to his estates on the Oise and Marne.

Fear of the Spaniards induced an attempt at reconciliation. The offer of Henri III. to mediate and to afford assistance was accepted, by the advice of the Prince of Orange. A new treaty was signed between the States General and the duke; but he returned no more to Flanders. The people no longer had any confidence in him, and he, repenting of his folly when too late, felt that he deserved none.

But while the Duc d'Anjou et de Brabant was endeavouring to play the despot in Flanders, Henri III., with his favourite *mignons*, was fêting the carnival more outrageously than ever. Both priests and people were highly incensed at the insults and wanton attacks this dissolute band nightly inflicted on peaceable and unoffending persons. Nor did these masked ruffians confine their profligate revels to the streets. They entered houses, destroyed or pillaged everything they could lay their hands on, and insulted the women.

L'Estoile speaks of the complaints, the indignation, the menaces, this shameful conduct inspired in the people against a sovereign by whom they were not only injured and insulted, but, as they said, bowed down to the earth by the burden of taxation, in order to supply him with the means of recklessly wasteful expenditure. But if the king, with his worthless companions, had been even more than usually hilarious this carnival, he was prepared to atone for it, and to reassure both clergy and people by Lenten devotions no less demonstrative than his carnival revels.

The Shrovetide orgies ended — at six o'clock on the morning of Ash Wednesday — the "compensatory works, which excused every sin," as Henri's Jesuit confessor told him, were then to begin. With the approval of the nuncio, the "White Flagellants" (*blancs battus*) were brought to Paris from Avignon, and named the Penitents of the Annunciation of our Lady. The king and his courtiers joined this brotherhood, and on the 25th of March made the first solemn procession in Paris with them.

They were covered with white linen sacks, having slits in them for the eyes. The rain was falling in torrents when they issued from the convent of the Augustines, and in double file proceeded to Notre-Dame, where, in their linen sacks drenched with wet, their mysteries and ceremonies were concluded. The king and his brother penitents are said to have inaugurated their first devotional masquerade in Paris by a very lively supper; and to have fortified themselves against any ill results from tramping in the heavy rain in their linen sacks from convent to church by many a bumper of the king's fine old wine of the Jurançon.

Shrove Tuesday had already usurped six hours of Ash Wednesday. Six more would not add greatly to the weight of the sin that so readily could be atoned for. A "compensatory work" was needed, which the king on this occasion found in ordering a hundred and twenty pages of his household to be flogged. These profane youths had amused themselves with a mock procession as White Flagellants. In lieu of linen bags, which were not attainable, they made eye-holes in linen cloths, threw them over their heads, marched in procession, and chanted the Miserere. The king thought that the most appropriate punishment for these impious mock flagellants was a severe flagellation.

The famous popular preacher, Poncet, who preached the Lenten sermons at Notre-Dame that year, thought that the king himself and his penitents merited the same punishment. Poncet was a man of dauntless character; distinguished for the warmth and animation of his style of preaching; often rising to eloquence when, in his indignation, lashing the vices of the period. At times, however, he would employ words or forms of expression that gave a rather grotesque turn to the comments which, in the pulpit, he fearlessly indulged in on the conduct of the king and the court.

On the day following the flagellants' procession, as Poncet was preaching before the king and the court and a large general congregation, at a point in his discourse suitable for what he was about to say, he fixed his eyes on the king and his favourites and exclaimed: "Ah! miserable hypocrites and atheists, you mock God under your masks, and for pretence carry a lash at your girdle. Par Dieu! it is not there you should have it, but on your backs and your shoulders, for there is not one among you who does not well deserve a good thrashing" (L'Estoile).

Many who were present, if they dared not laugh outright, could not repress a smile. Henri was more annoyed than his favourites. He said that for ten years he had always kept the carnival and the period of Lent in the same manner as the present ones, and no preacher had ever before found fault with him. He would have liked to send this presumptuous ecclesiastic to be hanged on the Place de Grève, as he had but a few weeks before hanged a poor gentleman of Beauce, who had written a pasquinade against him. But le Père Poncet was far too popular to be thus unceremoniously put out of the way. Henri was therefore compelled to be content with obtaining an order requiring him to retire for a short time to his convent.

Before he left Paris the Duc d'Épernon said to him, "M. le Prédicateur, I am told that people go to hear you preach because you make them laugh. That is not right. A preacher such as you should seek to edify rather than to excite mirth." "Monsieur," replied Poncet, "I would have you know that I preach the Word of God alone, and that none come to my sermons to laugh unless they are evil-doers or atheists; nor have I in all my life caused as many to laugh as you have caused to weep." *

The impression made on the people by the king's affectation of excessive devotion was usually the contrary to that he intended. Nevertheless he continued to take a prominent part in the festivals and processions of the Church, to visit the most famous shrines, and to spend a few days occasionally *en retraite* at one or other of the monasteries — his wife being similarly occupied in some neighbouring convent.

They were very solicitous for an heir to the throne, and together, on the 10th of April, set off from Paris on foot to pray the various virgins of Chartres and Cléry to grant them this blessing. But these unsympathetic virgins heeded not their supplications. Numerous as were the bribes, in the shape of jewels and expensive dresses, laid at their feet, their stony hearts remained unmoved. On the 24th they returned, both of them very weary. Henri, it was reported, would not have been unwilling to acknowledge a supposititious heir; but the queen was more scrupulous than her dissolute husband, and would consent to no such arrangement.

* Pierre de l'Estoile — "*Journal de Henri III.*" It was Poncet who accused the king and his flagellants with resuming their carnival orgies after the Ash Wednesday procession.

Yet Queen Louise seems to have regarded Henri III. as little less than a saint. "Nothing affects her so much as the king's presence," remarks the Venetian ambassador, Lippomano. "Her eyes are ever intently fixed on him, like a person deeply in love. At the solemn festivals it is she who with great reverence and deep curtsies presents the *serviette* to the king when he takes his seat at table. But, to speak the truth, he gives but little heed to his amiable queen. Almsgiving, prayers, and good deeds, visiting the convents, hospitals, and holy places fully occupy her; but for the end proposed hitherto in vain, her great grief still remaining — she has no children.

Henri III., as usual in want of money, yet desirous of calming the people's opposition to his ordinary methods of obtaining supplies, bethought him of issuing an edict against the too prevalent extravagance in dress. It was piously announced that "modesty in such matters appearing to be almost extinct, God was greatly incensed." Still further to induce the belief that the reforms he had promised but a few months back would be fully carried out, he cancelled an impost of two decimes which he had recently asked of the clergy.

But at the same time he caused inquiries to be made into the circumstances of the opulent merchants — wine merchants especially — and the upper *bourgeoisie*, for the purpose of levying a personal tax on them, varying according to what he considered, from the report made to him, the ability of each to pay. The sum thus levied was to be "paid within twenty-four hours, under pain of imprisonment, and without remonstrances." It was against this class that the edict censuring luxury in dress was chiefly directed. So that the saving effected by the economy he would have enforced on them, in the *toilettes* of their wives and daughters, he intended should pass into his own pocket.

While these reforms were proceeding Spain was regaining ground in the Netherlands, the Prince of Parma having retaken Dunkirk and other towns as soon as the Duc d'Anjou had left them. The duke was still at Château-Thierry, suffering greatly from phthisis, and lamenting his failures, matrimonial and political. Philip II., desiring to punish Henri III. for interfering in Flanders, renewed at this time his proposals to the King of Navarre. Money to pay his troops would be immediately forthcoming if he would consent to join him, and resume the offensive towards his brother of France. The infanta, Clara-Eugenia, was again promised, and a divorce from Marguerite of course. No abjuration was asked; an amazing concession, considering Philip's burning zeal against heresy. He merely advised Henri to pursue his temporal advantage, and to be satisfied with the privileges already granted to those of "the religion."

The divorce might well be considered a tempting offer, Marguerite's conduct since she left Nérac having given occasion for so much scandal and political intrigue that Henri III. would not allow her to remain at the Louvre, and even banished her entirely from the Court of France. The King of Navarre, however, neither accepted nor rejected the Spaniard's proposals. He thanked him for his good-will towards him, and at once warned Henri III. of Philip's designs. The bearer of this information was the young Baron de Rosny.

Philip II., when renewing his advances to Henri of Navarre, did not again press his suit on the Princesse Catherine. A second positive rejection would have been too humiliating; but in the interval other princes had made urgent proposals, and one or two, it was believed, at Philip's suggestion — Charles Emanuel of Savoy, for instance, to whom Philip afterwards married his daughter. But Catherine of Navarre held firmly to her religion, and also preferred romantically to marry for love rather than for political objects. The widowed Duc Charles de Lorraine offered his crown to her; but she naïvely informed him that his sons and daughters being about her own age, she thought him too old.

The duke therefore withdrew his proposal and offered his son, the Duc de Bar, in his stead. The duke was a handsome youth of seventeen, and Catherine was then in her twenty-third year, lively in disposition, pleasing in countenance and figure. The young duke admired her, and had no objection to her following her own religion. But no marriage ensued; Catherine probably objected to his youth, refusing the son's offer as she had refused the father's. Also, Henri and Plessis-Mornay — who was a chief agent in Catherine's matrimonial affairs — had other designs which seem to have clashed with those of the Duc de Lorraine.

They were desirous of marrying the Princesse Catherine to James VI. of Scotland, and the Duc de Lorraine, it appears, was no less desirous of securing the Scottish crown and eventually that of England for his daughter, in spite of the Scotch king's heresy. On the other hand, the zealous Mornay hoped to preserve the Navarrese princess from Catholic influence, by marrying her to a prince brought up in the severe doctrines of Scottish Puritanism. Queen Elizabeth was greatly in favour of this match, and wrote to Catherine on the subject.

Other suitors paid their court in vain, but Catherine was not put to the trouble of dismissing them; Mornay took that unpleasant duty upon himself. In Henri's absence, he informed him that "the Prince of Wirtemberg-Montbéliard had made an offer of marriage to the Princesse Catherine; but that he had replied to it in a manner to give the prince no hope whatever of its acceptance." He adds, "The prince has taken away the said lady's portrait." The portrait seems to have consoled him, as he did not renew his offer.

There were political reasons as well as religious ones for the desire to unite Catherine to James VI. The marriage was to be one of the first conditions of the League which Henri of Navarre and his advisers were meditating between Elizabeth and the Protestant German princes, as a sort of *contre-partie* to that of France. This negotiation was, however, frequently interrupted by the reported fluctuations in the health of the Duc d'Anjou, and by the troubles and intrigues of which the Château of Nérac had become the scene since Marguerite's return.

Henri III. had several times ordered his sister to leave Paris and return to her husband, which he told her would be "more decent and respectable than intriguing at the Court of France." As she seemed to have no intention of obeying, "he, in the presence of the whole court" (as the German ambassador informed the Emperor Rudolph), "said many affronting and scandalous things to his sister. So well did he seem to be informed of her numerous amours, that he named all the gallants she had had since her marriage, and those who were then in her good graces. He spoke of her having recently given birth to a son, and concluded his shameless address by again ordering her to leave France."

On the 8th of August she set out on her journey to Gascony, though on very bad terms with the husband to whom she was returning. At the Porte Saint-Jacques she and her ladies were unmasked by the captain of the guard, to ascertain if any of her lovers were with her. At Palaiseau sixty of the king's archers arrested three of her ladies, as the confidantes of her intrigues; also some of her gentlemen of her household, who, after being imprisoned at Montaigu, and questioned concerning their mistress's conduct, were released, and Marguerite and her retinue continued their journey.

A letter from Henri III. informed Henri of Navarre of his wife's infidelities. Fearing the result of the course he had pursued, this letter was speedily followed by another, begging him not to be prevented from receiving his wife by what he had already written respecting her. But Henri declined to receive Marguerite. She had absented herself for two years; had made an excursion to Flanders, and when it became necessary to quit that country, had returned to the French Court, where she had passed about eighteen months, taking part in all the cabals and intrigues of the time; quarrelling with the king, railing at and mocking his favourites, until, roused to violent anger, Henri resolved, if she would not go as he commanded, forcibly to eject her.

In consultation with his council, it was decided

that the King of Navarre ought to resent the extraordinary conduct of Henri III. The indefatigable Du Plessis-Mornay was despatched to Paris to inform the king that if Queen Marguerite merited the affront she had received, the King of Navarre required that full justice should be done him. But if unjustly accused, then he claimed to know, if only in the interests of the royal house, who were the authors of these calumnies. This affair, complicated with political questions, dragged on for months, Henri III. delaying either to withdraw or confirm the charges he had brought against his sister.

Consequently Marguerite was not received at Nérac, for the King of Navarre declared that "he could not acknowledge as his wife a woman covered with infamy." The Duc d'Anjou, whose deceptive malady now gave hopes of his recovery, endeavoured to effect a reconciliation. But in vain. Henri III. must give a satisfactory reply; and at last he did affirm that he had been deceived in the representations made to him. A few vague expressions of regret were added, and Henri was reminded that the most virtuous of princesses were liable to attacks from the tongues of the envious and slanderous.

The king desired Du Plessis-Mornay to thank his brother of Navarre for his fidelity to him, in informing him of Philip's designs. Also for consenting to again receive Marguerite on the faith of the explanations he had given him. It might be inferred from this that she was once more residing at the Château de Nérac; but if so, it was but for a very short time. For while Henri was then (as the memoirs of Sully and Du Plessis-Mornay relate) at the height of his passion for "La belle Corisande"—Comtesse de Grammont et Guiche—Marguerite had resumed her former relations with the head of the League, the Duc de Guise, and carried on an active correspondence with him, in which politics had fully as large a share as love.

Henri III., whose pleasures and devotions were interrupted by the turn events were taking under the influence of Philip and the Guises, had his spies on the alert, both in Gascony and the provinces of his kingdom. Henri of Navarre was by this means soon informed of Marguerite's amusements, and one of her servants who was the usual bearer of her mysterious despatches was arrested. This act excited strong resentment on her part. She accused her husband of persecuting her, and said that the superintendent of her household, Comte Ségur, had been ordered to conduct her to Pau as a prisoner.

This served her as a pretence for leaving Nérac, and, counselled by Guise it was believed, taking possession, in the name of the League, of l'Agenais and Quercy, part of her dowry. She then raised a small army and organised a petty war against

Henri of Navarre, who was menaced with assassination, to the great alarm of his sister Catherine. Marguerite was secretly supported in her warlike doings by Guise and the Leaguers; but as soon as information of the confusion and disorder she was occasioning in Gascony reached the French Court, Maréchal de Matignon was ordered to unite his forces to those of Navarre, which resulted in the defeat of Marguerite and her allies at Bec-d'Ambez. Marguerite then retired to Agen, where she seems to have intended to reign despotically.

Her friend, Madame Duras, was appointed first minister, and heavy taxes were imposed on the people. A revolt ensued, and the king's protection was claimed. Maréchal de Matignon then marched on Agen, whence the queen and her minister hastily made their escape. The former was taken *en croupe* by a cavalier, and travelled in that fashion for more than twelve leagues. At the end of her journey she was arrested, in the king's name, by M. de Cassillon, who conducted her to the Château d'Usson, in Auvergne, where, to beguile the tedium of captivity, she wrote her memoirs.

The petty war of Agenais lasted nearly two years, and compelled Henri of Navarre to make use of every expedient to raise money for the support of his troops. His sister Catherine, her ladies, and the Comtesse de Grammont, obtained a loan on the security of their jewels and sent it to him. But, during the continuance of this foolish yet troublesome war, Henri's position had materially changed. He had become heir-presumptive to the throne of France. The Duc d'Anjou had died; his death hastened by his own folly. He had felt so much better in the autumn of 1583, that he determined to pass the approaching winter in Paris, where he joined his brother and his court in the customary follies and dissolute revels of that season, and in the penitential mummeries succeeding them.

But ere they were concluded the duke was again taken ill. He hastened back to Château-Thierry, for he had a dread of his mother's attentions. On the 24th of March she left Paris to visit him, the physicians having reported that his spitting of blood was incessant, and that they could afford him no relief. But "Monsieur" lingered on yet for awhile, ever bemoaning the hardness of his fate and bewailing his lost hopes. As the physicians could give the queen-mother no hope of her son's recovery, she again visited Château-Thierry, and on the 1st of June brought away all her son's jewels and valuable works of art.

Henri III. also despatched D'Épernon with a retinue of a hundred gentlemen to Navarre, to inform the king of the Duc d'Anjou's critical state of health, and to urge him to come to court and to attend mass, that he might acknowledge him as his heir. But Henri declined to accede to these proposals. On the 10th of June the Duc d'Anjou breathed his last. Cough and slow fever had worn Elizabeth's gallant little lover to a mere shadow. "He had never felt well," he said, "since he spent the carnival with the king, and had had to pay very dearly for the riot and luxury he then indulged in." " He was French, both in name and nature; an enemy of the Spaniard and of the Guises. But he had the vices of his race, and no one regretted him." *

Du Plessis-Mornay, then at the Court of France, endeavouring to arrange for the greater security of the Huguenots in their cities of surety, was the first to inform the King of Navarre that he had become the second person in France, and probably at no distant period might expect to be the first. Henri III. was only thirty-three; but from his dissolute habits of life, which had told greatly on his constitution, he was regarded as almost an old man.

To his legitimate successor Mornay now wrote in eloquent terms, "exhorting him to show himself worthy of the destiny that God was preparing for him." "Those amours," he said, "to which you give so much time, and which have hitherto been so public, are no longer suitable or possible. It is now time, sire, that you should make love to the whole of Christendom, and especially to France."

* Pierre de l'Estoile.

François, Duc d' Anjou.
Photo-etching from an old print.

On the 24th of June the body of the Duc d'Anjou et de Brabant was brought to Paris, and placed in the Church of Saint-Ma-Gloire. The king after dinner left the Louvre to throw holy water on the body of his deceased brother. "He wore a long mantle of eighteen ells of violet-coloured Florentine serge, the train being of greater width than length, and borne by eight gentlemen. A considerable number of prelates, cardinals, princes, nobles, and gentlemen preceded him. The bishops wore their rochets with the scapulars and short mantles of black Florence serge; the cardinals their usual violet robes. The nobles and gentlemen were mounted on white horses, and wore mourning robes with the hood on the shoulder.

"The Swiss Guards, their tambours covered with crape, marched before the king, and the archers of the Scotch Guard surrounded him, all wearing their hoquetons (embroidered jackets) and usual livery, but with black doublets, hose, and hats, and their halberds covered with crape. The reigning queen followed the king, alone in a covered carriage of tan colour, her dress being also tan. Eight other carriages followed, full of ladies dressed in black.

"On the 25th the body was brought to Notre-Dame. The king, dressed in violet, with his face uncovered, remained for four or five hours at the window of a house facing the Hôtel-Dieu to see the funeral procession pass. The Duc de Guise was with him. It was remarked that he looked sad and melancholy. The third funeral procession from Notre-Dame to the late duke's final resting-place occurred on the morrow, the 26th, the king again witnessing it from the windows of a house in the Rue Saint-Denis.

"The funeral oration was delivered by the Archbishop of Bourges. It was the very worst he had ever spoken. Often he placed his hand on his beard, like a man abashed, or put out of countenance."

The queen-mother does not appear to have been present at any one of these three funeral processions. She had no regard for this youngest of her sons, and was suspected, as on two former occasions, perhaps unjustly, of shortening his last sufferings. She was certainly more affected by the recent death of her Chancellor Birago, who was one of the needy adventurers who followed her to France. Birago had received a cardinal's hat a few months before his death. It was generally believed that he poisoned his wife to enable him to enter the Church and attain at one bound to its highest dignity, save election to the papal throne. Catherine gave him an almost royal funeral, and a splendid monument.*

* Pierre de l'Estoile. The historians Mathieu and Davila; Du Plessis-Mornay.

CHAPTER XI.

Henri of Navarre Declared Heir to the Throne of France. — Prince of Orange Assassinated. — Spanish and Popish Plots against the Life of Elizabeth. — Henri III. Said to Be Becoming Insane. — The King and the Cardinal De Bourbon. — Gregory XIII. Sends Blessings and Plenary Indulgences to the Leaguers. — Elizabeth Sends the Order of the Garter to Henri III. — The "Demon of the South" Enraged. — The Queen-mother Seeks the Repeal of the Salic Law. — Pacificatory Edicts Revoked. — Treaty with the League.

WHEN the Duc d'Anjou's physicians pronounced his recovery hopeless, Henri III., in the presence of the court, declared Henri of Navarre his brother's rightful successor, and sole heir to the throne of France. Doubtless, he anticipated no refusal on Henri's part to embrace at once the Catholic faith, when with the question of his renunciation of heresy was involved the probable loss of that throne. But if later on the King of Navarre thought Paris, whose gates were about to be opened to him, "worth a mass," he appears to have been of a contrary opinion when his entry into that capital, as King of France, seemed but a remote contingency.

The hesitation he at first is said to have exhibited in his reply to the King of France's envoy proceeded less from religious than political considerations. If from motives of self-interest he should abandon the standard of Reform, would his conversion be believed in, and the Catholics abandon that of the Guises to enlist under his? It was doubtful indeed; and besides, Henri III. was not a man to be relied on. It was a point of honour also with Henri of Navarre that he should not debase himself by trafficking with his faith.

Some historians are of opinion that the League would have been disarmed, and the lengthened troubles of France avoided, had Henri at this period consented to reënter the bosom of the Church. "His decision, they say, was influenced by Du Plessis-Mornay, who, being at that time at the French Court, in his blind Calvinistic zeal repulsed the proposal in Henri's name. The struggle between the Guises and the Bourbons was then openly declared in the face of Europe — astonished at the audacity of one party, and the valour and perseverance of the other."

The League was reorganised, and its progress secretly extended. In towns where it had failed in 1567 it now succeeded — for to rouse the people it was diligently circulated, also announced from the pulpits, that "a heretic was about to become King of France," an announcement that stirred the souls of the fanatical Catholic masses to their very depths. Even the *bourgeoisie* and others who favoured a policy of peace and toleration stood aghast at the bare idea of heresy on the throne.

Further to inflame the minds of the people, the preachers described tortures of revolting cruelty and fearful forms of death, which they assured their hearers were inflicted on all good Catholics in England and other Protestant states. In order to impress these imaginary horrors more deeply on the agitated people, pictorial representations of them were affixed, at Guise's suggestion, to the walls of the churches of Paris, and laid on the graves in the cemeteries. "Behold! behold!" cried the Jesuit preachers, pointing to these prints, "behold your own fate! the fate of France under the ally of the English Jezebel."

The English ambassadors addressed some severe remonstrances to the king respecting these atrocious pictures. Inquiries were made, and after some search it was ascertained that the plates were at the Hôtel de Guise. The engravings were then withdrawn, having served their purpose — that of fomenting anarchy, and adding fuel to the flames of angry passion and prejudice already raging in the land.

On the 10th of July, one month after the death of the Duc d'Anjou, the Prince of Orange was assassinated at Delft, in Holland. Philip II. had offered 20,000 crowns to whoever should take the prince's life. Two previous attempts had failed; the third succeeded. He was shot in the breast by a fanatic named Balthazar Gérard, and fell dead in the arms of his sister and his wife, who were in the apartment when the assassin entered, on pretence that a letter he had brought must be delivered into the prince's own hands.*

Under torture, the wretched Gérard declared that a Jesuit priest had incited him to attempt the deed, assuring him that "although it was possible he might have to die for it, yet that his death would be a glorious and a happy one — angels attending to carry him to heaven, and place him near the Holy Virgin and her son, Jesus Christ." The tortures inflicted on him were terrible. The arm with which he had done the deed was burnt off to the elbow, and his painful death cruelly protracted. His family received the promised reward, to which Philip added letters of nobility to mark his sense of the service he fancied the poor fanatical assassin had done him.

Some cities were speedily, indeed, again brought under the yoke of Spain; but Holland and Zealand, in spite of the efforts of the Prince of Parma, remained firm, and elected Maurice of Nassau, the late prince's son, their hereditary governor. Wil-

---

* The Princess of Orange was the daughter of Admiral de Coligny and the widow of the Comte de Teligny, who, like her father, was one of the victims of the Saint-Bartholomew massacre.

liam of Nassau, his nephew, was elected hereditary Governor of Frise, and the sovereignty of the United Provinces, held by the Duc d'Anjou, was offered, with an extension of authority, to Henri III.

Expecting, probably, to go on from one successful murder to another, two attempts were made in the course of this year to assassinate the King of Navarre. Philip II. adopted at this time a policy so extreme towards England that even her nationality, and the life of her queen, were menaced by a series of plots and conspiracies sanctioned by the Pope. Gregory XIII., conjointly with Philip and his emissaries, endeavoured to incite a rebellion in Ireland; but succeeded only in bringing misery on its turbulent inhabitants.

The mission of the Guises was to obtain possession of the person of the young King of Scotland, James VI., in order "to turn him from the paths of heresy," and set him against Elizabeth. This, by many devices, they endeavoured through their agents to accomplish. But their schemes being discovered were defeated, as well as their attempt to induce the English Catholics to rise *en masse*; to depose or assassinate Elizabeth; to place her prisoner, Mary Stuart, on the throne; and exterminate Protestantism in England. To oppose these persistently hostile acts of the enemies of England and the queen, Elizabeth and her ministers were compelled to resort to very stringent repressive measures. But Philip did not yet despair of England becoming a province of Spain. Great maritime preparations were making for her downfall, the burdensome expense of which his new kingdom of Portugal was compelled to bear. He, meanwhile, though professedly unable to pay his debts, furnished the Leaguers and their chief, the Duc de Guise, with doubloons in abundance, for the furtherance of his designs on England, France, and the Netherlands.

The immediate object of the League was to declare the King of Navarre excluded from the right of succession, in favour of a Catholic heir. It then became necessary to designate which of the princes of the blood was rightfully authorised to take the place of the rejected one. Had the people of Paris been called on to name him, the claim of the princes of the blood would have been little regarded, and cries of "Guise!" "Vive Guise!" would have rent the air. This the duke knew full well. But the favourable moment for encouraging or yielding to it had not yet arrived.

Until then a stop-gap was needed. He was found in the person of the foolish, voluptuous, and incompetent old bigot, the Cardinal de Bourbon, Henri of Navarre's uncle. The cardinal was entirely governed by an intriguing and avaricious favourite domestic, who, though his master had but few secrets worth knowing, was quite willing to sell them, such as they were, and all the duke desired to know of the cardinal's affairs, his private life and general habits. This weak, vain, elderly prelate was flattered by Guise with the prospect of being released from his priestly vows, and marrying the Dowager Duchesse de Montpensier, the duke's sister.

Readily he consented to all that Philip II. might require of him, and promised "on his accession" to give him possession of his nephew's domains of Lower Navarre and Béarn, and to restore Cambray, which the Duc d'Anjou had taken and retained, and had left as a legacy to his brother. Hardly could a more accommodating candidate for the throne have been found to present to the League as the orthodox sovereign of France, or to fill the post of heir-presumptive, while the descendant of Pharamond and Charlemagne was watching and waiting for the opportune moment of placing the crown on his own head, instead of handing it to Philip as promised.

Miron, the king's physician, had whispered about that Henri III. was becoming insane. But without any apparent warrant for it, except that he began about this time to amuse himself with a cup and ball, and that his conduct was then, as indeed it ever had been, more remarkable for folly than wisdom. It may have even been so reported by the king's own order, as he was remarkably fond of mocking and jeering at those who did not stand high in his favour. The queen-mother, however, treated it seriously, and made her arrangements for ruling France under another regency, thinking that, aided by the Duc de Guise, she might succeed in abolishing the Salic law in favour of the children of her eldest daughter, the Duchesse de Lorraine.

Though ever speculating on the death of her children, as one by one they dropped around her, she seems to have thought only of succeeding to their power, of grasping the sceptre as it fell from their feeble hands; but never to have dreamed of being called away to join them in the tomb. Guise did, however, promise to aid the queen-mother in obtaining the repeal of this ancient law, which, but a few years back, the states of Pontoise had solemnly reaffirmed. He thus won her over to favour the views of the League in its purpose of eradicating heresy by the extermination of the heretics.

In order to free himself from the annoyance of persistent solicitation to abrogate all pacificatory edicts granted to the Huguenots, and to proclaim "the king's religion or death," Henri, with his wife, his dogs, his monkeys, and with several of his favourites, went to Gaillon "for a little diversion" at the expense of the "cardinal heir-presumptive." The splendid Château de Gaillon was a truly royal residence, built by Georges d'Amboise, and belonging at the period in question to the Cardinal de Bourbon. One morning during his visit the king, affecting, it would seem, to be unacquainted with the fact that his host was his heir-presumptive, asked him "if he would tell him the truth concerning what he was about to ask."

"Certainly," replied the cardinal, "if I know it."

"My cousin," said the king, "you see I have no heir, and I much fear am not likely to have. If then it should please God — everything, as you know, being uncertain in this world — that I should die to-day, the crown would fall in direct line to your house. Should that happen — though I well know that you do not desire it — is it not true that you would precede your nephew, the King of Navarre; the kingdom belonging to you and not to him?"

"I think, sire," replied the old simpleton, "that my teeth will have ceased to ache when that event occurs; and I pray God, with all my heart, to call me from this world before so great a misfortune happens. I have never given a thought to a thing so unlikely, and contrary to the order of nature."

"Yes, yes," said the king, "but how often is the order of nature introverted and changed as God pleases! I wish to know, and I pray you to speak freely, if such an event should happen, would not you dispute the succession with your nephew?"

The cardinal sought to evade a direct reply. But the king, with a sort of malicious pleasure, persisted in pressing it on him.

The cardinal could refuse no longer. "As you command me, sire, to tell you," he said, "although the possibility of such an event has never crossed my mind, it seeming to me utterly devoid of reasonableness; yet, if such a misfortune should occur, I will not deny the truth to you, sire. I think the crown would belong to me, not to my nephew, and I should firmly resolve not to give it up to him."

The king laughed heartily, and slapping the cardinal on the shoulder, said:

"*Mon bon ami*, the League might give it to you, but the court would take it from you."

He then left him, laughing, mocking, and jeering as he went.*

A distrust of the aims of the Guises and their partisans, Spanish and French, induced the king to begin the year with a change in the code of court etiquette, rendering access to him more difficult. He also instituted a new private body-guard of forty-five gentlemen, who were to live at court and receive each a yearly salary of 1,200 crowns, their sole duty being to guard the king

---

* Pierre de l'Estoile — "*Journal de Henri III.*"

The Cardinal de Bourbon had thoughts of supplanting his nephew in his rights so long before as 1562, when the King of Navarre died. He then solicited the Pope for several months to release him from his vows, and permit him to marry. The nuncio supported his request, urging that "astrologers were predicting the speedy extinction of the line of Valois." The Pope, however, refused his request.

night and day. At great expense he made an entire change in the livery of his household, and amused himself with inventing new fashions for the queen, who, always in adoration before her saintly husband, accepted with gratitude, and wore with pleasure, whatever it was his fancy to design for her.

But the troubles of his kingdom did not prevent him from passing a very joyous carnival, followed, of course, by the customary penitential processions, pilgrimages, and monastic seclusion. The promoters of the League, also at the opening of the new year, assembled at the Château de Joinville, near the scene of François de Guise's triumphant massacre of Vassy. There, on the 16th of January, 1585, the Duc de Guise and four of his brothers; the Captains Moreo and Tassi, representing Philip II.; and the Sieur de Roncherolles, the envoy of the "cardinal heir-presumptive," signed a secret treaty.

By it they bound themselves to contract a perpetual union for the purpose of exterminating the heretical sects of France and the Netherlands, and excluding heretical princes from the throne. The contracting parties undertook to prohibit heresy in France, and to pursue to the death and annihilate those heretics who refused obedience to the Church. The decrees of the holy Council of Trent were also to be received in France in their fullest extent, the cardinal binding himself to confirm and enforce all this and much more on his accession; to place France, in fact, so far as it depended on him, in the hands of Philip of Spain.

Gregory XIII. sent his blessing on the good work, and plenary indulgence to the contracting parties. He also gave them authority to take up arms, with or without the king's consent, against the heretics and those who favoured them, and promised to excommunicate Henri of Navarre and the Prince de Condé as soon as hostilities began. "He did not see that the death of the king was then desirable; but he had no objection to his being arrested, and placed in a monastery, well guarded."

Guise and the other chiefs of the League desired the holy father to give them his instructions and views on the matter in writing. The wily pontiff, however, refused to do more than state them verbally to the Jesuit priest, Mathieu — one of the League's most active intriguers. In the following month, Gregory XIII. died. The Leaguers then, in order to carry out their projects more effectually in Paris, divided the city into sixteen circuits, corresponding to its sixteen quarters, each having its chief and his committee. Thus was formed the powerful faction of "The Sixteen" ("*Les Seize*").

Henri III., since the Netherlanders had first offered him the sovereignty of their country, had been repeatedly implored to interfere ere the whole of Belgium was lost. An embassy was now despatched to Paris, at the instigation of Elizabeth, anxiously desirous of preventing the triumph of an enemy whose hired assassins were constantly seeking to take her life, and who was proposing to invade her kingdom. To induce him to send troops to their assistance, the envoys were authorised to offer the king 100,000 crowns per month — the greater part guaranteed by the queen — and to place in his hands ten or twelve cities of surety.

At Senlis, on the 7th of February, the ambassadors were met by messengers from the king, requesting them to proceed no further until he could name a day to receive them. He had not the courage to give them audience openly, but proposed to send for them secretly to Paris. When, however, the Spanish ambassador, Mendoza, whom Elizabeth had expelled from England, addressed the king in an authoritative tone, almost commanding him " to refrain from attending to what those excommunicated rebels had to say, unless he would draw upon himself the just vengeance of his Catholic majesty," then Henri, stung to the quick by the Spaniard's insolence, assumed an air of unwonted dignity.

" A King of France," he said, "trembled before no man, and neither menaces nor dangers would make him depart from the generous custom of his ancestors towards those who sought his protection." "Consequently a numerous escort was sent to meet the Netherlanders, who were promptly and very graciously received by the king, and treated with great hospitality." But, as usual, he could not overcome his indecision and utter a definitive yes or no to the proposals made to him. "He required time to consider them."

"This embassy, in the course of the same month, was followed by an English one. The Earl of Warwick was the chief ambassador. He and his suite were attended by two hundred horsemen, who found a resting-place in houses near at hand. They were hospitably treated at the king's expense, costing the royal treasury 500 crowns per day. The earl, with the gentlemen accompanying him, was lodged at the Hôtel d'Anjou, his suite in the neighbouring merchants' houses; but served at the king's expense.

"The Earl of Warwick had brought from Queen Elizabeth to Henri III. the collar of the Order of the Garter, which contained pearls and precious stones whose value was estimated at more than 100,000 gold crowns. On the 28th of February, the king's investiture took place, after vespers, in the Church of the Augustines, he making the oath of the Order in the hands of the Earl of Warwick. Henri was magnificently dressed in the costume of the chevaliers. In the evening he celebrated the event by a grand ball and *fête*. Under cover of this special embassy, the king was urged to take the Flemings under his protection, and offered, in the queen's name, a contribution of one-third of the expenses of the war.

"On the 2nd of March, being Shrove Sunday, the king entertained the embassy at a grand banquet, followed by a brilliant *fête* in the great saloon of the palace of the Bishop of Paris. To this *fête* the king invited a large number of the handsomest women of the city. In the latter part of the evening there was a ballet, in which eighty ladies and gentlemen joined; all sumptuously dressed, and in various colours. This entertainment is said to have cost upwards of 20,000 crowns. Yet another evening *fête* of still greater magnificence — a *fête d'adieu* — was given on the 10th.*

"A day or two after, the embassy left Paris." Its real object was not attained, though Henri had more than once seemed to be on the point of adopting the course suggested. Again "he thought it would be well, before giving his final decision, that the affairs of his kingdom should be more settled;" and finally, Elizabeth and the King of Navarre — two of whose agents were then at the court — were informed that "the king could do nothing until tranquillity was restored to France." It was, indeed, too true that he could do nothing. He had hesitated too long, instead of promptly acting when the sovereignty of the United Provinces was offered him on his brother's death.

* Pierre de l'Estoile — "*Journal de Henri III.*"

Yet so well aware was he of the intrigues of Philip and the Guises, and of the reorganisation of the League, that he had taken certain precautions for ensuring his personal safety. But he had very negligently omitted to place his army on a footing that would enable him to cope with these intriguers, and had passed the carnival in riot and debauchery.

Many persons, therefore, suspected that some secret understanding existed between him and the Guises. This suspicion was strengthened by the release of a vessel which had been seized on the Marne, conveying arms to Châlons, in charge of a member of the Cardinal de Guise's household. The King of Navarre's agents concurred in these suspicions, which coming to the knowledge of Henri III., he said "he hoped that God would destroy him, if he had anything to do with the Guises and this rising in arms." The king's indignant reply to Mendoza's menacing language, together with his investiture with the Order of the Garter, furnished the Leaguers with an opportunity of declaiming against him, and asserting that he was acting in concert with Elizabeth, in favour of the Protestant, against the Catholic religion.

Bigoted Catholics, generally, were scandalised at the reception the embassy met with from the king, and at the lavish magnificence of the *fêtes* in honour of the envoys of the heretic queen. The

THE DEMON OF THE SOUTH ENRAGED 195

enraged "Demon of the South" being fully informed by the Prince of Parma of Henri's daring reply to the menaces of the Spaniard Mendoza, at once called on Guise to fulfil his part of the pact of Joinville, or his schemes would be fully revealed to the king. Spanish infantry and German cavalry were already on their way to reinforce the army of the League. The Duc de Mayenne, pending their arrival, took possession of Dijon, while his brother surprised Châlons, and the Duc d'Aumale set off in all haste for Gaillon to bring their king, the Cardinal de Bourbon, to Péronne, the cradle of the League.

In the face of these demonstrations, Henri's new-found dignity soon vanished. He protested that he desired to maintain terms of peace with the Spanish king. He, however, adopted some measures of defence against the Leaguers; published a decree forbidding the levying of troops, and put Paris in charge of a military guard. The means of resistance were not wanting to him. Most of his troops were loyal, and 8,000 Swiss soldiers arrived to join his army, while but 4,000 responded to the demands of the Leaguers.

Queen Elizabeth proposed to send him 6,000 troops, and the State of Venice offered him a substantial loan. Hostilities had begun on the Loire, but with advantage on the side of the royal troops; and Henri of Navarre, who endeavoured to convince his brother of France that the aims of the chiefs of the League were directed towards his crown far more than against the reformed religion, offered him his services with those of the Protestant troops under his command.

But Henri III. feared the Guises less than the Huguenots. The murdered Coligny and other victims of the Saint-Bartholomew sometimes, it appears, rose up before him, unbidden, in mental vision, and the deeds of that dreadful day he firmly believed would yet be avenged when opportunity offered. The King of Navarre's proposal was therefore declined; and Henri enjoined him to refrain from taking up arms, in order to allow the Leaguers clearly to show their treasonable projects. He would then, he assured him, sign no treaty to his prejudice.

The queen-mother was despatched to negotiate terms of peace with the Duc de Guise; and as Protestant swords were not yet to be drawn, a vigorous onslaught was made in the interim by Protestant pens — the chief and the most able being that wielded by the Calvinist diplomatist, Du Plessis-Mornay. The intrigues of Catherine de' Medici with the duke concerning the repeal of the Salic law, contributed, with the renewal of hostilities, to paralyse the king's last feeble efforts against the ambition of the Guises.

The manifesto of the League, printed at Rheims — whither in great state the Leaguers had conducted their cardinal-king — was presented to Henri III. It was drawn up in the name of the Almighty God, King of Kings, and was signed by the Cardinal de Bourbon. It contained a long list of grievances and of abuses to be abolished, and required that the Holy Church of God should be reinstated in the one true Catholic religion. This, with other stipulations relating to the decrees of the Council of Trent, the Inquisition, etc., occupied the queen-mother and the Duc de Guise for two or three months in fruitless negotiation.

To the manifesto Henri feebly replied that he had given many proofs of his zeal for the true religion; that necessity had compelled him to make peace with the heretics; and, as though addressing the cardinal-king of the League, he mentioned that he was but in his thirty-third year, that his health was good, and that he yet hoped that God would give him an heir. He entreated, instead of commanding, the Leaguers to abstain from violence and illegal associations, and rather to rally around him and aid him in restoring the service of God and promoting the public welfare.

The chiefs of the League for reply presented their ultimatum to the king. "They demanded of him the issuing of an edict, enjoining all his subjects to make profession of Catholicism; the exercise of the 'new religion' to be forbidden under pain of death." The Huguenots were, in fact, to be attacked, crushed, annihilated, and to the forces of the League the immediate execution of this edict was to be assigned. Henri, as usual, a prey to irresolution, would neither consent nor refuse.

The queen-mother urged him to yield. His favourite, Joyeuse, a bigoted fanatic, pressed on him the advisability of conciliating the League. D'Épernon, his other favourite, inclined to the Politique party, therefore counselled him to take the offensive, his troops being more numerous than those assembled by Guise. Guillaume de Tavannes (son of the late marshal) gave the same advice. But the timid counsels prevailed, and Catherine returned to Nemours to conclude the treaty with Henri of Guise that was to plunge France into new and greater calamities. It was called the Peace of July, or Articles de Nemours, and was chiefly effected by the efforts of Guise and the physician Miron.

Soon after (18th of July), the king, in person, commanded the Parliament of Paris to publish the revocation of all edicts of tolerance granted to the Huguenots, also the proscription of the "new religion." On his way to the Palais de Justice, he said to the Cardinal de Bourbon, who accompanied him: "Mon oncle, against my conscience, but quite willingly, I ordered the publication of these pacificatory edicts; because they were a relief and solace to my people. I now publish their revocation, according to my conscience, but entirely against my will, because the ruin of my state and people depends on it."

"The secret of all this," says L'Estoile, "was that the king was on foot, the League on horseback, and that his penitent's sack was not so impregnable as the cuirass of the Leaguers. On leaving the Palais de Justice where the Parliament was assembled," continues L'Estoile, "the king was greeted with vociferous cries of '*Vive le roi!*' This astonished many persons; but none more than the king himself. But those cries came from people ordered by the Guises to make this demonstration, and who received payment for it — the little children being presented with sweetmeats to echo the cry."

It was chiefly to the queen-mother and her agreement with the Guises that the troubles again threatening France were believed to be due. And this L'Estoile declares was "pure truth; for she held up the Guises' chins with all her might, with the intention of depriving the Bourbons of the crown, that it might fall to the House of Lorraine and on the head of the children of the late Madame Claude de France."

CHAPTER XII.

Consternation of the Huguenots. — Priests Sent to Convert Henri of Navarre. — The Thunders of the Vatican. — Sixtus V. Opposed to the League. — A Reply to the Bull of Excommunication. — The Guises Use the Bull to Intimidate the King. — A Mania for " Bilboquet." — " Too Merciful to These Scoundrels." — A Vanished Army. — Elizabeth Joins in the Struggle for Religious Freedom.

GREAT was the consternation of the Huguenots when, beyond doubt, it was generally known among them that the king had capitulated to the League; that he had actually been prevailed on to sign a pact with the Guises, revoking all pacificatory edicts, and proclaiming death or exile to whoever did not embrace the Roman faith. Henri of Navarre was profoundly affected by the king's culpable weakness; for too plainly he foresaw the immensity of the evil his irresolution had brought on France, the suffering and distress into which the nation would be plunged, and the strife and bloodshed that inevitably must ensue.*

* The historian Mathieu says, with the view of impressing his readers with the intensity of Henri's grief, that "while he

But Henri of Navarre was not a man to waste time in pondering on misfortune, heavy though it was for France, for himself, and the cause of Reform. The Protestant party seemed to be in even greater peril than at the period immediately following the massacre of the Saint-Bartholomew. It was unfortunately not so united a party as then. Differences had arisen among its members, and jealousy had induced coldness towards its chiefs. But their common peril would, it was hoped, re-unite them, and petty differences vanish in their common endeavour to regain the liberty of conscience and liberty of worship within certain limits conceded them, and their right to which they had believed uncontested, until now despotically deprived of them by the enemies of the king and state.

Assisted by the able pen of his great negotiator, Du Plessis-Mornay, an eloquent appeal was addressed by the King of Navarre to Elizabeth of England for aid in money and for the assistance of her fleet. Also the principal English nobility, as well as the princes of Germany and other Protestant states, were reminded of the conjoint liability of the Reformers to support each other when attacked by their persecuting Catho-

sat, his head resting on his hand, musing on the above events, half of his mustache turned white." He gives this anecdote on the best authority, that of Henri himself, who, he says, told him of the fact.

lic enemies, and, as in the present case, in their pressing need for immediate action.

War, *à outrance*, was declared "against the League and its partisans, in the name of the King of Navarre, the Prince de Condé, the marshal, Duc de Montmorency, and other nobles, chevaliers, gentlemen, provinces, towns, and communities of both religions, associated for the preservation of the state." The Duc de Montmorency, chief of the Politique party, once more declared for the Protestant cause, having rejected with disdain the overtures of the Leaguers. "He cared not," he said, "to become a tool in the hands of the Guises for the furtherance of the ambitious views of those enemies of the House of Montmorency."

For similar reasons many of the nobility who joined the League in its first period now withdrew from it. The rising in arms against the king was also repugnant to many of the noblesse, amongst whom the monarchical principle was still strong, though the queen-mother and her sons had done their best to weaken it. The League was now most formidable in the populous provincial towns, though many of the largest of them — Marseilles, Bordeaux, etc., refused to recognise it.

The Cardinal de Lénoncourt, with other ecclesiastics and theologians, by the king's command, left Paris at this time to seek Henri of Navarre in Gascony, in order to induce him, if possible, to embrace Catholicism, "that he might escape the furious war about to be made on him and his party." He was also required to give up the cities of surety held by the Huguenots, and to prohibit in Navarre the exercise of the "pretended reformed religion" during the delay allowed by the edicts for the conversion of the people. Foreign troops, the king had heard, were about to march to the rebels' assistance. If Henri would prevent this, the king promised to recall the Catholic troops already in movement to the south of the Loire.

But Henri of Navarre refused to comply with the king's demands, or to yield to other inducements held out to him — even a vague promise to appoint a council of priests for his conversion. "Many," says L'Estoile, "thought the instruction to be given for his conversion rather extraordinary, as close on the heels of the party of priests an army was supposed to be following. That Béarn would be immediately blockaded and taken was firmly believed, and Henri's epitaph was already written in Paris."

But the Leaguers were not in a position immediately to realise by force of arms those measures they had extorted from the weakness of Henri III. for the extermination of heresy; and the king himself showed great unwillingness to supply their deficiencies from the military resources of the crown. The ardour of the Catholic king, too, was so deeply absorbed in the preparation of his formidable armada for the conquest of England and destruction of her heretic queen and people, that his zeal for shedding heretic blood in France seemed slightly less fervid than usual. At all events, his promised liberal contributions towards that holy purpose came into the Leaguers' hands rather slowly, and already were considerably in arrear.

But while fire and sword were in abeyance, the thunders of the Vatican burst on the devoted heads of Henri of Navarre and the Prince de Condé. The Bull of excommunication, prepared by Gregory XIII. very shortly before his death, was now fulminated by his successor, Felix Peretti, Cardinal de Montalto, who, as Sixtus V., was elected to fill the vacant Chair of Saint-Peter.

Sixtus was a man of very different character from the feeble-minded Gregory, who was devoted to Philip of Spain, and as anxious to please him as to serve God, in ridding the world of heretics. He had celebrated the Saint-Bartholomew massacre as a great and glorious deed, and had sent his solemn benediction to its authors. He had approved all Philip's atrocities in the Netherlands; had promoted the formation of the League and promised it substantial aid, both in money and men. But before the Bull could be launched, before the active operations of the Leaguers could be begun, or the 60,000 gold crowns be despatched from Rome,

Gregory XIII. was called away from this to some other world.

Sixtus V. was no less desirous than his predecessor for the extinction of heresy and the heretics. His temper was impetuous, and he was severe to mercilessness, yet throughout his career he had been very exact in fulfilling all the duties of his position, — from the humble one of his boyhood, when he was a keeper of sheep, to the elevated one of shepherd of the flock of the faithful or Pontiff of Rome, to which dignity he attained after passing through all the gradations of the Order of the Cordeliers.

But it is doubtful whether he would ever have sat on the papal throne had the bishops been able to agree at once on the choice of Gregory's successor. They were not; therefore, as a temporary expedient, they elected the Bishop of Montalto, who was supposed to be in a state of such extreme weakness that he could not long survive; yet, perchance, long enough, they thought, to enable them to make up their minds on the claims of a more eligible candidate. Peretti being elected, his health speedily improved, — illness having been counterfeited.

He wore the tiara five years, and reigned rather despotically. But he was not the humble servant of Philip II. or of the Guises, and to the League he was strongly opposed. "Gregory," he said, "by encouraging it, had sown discord throughout

Christendom." From Sixtus, therefore, the Leaguers received neither money nor troops, though he thought it incumbent on him to launch Gregory's Bull against the heretic Bourbon princes.

It was issued in the name of "Sixtus, servant of the servants of God, against Henri de Bourbon, pretended King of Navarre, and Henri de Bourbon, pretended Prince de Condé, in virtue of the authority — surpassing that of all terrestrial kings and princes — given by God to Saint-Peter and his successors." Against those "two children of wrath, a bastard and detestable generation of the House of Bourbon, the sword of vengeance was declared unsheathed," and the two "relapsed heretics pronounced guilty of treason towards God." Therefore, they and their heirs " had forfeited all principalities, domains, honours, dignities, and offices whatsoever, and were incapable of succeeding to any duchy, principality, or kingdom, and especially the kingdom of France, against which they had committed such heinous crimes."

Their officers, vassals, and subjects were absolved from their oath of fidelity, and commanded to "render them neither service nor obedience, under pain of being included in the anathema pronounced on the princes."

A short exhortation, addressed to Henri III., was added by Sixtus to this denunciatory document. "Henri, most Christian King of France, Sixtus's dear son in Jesus Christ," was exhorted to bear in mind the oath taken at his coronation to exterminate the heretics; "in order that by his authority, power, and virtue he might ensure the due execution of that most just sentence."

Henri III. did not, in fact he dared not, protest against this Bull. He sent it to the Parliament for verification, which, as he desired and expected, was refused, the refusal being accompanied by a strong remonstrance to the king for not having instantly rejected it. "It merited only," they said, "to be thrown into the fire in the presence of the whole of the Gallican Church; and, rather than register this arrogant Bull, the Parliament declared they would resign in a body. They denied that the princes of France were amenable to the Pope. But stronger still, they denied that the prince's subjects had any right to take cognisance of his religion."

This seems scarcely consistent with what was then taking place in France with reference to the religion of the heir-presumptive to the crown. However, in declining to verify the papal Bull, the Parliament vindicated the honour of the crown, which Henri III. failed to do, and also made it plain to the Pope that they recognised no right in him to dictate the course that should be pursued towards the heretic princes.

But amazement was great and general at Rome when, some days after the rejection of the Bull which was to have struck terror into the hearts of the excommunicated princes, and brought them on their knees before his holiness, placards appeared affixed in all the public places of the holy city — even on the gates of the Vatican. They were the protest of "Henri, by the grace of God, King of Navarre, Prince of Béarn, first peer of France and prince of the blood, and of Henri de Bourbon, Prince de Condé, against the Bull of Sixtus V., calling himself Pope of Rome, from whom they appealed to the Council of Peers of the Court of France. As to the charge of heresy, they declared that he had maliciously lied, and that it was 'Monsieur Sixte' himself who was a heretic, a tyrant, a usurper, leagued with the conspirators in France,— enemies of God, the state, the king, and perturbers of the general peace of Christendom."

Stupefaction fell on the Papal Court when this reply, with much more in a similar tone of defiance, was placed in the hands of the Pope and cardinals. Sixtus was the first to recover from the angry excitement the reading of it occasioned. Instead of displaying any rancorous feeling towards the King of Navarre, he is said to have allowed it to appear that he felt some esteem for the man who so valiantly returned blow for blow, and that he was inclined from that time to augur well for his fortune in the future.

The Bull, however, was turned to account by the Leaguers to force the king to pursue Henri of Navarre, who had offered his services to him, and to second the views of the Guises, who were secretly endeavouring to dethrone him. Henri feared both Huguenots and Leaguers. His policy was to let them, as he hoped, destroy each other, while he by dilatoriness and a pretended want of funds would interfere but little in this new war, and thus be able to continue his customary pleasures and devotions with but slight interruption.

But the Duc de Guise, who required for himself the chief command of the larger division of the royalist army, and that of the second for his brother, the Duc de Mayenne, called on Henri — being secretly supported by the queen-mother — to hasten the arrival of the Germans and Swiss then on their way to France; but, as it seemed to the duke, marching far too leisurely.

When he arrived at the Louvre to make this request, he found the king and three or four of his favourites playing eagerly against each other with their cups and balls.* From Henri's neck, suspended by a silken cord, hung a small basket, in which he carried two dogs of diminutive size and rare breed and beauty. Several birds and monkeys, some caged, others in the enjoyment of their liberty, warbled, screeched or flitted about at

* Such a mania had "bilboquet" become, that not only the king, the ladies, and the courtiers, the pages, and other members of the household, passed much of their time in this puerile amusement, even when they walked in the streets, or took an airing in their coaches, but the taste for it had extended beyond the palace, and the *bourgeoisie* had adopted it.

their own good pleasure — his menagerie being completed by three or four hideous dwarfs.*

Guise, who bore himself rather haughtily, as well he might, in the presence of his contemptible sovereign, was desirous of pressing on him the expediency of immediately summoning a council, for the purpose of enacting severer decrees against the unfortunate Huguenots. For "many of them were," he said, "robbing the king of his confiscatory rights." They were, in fact, disposing of their possessions for anything they could obtain for them, and with the proceeds were preparing with heavy hearts to leave their country with their despairing wives and children. The time allowed for their conversion, or the alternative of death or exile, was six months. But on reflection the Leaguers considered that they "had been too merciful towards those scoundrels," and proposed that to make up their minds which to accept of the choice of evils offered them, the term of six months should be reduced to fifteen days.

Whether willing or not, the Guises, aided by the queen-mother, compelled the king to assemble the private council and to accede to whatever was proposed to him. The new edict enjoining con-

---

* His dogs of various breeds, of which he had an immense number, cost, with their numerous attendants, not less than 100,000 crowns yearly. For his parrots, monkeys, and other animals, which accompanied him in his changes of residence, the expense was as great.

version to the true faith within fifteen days, or confiscation of property, with death or exile, was sanctioned by the council, and sent for registration to the Parliament of Paris, who positively refused to give effect to it.

The Parliament had often shown a refractory spirit when required to register concessions not approved by them to the Protestants. They now separated themselves from the Catholic faction, and opposed the Guises and the League with its "Council of Sixteen," openly treating it as seditious, and hostile towards the state. The king, however, commanded them to register the edict, which at last, after vehement remonstrances, was done, but under protest.*

The Parliament now advocated tolerance; for amongst that body of magistrates were several moderate Catholics and members of the Politique party, who were decidedly opposed to forcing the conscience, or of punishing with either confiscation, exile, or death, those who were unwilling to embrace Catholicism. One of those magistrates, Pierre de l'Estoile, "*conseiller et grand audiencier du roi*," assisted Du Plessis-Mornay in preparing the Bourbon princes' audacious reply to the Bull of excommunication.

Henri III. had begun his usual dissolute car-

---

* A six months' delay was afterwards granted to the women, who cared not to accept it, preferring to follow the fortunes of their husbands and relatives.

nival revels, when the nuncio, in an assemblage of the clergy, proposed the reception in France of the oft-rejected decrees of the Council of Trent. Sixtus V. thought the moment opportune for the purpose. The Inquisition would probably soon have followed. But Henri shared the general feeling against both the Council of Trent and the "Holy Tribunal," which the Guises were so anxious to inflict on the nation. Pleading the inconsistency of the decrees with the liberties of the Gallican Church, he refused to listen to a proposal that, adopted, might lead to other encroachments. Thus, while greatly offending the League, he gratified the Parliament.

Meanwhile Henri of Navarre and his Huguenots had taken the field, and with some success in Poitou and Dauphiny. On the other hand, the Prince de Condé, jealous of his cousin of Navarre and desirous of rivalling him by some independent and brilliant feat of arms in this campaign, attempted to relieve Angers, then besieged by the Duc de Joyeuse. To achieve his purpose, great expedition was imperative; but the prince, who would have no one interfere with his project, lost so much time in making preparations, that when he arrived at Angers, he found that the governor was killed, and that the garrison had surrendered.

Condé's small force, together with the cavaliers who accompanied the expedition, in order to avoid being hemmed in between the army of Joyeuse and that of Mayenne, who was marching towards them, gradually dispersed in various directions; vanishing, as it were, before the pursuing armies, which on their junction, no enemy appearing, seemed to have been following a shadow. Condé made for the coast, and crossed to the island of Guernsey. Though he reaped no laurels from his ill-advised adventure, fortunately scarcely any lives were lost, and no person of note was made prisoner.

Yet it had for a time an unfavourable effect on the prospects of the Huguenots. The places Henri had taken were again besieged by the army of the League; while of both money and troops he was almost destitute. The German auxiliaries had not yet arrived, and famine in Navarre added to his difficulties and to the miseries of war. Yet this cruel war dragged on; the King of France doing his best to protract it, and with the hope of discouraging the League, giving as little aid to its chiefs as possible, but dividing his troops into small detachments amongst his favourites.

The winter of 1586–1587 was of unusual severity; and suffering, with the discouragement of, at best, partial success, demoralised the King of Navarre's and the Vicomte de Turenne's small army. The former was advised to pass over to England and thence into Germany, to hasten the march of the German reinforcements. But this advice he promptly rejected. It was not in his nature to be cast down by the buffetings of adverse fortune. His Gascon gaiety never failed him, and he was of opinion that *"qui quitte la partie, la perd."* He therefore determined to remain, and dispute Gascony, step by step, against Mayenne.

His sister Catherine made an effort to send him aid in money. Her own resources were exhausted; but she asked of the jurats (the Municipal Chamber of Pau) the trifling loan of 15,000 *livres*, which they declined to grant. But when the people of the town heard that their princess's request had been ungraciously refused, they raised by subscription amongst themselves a sum of 16,000 crowns, and presented it to her. It was immediately sent to the Huguenot army.

The Prince de Condé had in the meantime returned to La Rochelle, escorted back to France by a squadron of English ships, and bringing with him money for "the cause" from Elizabeth. The English queen had in the preceding year accepted the protectorate of the United Provinces, and but that Antwerp had succumbed, after a siege of great horror, the sovereignty would have been offered to her. She now took a prominent part in the great struggle for religious freedom, and despatched a small body of troops to the Netherlands; but chose not wisely when she placed it under the orders of Leicester.

Navarre and Condé being again united, the

affairs of the Huguenots seemed likely to improve. But yet another attempt was made by Henri III. to constrain the King of Navarre to return to the flock of the faithful. The Duc de Nevers was chosen for this mission. He was well received by Henri, whom the duke appears not to have met since 1576, when he escaped from Vincennes. He describes him to Henri III. as "unchanged by cares and increase of years from what he was in his earlier youth when at court; pleasant in manner, and of lively humour. He listened courteously," he says, "to all the arguments laid before him, and replied to them in the same way; took no offence at anything, but yielded nothing."

The queen-mother fancied that she would succeed, if not in again requiring him to separate himself from the heretics, at all events in negotiating with him a peace or truce that might last a few months, and thus render the services of the troops on their way to invade France unavailable. The means on which she relied completely failed in obtaining any power over the King of Navarre. La belle Corisande held him then in fetters far too strong to be broken by the wily nymphs of the squadron.

CHAPTER XIII.

Plots against the Life of Queen Elizabeth. — The Spanish Invasion Deferred. — Henri III. Asks the Consent of Guise to Make Peace with the Huguenots. — Henri Compounds with His Defaulting Treasurers. — The Marriage of the Duc d'Épernon. — Balls and Banquets. — Joyeuse Inclines to the Leaguers. — Revolting Barbarity. — The Catholic Bourbons Join Their Protestant Relatives. — Battle of Coutras. — Great Victory of the Huguenots. — Joyeuse and His Brother Slain. — Gallantry and Romance.

THE folly, the cowardice, and the disorderly conduct of Henri III., together with the intrigues of the League and its Council of Sixteen under the rule of the Guises, had reduced France to such a state of confusion and tumult that the kingdom was threatened with dismemberment and ruin. Plots, too, against the life and the throne of the English queen were constantly being concocted, with the connivance of those zealots for the glory of God — the Pope and the Spanish king — at the English Catholic college of Rheims. This establishment was under the spiritual guidance of the Cardinal de Guise, a younger brother of the duke, who had succeeded to the archbishopric of Rheims on his late uncle's death.

As there was always either a traitor or spy assisting at these political or religious reunions, many foul plots, arranged at Rheims and elsewhere, at that intriguing and bloodthirsty period, were by such secret counterplotting betrayed and baffled. Henri III. had a very diligent spy even amongst the fanatical Council of Sixteen — Poulain, the Lieutenant-General of the Provostship of Paris — who seems never to have been suspected, as he was never denounced, and who several times prevented the king from being surprised, arrested, confined in a monastery, or murdered.

Spain, Rome, and the Guise faction, in their schemes to depose and murder Elizabeth, of course aimed at releasing the Scottish queen, and placing her on Elizabeth's vacant throne. They planned for England a sanguinary festival, to take place on the 24th of August; their enterprise being placed "under the invocation of the Furies of the Saint-Bartholomew." To these perpetual menaces against her life and her crown, Elizabeth replied by Mary's trial and her condemnation to death. Yet some months elapsed before the sentence was carried into effect, and during that interval Henri III. sent his chancellor, Pomponne de Bellièvre,* to England solemnly to remonstrate

* He was saved by the Duc de Guise from the massacres of the Saint-Bartholomew, and afterwards abjured.

and to request the queen to refrain from sending a queen-dowager of France to the scaffold.

A plea to save life from one who in cold blood and with excessive cruelties had sacrificed the lives of so many innocent and unoffending people, could indeed carry little, if any, weight with it. It was reported by the Guises amongst the people that, instead of seeking to save, Henri had urged the queen not to spare her captive. This, however, was not the fact; but it served the purpose of the chief of the League to paint the king's acts at this time blacker than they really were.

"Elizabeth received the French envoy graciously, and listened with attention both to the king's remonstrances and his request. Then replied at some length, justifying the course she had taken." "If I were to grant your request," she said, "I should perjure myself and take the holy name of God in vain. I would not make a similar request to the king, my good brother, your master, or to any prince or potentate in Christendom, where it concerned the safety of the state, as it does mine in this affair, as I desire that they may be preserved and protected from all their enemies, and that I, who am but a poor weak woman, may be enabled to resist the many snares laid for me, and the attacks upon my throne."

Still Elizabeth hesitated, and Mary did not lay her head on the block until the 7th of February, 1578. On the 30th a solemn service for the repose of her soul was said at the Abbey of Saint-Denis and at Notre-Dame de Paris. The Catholic party, whose murderous zeal was so baneful to her, professed to regard Mary Stuart as a saint, and, no less erroneously, as a martyr who had died for her faith, which of course she had not. The populace called aloud for vengeance on the English she-wolf and her Huguenot allies. But the Protestant princes, whom Elizabeth is said to have consulted, made the Scottish queen's death a question of public safety. In that light it seemed to Henri of Navarre, to the Prince de Condé, and other chief men of their party, to be fully justified, as affirmed by D'Aubigné.

Besides this defiance, cast, as it were, in the face of the "Demon of the South," his project of speedily invading England was for a while also thwarted by the great English navigator, Francis Drake. While cruising during May with a squadron off the coast of Spain, watching the proceedings in her port, and on the lookout for Spanish galleons, he found an opportunity of surprising Cadiz, and making terrible havoc amongst the armaments preparing in that port; also in the mouth of the Guadalquivir and the roadstead of Lisbon. The "stronghold of heresy" was therefore safe for upwards of another year from the attempts of "God's avenger" to invade her.

The kingdom of Portugal was utterly drained

of her resources, and her people heavily taxed, to supply Philip with funds to repair the damage done to his fleet. While this was in progress he was desirous of securing the port of Boulogne for his armada. The Spanish ambassador mentioned his Catholic majesty's wish to the duke and his Council of Sixteen, and forthwith a *coup-de-main* was arranged at a meeting held at the Jesuits' seminary in the Rue Saint-Antoine.

The Duc d'Aumale was chosen to carry out the scheme, and the provost-marshal — who was prevailed on by the League to join in it — promised that, when he made his quarterly inspection at Boulogne, he would seize one of the gates of the town, and give it up to Aumale. The king was informed of the plot the same day by Poulain, who had been present at its discussion. The officer in command of the fortress, in the absence of the Duc d'Épernon, who was Governor of Picardy, was communicated with; and when Aumale and his detachment made their appearance, they met with so warm a reception that they at once abandoned their project and beat a hasty retreat.

From the preparations making by all parties, war on a larger scale than in previous years appeared to be contemplated. Henri of Navarre and his Huguenots were the most active, and maintained the upper hand in Guyenne and Poitou. A large *corps d'armée*, composed of Germans and Swiss, was assembling in Alsace to join them, and the League was endeavouring to raise an independent force of its own.

The king, feeling himself taken as in a vice between the two parties, made a last effort to effect a peace. But Guise and the League had so humiliated him, that it was not he who offered terms of peace. He simply pressed the duke to consent to his offering some concessions to the Huguenots. Guise sternly refused, and was not induced to yield by the promise of great advantages for himself and family, which the king urged a desire to lavish on his powerful subject. Peace would have been fatal to his designs. "He and his," as he wrote to his brother Mayenne, "had forever espoused the cuirass."

He whom the people, frantic with delight whenever he appeared in public, called on to place himself at their head — vociferating "*À Rheims! à Rheims!*" whither almost by force they more than once would have carried him to be crowned — could afford to smile contemptuously on any proffer of favours from a king who was execrated by his people, and who, with his effeminate favourites, was the object of their gibes and jeers. Henri III., then, with rage in his heart, yet shrinking from asserting his kingly authority, bowed to the will of the arrogant chief of the League.

But as Guise was eagerly anxious to prevent the junction of the Germans and Swiss with the army of Henri of Navarre, he condescended to allow the king to divide the command of his army with him, that, by marching on opposite sides of the Loire, the approach of the foreign auxiliaries might be arrested. In the meantime the Duc de Joyeuse, it was proposed, should be despatched with a body of troops to give battle to the King of Navarre, before any reinforcements could reach him.

If the queen-mother did not wholly approve all the acts of the League and its chief, she yet opposed the king's interference with them, putting faith in the duke's promises to obtain the repeal of the Salic law in France, which she had set her heart upon, in favour of her grandchildren of Lorraine. Her usual quick discernment is said to have partly failed her at this time, and she who had spent her life in deceiving others, was now completely duped by the Guises, who made use of her to subdue the king to obedience, when, at times, he was partly roused by the counsels of his favourite D'Épernon to resent the indignities offered him.

But money was wanted for the wars, and one expedient the king resorted to was to compound with the defaulting treasurers and financiers of France. He pardoned all their former robberies of the state, provided that the sum of 200,000 crowns for the principal, and 40,000 for the expenses of justice, were paid to him by all who, whether for little or much, had had the management of the king's finances. "Thus," says L'Estoile, "giving encouragement to those who had been faithful to the king and his interests, to do as those others had done who had found more advantage in thieving than in acting as honest men."

"The king also assembled at the Louvre several presidents and counsellors, with the provost of the merchants, aldermen, and other persons of note of the municipality of Paris. Then, in presence of the Guises, and several cardinals and nobles, he informed them that he had resolved to pursue the war against 'those of the new opinions' until they were wholly exterminated. He hoped, he said, to accomplish this good work in two years; and proposed to head his army himself, and to die if needed."

His majesty, who had the gift of eloquence, and could speak, when he chose, with much effect, then made a pause, when his harangue, as he seemed to expect, was duly applauded. The acclamations having subsided, the king resumed his oration. "Turning towards the provost and merchants, he reminded them that war was expensive, and could not be carried on without money. But as he found they so thoroughly approved the war he proposed, he would ask them to enable him to fulfil the promises he had made them respecting it. He would suggest a subvention of 600,000 crowns to be taken *à rente* on the most affluent merchants, and a further sum of 720,000 crowns on the whole kingdom."

His audience, who had so loudly praised his determination to die on the battle-field, if needful, had not a single word of approval to bestow on his heroic resolve when asked to pay the cost of it. Many dissentient voices were raised against his suggestion; and, although he eventually obtained the greater part of his demands — for if they were not readily complied with, he, without scruple, forcibly appropriated the *rentes* of the Hôtel de Ville — the assembly broke up in a very dissatisfied and angry mood.

Henri himself probably enjoyed the discomfiture of the provost and merchants of the municipality, as they listened to the second part of his proposal. There was always a vein of mockery running through his addresses, and when he perceived that it had given offence to any person opposed to him, he seemed to derive from it a secret malignant pleasure. His preparations for war were, however, made so leisurely, with the intention of annoying the Leaguers, that the duke was in a state of feverish anxiety lest Henri of Navarre, whom he hoped to reduce to the direst distress by cutting off his reinforcements, should by the king's dilatoriness yet effect his junction with them.

Yet Henri hurried not himself. Having a fair supply of cash in hand, he thought the moment propitious — not knowing what dangers his desperate valour on the battle-field might lead him into — to marry his favourite D'Épernon, whom he was accustomed to call his eldest son, before setting out for the wars. Le Duc d'Épernon, some few years before, had been betrothed to the queen's youngest sister at the same time that the other newly created Duc de Joyeuse was married to the queen's second sister, Marguerite de Vaudemont. D'Épernon's *fiancée* was then a mere child, and her marriage was in consequence deferred. The betrothal was set aside as the princess grew up, her family seeking a more suitable alliance than this recently ennobled king's favourite.

But the king is said to have declared that the House of Lorraine, root and branch — thus including the Guises — had become abhorrent to him. Another bride must, therefore, be sought for D'Épernon. The lady honoured with the royal approval was the young Comtesse de Foix-Candale. The king, queen, and queen-mother, princesses, and ladies and gentlemen of the court, were all present at the celebration of the marriage, and at the balls, banquets, and *fêtes* that followed; the costly extravagance of the gentlemen's embroidered and jewelled costumes vying with the unparalleled magnificence of that of the ladies. Henri, with his chaplet of death's-heads, which, dangling at his side, he now constantly wore, danced all night with great glee.

He was unmindful, apparently, that the drawbridges were raised, the number of guards increased, and the military patrolling the streets of the city — rumours having reached the palace of an intended attack on the king and the capital that night. There was a famine also in the land. The crops had failed, and the starving people were rioting for bread. But to return to the palace. In the banqueting-hall, a grand supper was awaiting the bridal party, but there was no bread for the famishing poor.

The bride wore the king's marriage present — a necklace composed of a hundred fine large pearls, their value estimated at 100,000 crowns. When the Duc de Joyeuse was married, and the Duc d'Épernon betrothed, the marriage portion — 400,000 crowns — given by the king to each of the princesses was paid to both the married and the betrothed duke at the same time; "that there might," the king observed, "be no jealousy on the part of D'Épernon because of its delay. Yet, another 400,000 is referred to as paid on the present occasion.*

At this marriage there took place another of those sham reconciliations that Henri III. was fond of effecting on festive occasions. He desired the Ducs de Guise and D'Épernon to embrace each other and be friends. They obeyed so far as the embracing went; but probably being

* Pierre de l'Estoile — "*Journal de Henri III.*"

annoyed by that act, became even greater enemies than before. D'Épernon was entirely opposed to the League, consequently to Guise and his aims; also to the queen-mother who supported them. It was D'Épernon only who could awaken in Henri any spirit of resistance to the League. But unhappily his spirited resolves died away when more timid counsellors appeared.

Except that Guise was compelled to show a sort of deference to the king and to appear at court — being Grand-Master of the Household — when required to do so on ceremonious or festive occasions, it would seem strange that he should be present at a grand banquet in honour of a favourite's marriage. Had it been that of Joyeuse who so furiously hated the Huguenots, it would not have been surprising, for he indeed appeared disposed to join the League. For this Henri justly thought him ungrateful, and reproached him for inclining towards an enemy who was seeking his life, and putting forth pretensions to his crown.

Joyeuse was then absent in command of a small *corps d'armée*, the war being still carried on in Poitou and Saintonge. Some slight successes were achieved by him over the Protestants, and one or two small towns were taken; but the unfortunate prisoners who fell into his hands were all massacred with revolting barbarity. Amongst them was one of the most respected of the Protestant ministers, whose life Joyeuse was entreated to save; he, however, refused, saying, "he was anxious to deserve the praises of the Paris preachers."

The heat of the weather — it was the month of August — began to affect the health of his troops. Many deserted to avoid the misery of dying on the roads, when, exhausted by sickness and fatigue, they fell out of the ranks on their march. But information reaching Joyeuse that his favour at court was in peril, he instantly left his army, and travelled with all speed to Paris. He was not very cordially received by the king; but some of the Leaguers, for that reason, gave him a warm welcome.

The favour of the League, however, would not compensate him for the loss of the king's good graces. He was jealous, too, of the strange influence exercised by the Duc de Guise and of his popularity with the people, and resolved to raise himself to the level of the duke in influence, by a great and decisive victory over the Huguenots, or to perish in the attempt. He therefore solicited and received permission from Henri III. to give battle to those heretics at the first favourable opportunity. He vowed to the king that he would bring back as trophies of his victory the heads of the King of Navarre and the Prince de Condé.

Above a thousand cavaliers and between two

and three hundred of the flower of the young Catholic nobility, with whom Joyeuse — reckless in disposition, lively in temper, and prodigal of the wealth with which the king so lavishly provided him — was a great favourite, followed him to the wars. They set out on their expedition as though on a party of pleasure, with very light hearts indeed, all looking forward to a great victory and corresponding massacre.

But while Joyeuse was absent, the King of Navarre very actively assembled all the troops that could be spared from the garrisons of Guyenne and the Poitevins provinces. The lieutenant with whom Joyeuse had left his army Henri compelled to fall back a few leagues. His troops being also wasted by fatigue and sickness, he was unable any longer, either by promises or threats, to prevent great numbers of them from deserting.

Unexpectedly the Prince de Conti and the Comte de Soissons, the two young Catholic brothers of the Prince de Condé — being dissatisfied with the course taken by their uncle, the Cardinal de Bourbon, in allying himself with the seditious faction of the League — had decided on joining their Protestant cousin and brother, and drawing the sword against the Guises. The Vicomte de Turenne was despatched by Henri to the north with a detachment of troops to receive the count, who joined the army at Rosiers, attended by three hundred gentlemen and a thousand arquebusiers levied on his own domains.

A second motive, unknown to Henri, had influenced the Comte de Soissons in determining to join the Huguenot army. He was one day complaining, in the presence of the Abbé del Béné, of the weakness and injustice of Henri III. in passing over the claims of the princes of the blood in order to elevate his favourites. The *abbé*, whose religion and political morality were both regarded as equivocal, though professedly inclining to the Politiques, undertook to bring Soissons over to the party of Henri of Navarre. He represented to him that the interests of religion were but of very secondary importance compared with those of the state. He also pointed out what great advantages might accrue to him by joining the Protestants, and aspiring to the hand of Catharine of Navarre.

As Comtesse de Soissons she would bring the prince, he said, very considerable estates as dowry, and should Henri die without legitimate heirs, Catherine would inherit his domains, and the rights of the House of Bourbon to the throne of France pass to her husband and children. The count yielded to the *abbé's* reasonings. It was an intrigue of love, war, and politics which pleased him. He therefore wrote to his uncle the cardinal, simply stating — being a very independent young gentleman — that "he and his brother had left his party to join that of Navarre and the Huguenots." The Prince de Conti thought, with Soissons, that the cardinal was promoting the views of those who meditated the ruin of the House of Bourbon; consequently, that it was their duty to unite with their relatives in their struggle against them. The prince, accompanied by François de Châtillon, the late admiral's son, proposed to take a different route and join the advancing Germans.

Henri III. had arranged a sort of programme of the events of the impending war, according to the turn he desired they should take, and believed that, guided by him and his instructions followed, they could not fail to do. The brilliant Joyeuse and his staff of ardent young nobles, eager for the fray, and reinforced in Guyenne by the army of Maréchal de Matignon, must surely gain a victory over the forces, scanty in numbers and ill-provided, that Henri of Navarre would be able to oppose to them. But even should fortune be perverse, at least the heretics would receive a check that must cripple them severely, and from which they would not recover quickly.

As to Guise, the king determined that he should not have sufficient troops to achieve a victory over the numbers then advancing from Alsace. He hoped that they would overwhelm him, and that the Germans in their turn might suffer from the desperation of the Leaguers, and thus utterly, in fact, destroy each other. So much had this idea possessed him that the queen-mother's secretary, Davila, says he would pace his apartment hastily and at frequent intervals, muttering in Latin, " *De inimicis meis, vindicabo inimicos meos.*" ("I will destroy my enemies by my enemies.")

But events did not arrange themselves in exact conformity with the king's expectations. After some skirmishing with little loss and less advantage to either party, Henri perceived that without his expected reinforcements he would not be able to resist the royalist army when joined by De Matignon's corps. He therefore determined to make his way by Guyenne and Languedoc towards the source of the Loire, to await the arrival of the Germans. But Joyeuse, fearful that the Protestant army might escape, set out in pursuit without waiting for the army under De Matignon. Henri, being anxious to secure the important post of Coutras to assure his passage of the Drogne, had sent on General de la Tremouïlle with a detachment of troops to take possession of it.

Joyeuse, divining that Henri's object was to place the river between him and the royalist army, also sent forward a small body of troops, under Captain Lavardin, to endeavour to forestall him. And lest Henri should succeed in effecting his retreat in the way he proposed, Joyeuse resolved to give him battle on the morrow (October the 20th), though De Matignon's reinforcement was not expected until the 22nd, so eager was he to secure the trophies he had promised the king. The young nobles who formed his brilliant escort and staff were in the highest spirits.

"No quarter," they declared, with one voice, "should be given to those accursed heretics."

A slight disappointment awaited them on the evening of the 19th. La Tremouïlle had reached Coutras, by a forced march, an hour before Lavardin. A very sharp encounter ensued between the two small detachments, La Tremouïlle maintaining the advantage he had gained against all attempts to dislodge him. Holding this fortress, situated at the confluence of the Drogne-et-l'Isle, the King of Navarre thought he might safely attempt that night the passage of the river.

A portion of the baggage with the artillery was already on the opposite side, when scouts brought in the intelligence that Joyeuse had left his camp in the night, and with his army would be "in presence" at the latest by eight in the morning. The method of fortifying a *tête-de-pont*, and preparing the means for an army to cross a river with impunity, was unknown, it appears, in the warfare of that stormy period, and Henri's army was too small to run the risk of crossing in the face of an enemy so superior in numbers. His arrangements for the retreat were rapidly changed; the artillery was brought back. It consisted but of three small pieces of cannon, which were, however, advantageously placed, and at daybreak his troops were drawn up in order of battle. Shortly after the two armies were face to face, and for a time seemed scanning each other's means and arrangements.

They were compared, as they stood waiting for the signal to attack, to the armies of Darius and Alexander, — that of Joyeuse by far the more numerous, especially in cavalry, but composed of effeminate courtiers — soldiers arrayed in satins, velvets, gold, and embroidery; with flowing plumes and jewelled cuirasses, and led by a general debilitated by the enervating pleasures of a licentious court.

On the side of the Bourbons, fewer combatants; but its squadron of cavaliers composed of nobles inured to fatigue, men encased in iron, and at their head a young hero brought up in camps, familiar with reverses, and animating all hearts with the military ardour that glowed in his own. Yet it was evident that if victory was to declare for him, it must be won by the superior disposition of his troops, his dexterous manœuvres and military genius.

A few shots were exchanged, and the Catholics began to move. Instantly the Protestant ministers who accompanied the army intoned the 12th and 13th verses of the 108th Psalm, and the Huguenots fell on their knees.

"Ah! the cowards!" exclaimed Joyeuse and his cavaliers; "they tremble, and are confessing!"

"Not so," replied one of their more experienced captains; "they show us that they mean to vanquish or die."

Having then bowed the knee to the God of armies, this act of devotion occupying scarce a minute, the cavaliers without delay were again in the saddle, and the battle began.

"Cousins!" cried the King of Navarre, as he passed Condé and Soissons to take up his own position, "bear in mind that you are of the blood of the Bourbons, and, God willing, I will show you that I am your senior!"

"And we," replied Condé, "will convince you that you have worthy juniors!"

The battle of Coutras has been more or less fully described by several contemporary writers. It resulted in a most complete victory over the Catholic army. Those who were not killed took to flight, though few escaped with their lives. Joyeuse received a fatal wound; his brother died also. The booty it seems was immense, exceeding, with the ransoms, 600,000 crowns in value.

Henri displayed on that day all the bravery of a soldier as well as the sagacity of a great captain. It was the first regular battle the Reformers had gained in France, and the glory of the triumph was increased by Henri's humanity and great moderation. He displayed no more pride after his brilliant achievement than he had displayed fear before the battle ensued. To his prisoners, many of whom were taken by his own hand, he showed much courtesy and affability. To some he restored their arms; others he dismissed without ransom. He was very anxious that the wounded should be speedily attended to and well cared for; and declared, as he had done before this encounter took place, that he sought nothing more than a renewal of the pacificatory Treaty of 1577.* The Huguenot losses are said not to have exceeded forty men; from which circumstance the Protestants believed that they had been especially protected by heaven. Their joy was therefore extreme. But some disappointment was afterwards felt when this great victory, from which important results were looked for, really led to nothing of immediate benefit. Henri was greatly blamed for not following up without delay the advantage he had gained. But instead of doing so — though many excuses have been suggested for his conduct — he partly disbanded his army.

Laden with the rich spoil of the Court of Henri III., the men returned to their homes, promising to reassemble at the end of November; while, after the grand feat of arms that revealed to France a great general in the already well-known

* D'Aubigné; Mathieu — "*Histoire de France;*" F. Servan — "*Guerres des Français.*"

brave soldier, Henri, accompanied by the Comte de Soissons, set out for Sainte-Foy. Leaving there the command of the troops he retained to the Vicomte de Turenne, he continued, with Soissons, his journey to Béarn, followed by a detachment of cavalry. The object of his journey was to present the count to his sister — to whom, unknown to his council, he had promised her in marriage — and to lay the twenty-two standards taken at Coutras at the feet of the Comtesse de Grammont, "*La belle Corisande.*"

Thus he gallantly "assigned to love the victory" that opened to him the road to the throne of France, and to his sister the romance of her whole life. Yet there were many amongst his warmest partisans who reproached him with sacrificing the serious interests of "the cause" to this "*folie chevaleresque.*"

CHAPTER XIV.

Charles de Bourbon, Comte de Soissons. — Promise of Marriage Exchanged between the Count and Catherine of Navarre. — Count Suspected of Being a Magician. — The King of Navarre's Allies Waylaid and Murdered. — A Governor's "Word of Honour." — Henri III. Capitulates with the German Troops. — A Thanksgiving for Victory. — A Saint of Saints. — Great Events Predicted for 1588. — The Armada. — Death of Prince Henri de Condé.

CHARLES DE BOURBON, Comte de Soissons, was the youngest of the princes of the branch of Condé. He was just twenty-three, and already celebrated for his valour, and his success at the Court of France — not that success at the Court of Henri III. would seem to bespeak the possession of any very noble qualities. It was said of him that "he loved glory like a Bourbon, intrigue like a Valois, and the arts like a Medici."

He excelled in all the bodily exercises and warlike pastimes of the day. He shone in conversation, being exceedingly intelligent and witty. His manners were very distinguished, his person handsome, and he wore the rich and dazzling costume of the period with remarkable grace and dignity.

Soissons had won the good opinion and esteem of Henri of Navarre by the courage and audacity he had displayed at the battle of Coutras; while the dangerous step which he and the Prince de Conti had taken in joining their heretic relations — thus braving the old cardinal's heavy displeasure and the king's resentment — was, of course, another and a very forcible reason for meeting his advances with favour. Had Henri known that he owed his new ally in any measure to the attraction of Catherine of Navarre's supposed rich dowry, he, doubtless, would not so readily have promised her in marriage to him, or even have been willing to present this dangerously fascinating Prince Perfect to his sister.

Certainly Henri had promised her hand to many suitors, all of whom she had hitherto not scrupled to reject. Generally, it was on the ground of difference of religious belief, for Catherine clung to the faith she had been brought up in by her mother far more tenaciously than did Henri. He, it has been apologetically suggested, being compelled to live and act from day to day as circumstances urged him, promised his sister first to one prince, then to another, and secretly negotiated with two or three suitors at a time — whether princes or simply private gentlemen — just as they joined or withdrew from " the cause."

There was some probability that the suitor now presented to the princess might renounce Catholicism for "the new opinions," though neither he nor his brother had spoken of abjuration. Religion was probably a matter of indifference to these Catholic brothers of a Huguenot prince; friends both of Henri III. and the Guises, and cousins of Henri of Navarre — allied, in fact, to all parties. Soissons especially associated himself with their aims and aspirations, shared in their dangers and triumphs, and passed from one to the other with a levity which induced L'Estoile to refer to him in his journal as the "Proteus of his times."

"All the qualities, the seductions, and also a very fair share of the vices of the great contemporary races" are said to have been united in him; while nature had endowed him with a charm of manner whose influence was especially felt, as one can well understand, by the more impressionable of womankind. To this dangerously seductive young cavalier Catherine of Navarre gave her heart; and in the process of winning it, the cavalier lost his own. "If not formally betrothed in the presence of the King of Navarre, a promise of marriage was exchanged with his consent. It was decided that their union should take place at no distant period — the precise time to be named as soon as the troubles of war allowed."

Yet Mornay was then in England negotiating the Scotch marriage; and Henri's secretary, Rosny (afterwards Sully), having probably heard of the

Abbé del Béné's advice to Soissons, suggested to the king that the count sought Catherine from mercenary views. This created a coldness between the king and the count. The latter, though the youngest of the branch of Condé, was very wealthy, and as Catherine's dowry would necessarily be but a small one, the imputation cast upon him was scarcely well-founded.

But when Du Plessis-Mornay returned from England with Melville, who came in the name of James VI. to ask the sister of the King of Navarre in marriage, and Catherine was desired to receive the Scottish king's envoy graciously, then an open rupture took place between Henri and Soissons. The count overwhelmed the King of Navarre with reproaches, which he certainly merited, and immediately left Béarn for the Court of France. That some misunderstanding, though not its exact nature, had taken place between her lover and her brother, was made known to Catherine by Mornay. Having arranged the Scottish marriage, which had Elizabeth's sanction, he naturally was anxious for its successful issue. He expected "the cause" to benefit from it greatly; therefore pressed Catherine to make a slight sacrifice for the sake of her religion and her brother's interests.

The princess did not regard it as a slight sacrifice. She was devoted to her brother, and ever eager to promote his views; but when, as more than once occurred, he sought unduly to urge her to renounce her engagement to Soissons, she would very firmly assert her right, at least, to be faithful to the only *fiancé* her heart recognised. The Scottish envoy was, therefore, coldly received, and Catherine declined the honour of becoming Queen of Scotland, and eventually of England. She gave as a reason for refusing the king's offer, her doubt that the delicacy of her constitution would allow of her enduring the rigour of the northern climate.

This affair was thus brought to an end; and in the following year James married the Princess Anne of Denmark. Both Henri and his minister were displeased with Catherine; but Mornay, great as was his disappointment, was more disposed than Henri to treat her offence with gentleness. Yet, as a strict Calvinist, he could not quite understand that this frivolous young courtier, as he considered him, should inspire in her so deep an interest as to overcome the objections to his religion.

She had refused, on account of their faith, several princes, who would otherwise have been more eligible suitors than Charles de Bourbon. On the same grounds she had declined to share the Spanish throne with Philip II., to which exalted position he was anxious to elevate her as his fifth queen. But as regarded the persecutor of "the cause" there was no question of eligibility, even had there been no mystery connected with "the Demon's" disposal of the four predecessors.

In that age of superstition it was not uncommon for Catholics, far more zealous than Catherine de' Medici, to have recourse to astrologers and magicians to read the decrees of Providence in the stars, or to discover them by incantations. The Comte de Soissons had the reputation of not only being addicted to studying the course of the stars, but of holding intercourse with the powers of darkness. Strange stories were told by the peasantry on his domains of what somebody was believed to have seen or heard in the subterranean passages or vaults of his Château de Nogent, as well as of flickering lights and fantastic shapes that sometimes on dark nights were visible on the towers of Blandy, and believed to be indications of his relations with the invisible world.

These silly tales inspired — and not alone amongst the ignorant peasantry — a sort of timid superstitious curiosity, and on his own domains surrounded him with a marvellous *prestige*. Yet he was very popular with his dependents, and made a liberal use of his wealth. His hospitality was princely, and "he was ever ready to support the feeble, to combat the abuse of power, and to raise his voice against that oppressive taxation under which the people groaned." His hôtel in Paris was celebrated for the fine collection of *objets d' art* he had collected there at great cost.

Soon after the death of the queen-mother the

count became the possessor of the hôtel, which Jean Bullant had built for her — chiefly according to her own designs — with the beautiful chapel, and the Doric column still standing, which served her as an observatory. From that time it was called the "Hôtel de Soissons;" and the count is said to have made use of the tall column for a similar purpose to that for which the queen-mother constructed it — close observation of the course of the heavenly bodies, with the hope of diving into futurity.

All the defects of his character, his volatility and caprice, were duly laid before Catherine, as well as his suspected familiarity with the arts of the magician. But she disdainfully refused to give heed to imputations so absurd. They had mutually determined to adhere to their plighted faith, trusting that their union would ultimately follow, and in the meantime to seek consolation in correspondence.

Whilst Soissons was residing at Béarn, the army marching to the assistance of the King of Navarre was partly massacred, partly dispersed. It consisted of 15,000 or 16,000 German cavalry and infantry, and about 10,000 Swiss. Their march lay along the banks of the Loire, which should have been crossed at La Charité; but the king, with a body of troops, was stationed there to prevent this. On the opposite bank Guise and the Marquis de Pont followed with another detachment to harass the Protestant army.* Arrived near Montargis, the duke, in the middle of the night, fell suddenly on the cavalry who were lodged in the adjacent village of Vimori, killed as many as possible, seized their baggage, and decamped before daybreak — fearing to be surrounded.

Worn out with fatigue, wanting provisions, deprived of their baggage, attacked by the peasantry, who savagely murdered all who wandered from the main body, their number daily diminished, and they loudly accused the King of Navarre of treachery. The Swiss were inclined to return at once to their country, but, hearing of the victory of Coutras, continued their march with the Germans to Anneau, a small town in Beauce, where they hoped to obtain provisions, and perhaps to be joined by the King of Navarre.

The Governor of Anneau entered into an arrangement with Baron Dohna, who commanded the Germans in the place of Jean Casimer, to observe a strict neutrality towards them if he was not himself attacked. The baron thought he might confide in "his word of honour." This governor's "word of honour" had, however, been previously also given to the Duc de Guise. It had been concerted between them that he should

* The Duc de Pont was the eldest son of the Duc de Lorraine, and the queen-mother's grandson, for whom — the Salic law being repealed — she destined the Crown of France.

admit a thousand of Guise's soldiers into the fortress during the night, while the duke surrounded the town with his troops to prevent any escape, when his brutal soldiers issued from the fortress to fall upon and massacre the sick and weary Protestant army, while resting for a brief space from its fatigues, in reliance on the infamous governor's " word of honour."

Guise in person animated his assassin band, both by word and deed, to do their work thoroughly, and kill and slay vigorously for " the glory of God." The German commander-in-chief and ten or more of his cavaliers with desperate valour cut their way, sword in hand, through the murderous mob that attacked them. The Swiss that day abandoned the army. The Germans and French, reduced from 16,000 to about 10,000 men, hastened their march to escape, if possible, D'Épernon's large army manœuvring around them. Their numbers were daily diminished by death and desertion. Their baggage and artillery were lost. The roads were strewed with men and horses exhausted and dying, their arms abandoned, chariots broken, and stragglers unpityingly murdered by the peasantry.

Plunging into the woods of Morvon, the remnant of the army with pain and difficulty reached the Mâronnais. A handful of scouts of the king's vanguard having defeated a party of the German infantry, Henri, who was not willing that Guise's victory should be too complete, offered the Germans permission to return to their country in safety, and to the French Protestants leave to quit the kingdom. The Comte de Châtillon and Prince de Conti, who had now joined them, strove to prevail on the troops to decline this offer. But courage as well as strength was exhausted, and the king's conditions — that they should swear never again to bear arms in France without his permission — were generally accepted.

Châtillon and Conti refused to follow this example. The latter escaped in disguise. But Châtillon, rallying what remained of his scattered Languedocians, conducted them safely, as he promised he would do, over the snowy and mountainous district of Velay to Vivarais. Their sufferings, however, were great. Other Huguenot chiefs, amongst them the Duc de Bouillon, reached Geneva with difficulty, and died there of grief and fatigue.

The confederate army being destroyed, Henri III. returned to Paris, where (23d of December) he made a sort of triumphal entry. At Notre-Dame he alighted, fully armed, to thank God for his victory. A number of the lower order of the populace assembled, and hailed him as he left with clamorous cries of "Long live the king!" their vociferations overpowering all others — "a service," says L'Estoile, "for which they were liberally paid." For the mass of the Parisian population looked with disdain on the vain pomp with which Henri had surrounded himself, and responded to "*Vive le roi!*" by "*Vive Guise!*" "*Vive le héros d'Anneau!*"

With eager eyes they sought their hero amongst the brilliant staff in glittering cuirass and plumed casque, as if ready armed for the battle. But they sought in vain. Henri, at the end of their expedition, had forbidden Guise to return to Paris. Honours, however, were heaped on D'Épernon, to whom the king also gave, besides the important post of Admiral of France, all the lucrative offices and governorships held by his favorite Joyeuse, for whom he was preparing a funeral and tomb of royal magnificence. This irritated "the Sixteen" beyond measure. They accused the king of heading his army only that he might compound with heretics, and contrasted his conduct with that of their glorious hero at Anneau,— this massacre being the one event of the war to which they would give any heed.

The Sorbonne, on learning that Henri had offered the Germans terms of capitulation, secretly, in their righteous wrath, decided that "the government might be taken out of the hands of a prince who did not do what was required of him." This was for the information of "the Sixteen;" therefore, was not long in finding its way to the king's ears, through the agency of his faithful Poulain. The Sorbonnists of the Faculty of Theology were summoned to the Louvre. The king then informed them that although they "all deserved to be sent to the galleys, or even something worse, he yet would pardon them, on condition that they came to no more such resolutions."

"The Sorbonnists were less alarmed than irritated, and rightly believed that the king's clemency was attributable to his fears." Yet Henri III., bad as he really was, and generally and deservedly detested, often publicly insulted, and the subject of as many disgraceful and libellous rumours as of others equally disgraceful but well founded, was at this time described by an enthusiastic panegyrist as "a saint of saints." This ardent admirer of the "king's many virtues, sincere piety and holy zeal in the service of God," was the advocate-general, who, in an address on the occasion of the Duc d'Épernon being installed as admiral (11th of January), took the opportunity of descanting on the noble qualities that characterised the king, declaring, in conclusion, that none of his predecessors on the throne of France were so deserving of canonisation as he.

Henri was then engaged in his usual carnival orgies. The customary penitential masquerading and convent seclusion were of course to follow, after which he proposed, he said, to besiege La Rochelle. He seemed blind to the actual condition of Paris, unmindful of the public feeling towards him, and, indeed, of the situation of France generally.

Wonderful events were looked for during the year 1588 — several ancient predictions having announced great revolutions throughout the states of Europe. Those who were weak enough to give any credence to them, soon found in the troubles of these agitated times, and the disasters political, religious, and domestic incidental to them, a sufficient confirmation of such very trite prophecies. One that the League and all good Catholics laid much stress on, as indicating the anger of God against the heretics, was the unexpected death of Prince Henri de Condé, on the 5th of March. This catastrophe, which caused great consternation amongst the Huguenots, was rendered more distressing from the fact that the prince owed his death to poison, administered by a page and "another member of the household of the princess" (Charlotte de la Tremouïlle).

Both of those suspected persons effected their escape; but one of the prince's domestics was condemned and executed as an accomplice, and the princess herself, at the instance of Condé's brothers, was arrested and imprisoned. The prince was said to be a jealous husband; but not without very sufficient reasons. The fugitive page was believed to be the princess's lover. Six months after the prince's death, she gave birth to a son in prison. She then appealed from the ordinary tribunals to the Parliament of Paris.*

The death of Henri of Navarre would have been far less felt by zealous Calvinists as a great calamity than was the untimely end of Henri de Condé. His religious convictions were deeper, and more in sympathy with the ardour of the Huguenot people than were his cousin's of Navarre. He would have been much more likely to die a martyr for "the cause" than to have abjured, gaily declaring that "Paris was worth a mass." By Condé's death, as many thought, Henri of Navarre was freed from an ambitious and jealous rival, rather than deprived of an able and active lieutenant who cordially coöperated in his views. Nevertheless, he naturally greatly lamented the sad fate of his cousin, his coreligionist and companion-in-arms.

* Events, political and religious, and the varying success of the civil war between the League and Henri of Navarre, prevented the princess's appeal from receiving the attention of the Parliament for a space of seven years. During that time she remained a prisoner. The Parliament then declared her innocent of the crime imputed to her. This, probably, was through the influence of Henri IV., who had then abjured, and may be said to have been really King of France.

CHAPTER XV.

Great Events Predicted by the Astrologers in 1588. — Guise Forbidden to Enter Paris. — The Queen of the League. — The Duke's Entry. — He Visits the Queen-mother. — Rage of Henri III. — King Sends for an Italian to Assassinate Guise. — Guise Feels that He Has Barely Escaped Assassination. — Prepared for Action, but no Orders Given. Fighting in Paris. — The Day of Barricades. — Terms of Reconciliation. — Threat of Invading the Louvre and the Tuileries. — Flight of the King from Paris.

NOTHING that the starry heavens had revealed to the astrologers Nostradamus, Ruggieri, and others of earlier date, of the events to ensue, whether for good or evil to France or other European power in 1588, was looked forward to with equal anxiety or equal hopefulness of its entire success, than the subjugation of England and the destruction of her heretic queen and people by Philip II.'s armada — already, rather prematurely, named the "Invincible." Drake's ravages in the Spanish ports in the preceding spring were nearly repaired. But before this mighty fleet set sail, Philip desired that the King of France should be reduced to complete powerlessness to interfere with his projects, as he knew that Henri III. had promised Elizabeth considerable aid in case of invasion.

Disturbances, political and religious, were, therefore, to be fomented in Paris and the faubourgs by means of the League and its Council of Sixteen, and the king, if possible, was to be kept in "strict seclusion" at Vincennes or elsewhere. But Guise seemed rather disposed to draw back, as if fearing the audacity of his own aims, and their possible failure. He may, too, as has been also suggested, have been unwilling to risk their fulfilment by too assiduously promoting Philip's schemes. Philip, however, called upon him to perform his part of the compact of the League with Spain. Money and troops were ready for him, and Philip proposed to withdraw his ambassador from the Court of France, and to send an accredited envoy to the League. Guise and the chiefs of the League then assembled at Soissons, and forwarded thence a request, or, more correctly, a command to the king, to order the publication of the decrees of the Council of Trent; to establish forthwith the Inquisition in France; to issue an edict authorising the confiscation of the property of all heretics; and finally, to banish his favourites.

Though Henri did not at once consent to these audacious demands, he did not, as he should have done, at once refuse them. As usual, he was desirous of gaining time to make up his mind, — a process become more difficult than ever, since the queen-mother, with her own objects in view, had given her support to the Duc de Guise and the League and opposed D'Épernon, who advised the adoption of stringent measures against them.

The Leaguers of Paris were not satisfied that Guise should so long absent himself from the capital. To their message to that effect, he replied that he would soon be with them, and desired "the Sixteen" to see that arms were provided for the people in all the quarters. It was arranged that, accompanied by a detachment of cavalry, he should enter Paris on the night of the 25th of April by the Porte Saint-Martin, of which "the Sixteen" possessed the keys. It was expected that D'Épernon, as Governor of Paris, would then be going his usual nightly round, when he was to be fallen upon and put to death. Guise, with his Leaguers and his cavalry, was then to attack the Louvre, and compel the king to place himself at the discretion of the League.

On the 22nd, Poulain had warned him of his danger. Immediately 4,000 Swiss, in garrison at Lagny, were ordered by Henri to occupy the faubourgs; from which the Leaguers understood that their plot was discovered. Until another could be concocted, the turbulent and intriguing Duchesse de Montpensier, Guise's sister, active, resolute, and intense in her hatred of Henri — who is said to have wounded her vanity by rejecting her as a mistress — undertook to entrap him

Duchesse de Montpensier.
Photo-etching from an old portrait in the Louvre.

in the Faubourg Saint-Antoine as he returned from Vincennes, accompanied, as was expected, by two or three only of his favourite courtiers.

Several men lying in wait were suddenly to rush forward and seize the horses' heads, while others entered the carriage and forcibly conducted the king to Soissons. But again he was warned in time; and to the great disappointment of the "Queen of the League," as the duchess was called, he returned with an escort of cavalry. Poulain was ever on the alert, determined, it would seem, to earn by his diligent watchfulness the 20,000 crowns Henri had promised him.

On the 24th of April, the king sent M. de Bellièvre to Soissons to endeavour to negotiate with his "cousin of Guise" and the other princes of the League; also to inform him that he had placed the Swiss in the faubourgs, and his regiment of guards at the Louvre, "because of very strange rumours then circulating in the city." But the more humbly the wretched king addressed his "cousin of Guise," the more haughty, arrogant, and exacting he became. Henri's submissively expressed wish that they might together "complete the extermination — by the blessing of God so happily begun — of those of the new opinions," was met by severe remonstrances concerning the treatment experienced by the "good Catholics." M. de Bellièvre had, therefore, little more to report to his majesty than that the duke was coming to Paris to justify himself in person.

The king at once sent back his messenger, "to beg the duke to suspend his journey." An ambiguous answer was returned. This at length roused the king's anger, and M. de Bellièvre had instantly to retrace his steps with a positive command — yet a verbal one only — to the Duc de Guise to remain at Soissons. The queen-mother desired Guise's presence in Paris, and at her suggestion the king's command was moderated in tone, and announced to the duke as his majesty's wish.

The haughty duke cared not what were his wishes. It happened, too, that one of the chief Leaguers was urging him to go to Paris when the king's messenger arrived positively to forbid him. To disobey the wishes of even so contemptible a king as Henri III., was considered an act of so great temerity that even the ambitious Henri of Guise himself — bent on usurping the sovereign power — momentarily hesitated to defy him. M. de Bellièvre, however, returned with so vague an answer that Henri despatched his secretary, and following him the grand-master of the artillery, with renewed orders to the duke not to enter the capital.

He was already on his way thither, accompanied only by fifteen of his partisans. Suspecting, probably, that other messengers and stricter orders would be despatched to him, he avoided them by taking the less frequented by-roads, and on the 9th of May entered Paris about noon, by the Porte Saint-Martin.

Feigning a desire to conceal himself, he rode a few paces with his hat pressed low on his forehead and his face concealed in the folds of his cloak. Then (a little manœuvre agreed on beforehand) a young gentleman of his party, as they turned the corner of the Rue Saint-Denis, rode up to him, and, as if in jest, raised his hat and drew his cloak from his face. "It is time," he said, "that Paris should know who is in her midst." No sooner was it known, than *"Vive Guise!"* resounded through the city, caught up and repeated from street to street. *" Vive Guise!"* "The defender of the state, of the Catholic religion, and the saviour of Paris!" Nearly the whole of the population rushed from their houses to gather around him.

The ladies from the windows covered him with flowers and green branches, as slowly he moved along, smiling benignly on the infatuated mob; some of whom were on their knees, as though in adoration of a saint. Those who had strength and persistence to get near enough, devoutly kissed the border of his cloak, or touched him with their chaplets, afterwards pressing them to their lips and forehead. "Had he as diligently sought to serve his country as he had striven to degrade her, and place her in the power of a foreign despot, who promised him his aid to usurp the throne, he could not have received a more frantically enthusiastic welcome." The duke alighted at the queen-mother's hôtel. Even she was amazed at this extraordinary display of enthusiasm, and some fears for the result began to trouble her.

As Guise entered, she said, "I am glad to see you, but would rather it should have been on some other occasion." Henri, when his secretary informed him that Guise had arrived, stamped and raved with passion, like Charles IX. "He shall die for it!" he exclaimed, with an oath.

One of the queen-mother's gentlemen, sent from her hôtel to the Louvre, now entered, to ask leave to bring M. de Guise to the palace. "Let her bring him!" he cried, stamping with rage. The queen-mother had not been to the Louvre for nearly three years. She was residing at her new hôtel, and on Guise's arrival, being slightly indisposed, she requested Henri to come to her. He replied by a positive refusal.

Catherine in a litter, and Guise on foot beside her, then made their way to the palace, followed by six of his gentlemen and a vast crowd, whose acclamations reached the royal ear, mingled with the frequent cry, "*À Rheims! à Rheims!*" Whether the chief of the "Holy League" should live or die was then being warmly debated. Henri was for instantly despatching him, and sent for an Italian officer, Alfonso Corso, a Corsican, to do the deed for him. Being devoted to the king, he was willing to obey; promising to arrest the rebel as he entered the *salle d'armes*, and speedily to bring his head to the king.

Another Italian, the Abbé del Béné, supported his countryman's suggestion. But Henri's secretary, M. de Villeguier, with the Chancellor Cheverny and M. de Bellièvre, implored the king not to hazard so dangerous a step. They bade him listen to the clamour of the multitude who had now reached the Louvre, and to consider the fearful scenes of bloodshed that would inevitably ensue when the assassination of this hero of the populace became known. With but a few of the household troops in the Louvre and with no immediate means of bringing others to his aid, "the king," they said, "would not be safe in his palace."

This allusion to probable danger to his own person seemed to have a moderating effect on his anger. He had also exhausted himself by the violence to which he had given way. Languidly he threw himself on a sofa and snatched up his cup and ball, but apparently without any intention of solacing himself with a display of his skill in that harmless amusement. Two of his dogs jumped on his knees, and whined a request to be noticed by him. He began to fondle and caress them, when the door of the apartment was opened, and the queen-mother and M. de Guise were announced.*

The sight of his enemy roused him from the calmer mood into which he was subsiding. Nor could Guise wholly conceal a certain restlessness, as though he suspected some design to entrap him.

"I sent you word not to come to Paris," said the king harshly.

"Sire," replied Guise, bowing profoundly, "I have come to place myself in your majesty's hands. My enemies have calumniated me, and I seek to justify myself. Though had I been expressly forbidden, I would not have come to Paris."

"Did not I send you," exclaimed the king in an angry tone, and turning to Bellièvre, "to tell the duke that if he came to Paris, he should be held responsible, being considered their author, for all the seditious movements in that city?"

Bellièvre attempted, not daring to name the queen-mother's interference, to excuse himself. But Henri, interrupting him, raved out:

"I told you much more than that."

The queen-mother, alarmed at the king's visibly increasing anger, took him aside and described the popular excitement she had witnessed while passing from her hôtel to the Louvre. This interruption was probably intended by Catherine to afford

* Mathieu; L'Estoile; Davila.

the duke an opportunity of taking leave. He at once availed himself of it, bowing low as he was leaving the apartment. But the king, very unceremoniously putting aside his mother, and with difficulty suppressing his rage, said to Guise, whose exit was thus for a moment delayed:

"If you have been calumniated, of which I am not aware, your innocence and the uprightness of your intentions will appear, if your presence in Paris should occasion no further disturbances, riotous assemblages, or discord in the state."

Guise made no reply; but it was noticed that he was extremely pale. He evidently felt that a great danger had menaced him, and when he rejoined the gentlemen who accompanied him, and who awaited his return in an outer apartment, it was very clear, as he passed with them through the gates of the Louvre to regain his own hôtel, that he was relieved from much mental anxiety.

Scarcely, however, had the duke left the royal presence, than Henri lamented that he had forborne to arrest and imprison his hated rival, even had he refrained from immediately ordering his assassination. He would make himself full amends, he declared, for that oversight on the following morning, when Guise, as was customary, would attend his *lever*. To his forty-five guards should then be entrusted his effectual deliverance from his enemy. Again, efforts were made to dissuade him, and he was prevailed on to defer his purpose for awhile.

The city was kept in a state of great agitation through the night. Guise and the Leaguers, with "the Sixteen" and their chief partisans, assembled in council, and as far as was possible the Hôtel de Guise — as a precautionary measure against an expected attack on it by the king's troops — was hastily transformed into an arsenal and fortress. The Louvre was also as closely guarded as a besieged city. "In the morning (10th of May) the Duc de Guise appeared at the king's *lever*, but escorted by four hundred gentlemen, all wearing breastplates, and armed with pistols under their mantles." Henri received him, if not very cordially, at least without any appearance of displeasure.

Preparations for vigorous defence, if not for offence, continued during the day. Consequently, when on the morrow the duke again presented himself, the king gave him a very frigid reception. The queen-mother, to whose vain schemes much of the present disastrous state of things was due, becoming alarmed, now strove to allay the hostile feeling existing between the king and the duke. She arranged that they should meet in the afternoon in the garden of her new hôtel.

It has been described as a charming garden, and as it was then the season of flowers, she may possibly have thought that the beauty and fragrance of her gay parterres would exert a soothing influence on both duke and king; and a discussion in a garden be less likely to be carried on with the excitement of ruffled feelings than in a sombre *salon* of the Louvre.

If it was so, her expectations were disappointed. Their interview was a long one. Recriminations and justification on both sides took place; but without any satisfactory result. They separated as irreconcilable enemies as when they met.

At three o'clock on the morning of the 12th of May the Porte Saint-Honoré was opened by the Superintendent of Finance, François d'O, to the regiment of French guards and the 4,000 Swiss. The king on horseback was there to receive them, and to assign them their posts. He impressed on them that they were to refrain from all unnecessary violence, or they would answer for it with their lives. A *corps d'élite* of 6,000 infantry also filed before him from the Porte Saint-Honoré to the Cimetière des Innocents. There the troops separated, and marched off, preceded by their drums and fifes. French troops occupied other parts of the city, and the cannon mounted on the towers of the Bastille was pointed on the Rue Saint-Antoine.

The king had not informed the queen-mother of his intentions. She was extremely uneasy and anxious, and with Queen Louise entreated him not to allow fighting in Paris. She urged that

Guise should be communicated with. Henri consenting, she despatched one of her confidential secretaries to implore the duke to leave Paris, offering, as an inducement, pardon to all his friends and partisans. Agitation and anxiety reigned at the Hôtel de Guise no less than at the Louvre; but the duke, though expecting momentarily to be attacked, would not immediately give a positive reply. He first desired to assure himself of the real sentiments of the people.

The people had looked on the marching of the troops in silence, but with extreme disquietude and astonishment. As the morning advanced, many noisy groups began to assemble; the students of the university were very clamorous, one of "the Sixteen" having sent a messenger there to say that the Comte de Châtillon with his Huguenots was in the Faubourg Saint-Germain, for the purpose of avenging on the Parisians the death of the admiral.

But Henri, now that his preparations were made for reducing the "rebel duke" and his partisans to obedience — his troops being posted by himself and waiting only his orders to attack the fortified Hôtel de Guise — had fallen into his usual state of irresolution, and gave no orders whatever. For some hours the people and the troops gazed angrily at each other, the latter weary of inaction, and annoyed with the king for exposing them to the taunts and jeers of the populace as they "stood ranged before them, immovable as statues of iron."

Suddenly some threats being uttered by the soldiers, or one of their officers, a cry of fury arose, and the dense mass of people then crowded together was instantly in movement. Barricades were speedily formed on all sides, and around the troops. Chains were fastened across the corners of the streets, supported by blocks of wood and barrels filled with earth and stones. Furniture, carts, litters — anything that came to hand was thrown together to strengthen the defences. Men and women appeared at the windows armed with stones and other projectiles, the women wearing breastplates, like the men, and attacking the soldiers with the frenzy of furies, hurling on them stones torn from the streets, tiles from the roofs, brickbats, broken bottles, and even showers of sand and earth when other ammunition was exhausted.

The anger of the people was most violent towards the Swiss, who, as foreigners, they thought had no right to a part in this domestic quarrel, however willing they were to employ them to fight their foreign enemies. Thirty or forty were killed or wounded. Their officers meanwhile were imploring the people to believe that they were "good Christians, friends of the Parisians, and that they had been placed there quite against their will." Barricades continued to be pushed forward at every fifty paces until they approached within that distance of the Louvre, where the last was defiantly placed directly opposite the guard-house.

Each was guarded by a company of arquebusiers of the League, who now began to use their weapons with effect on the several detachments of French guards, who, being unable to return the attack, hampered as they were by the barricades, were in several instances glad to capitulate on condition of retiring at once to their quarters. The cry "To arms!" was generally responded to. Many of the upper *bourgeoisie*, though strongly opposed to the League, yet dared not refrain from appearing at the barricades, armed either with hallebarde or arquebuse.

The merchants of the Rue Saint-Denis, before joining in the fray, went in a body to confess and receive the communion. They then armed themselves with cuirass, helmet, and pike, and joined the people of the Halles. The tocsin sounded in the quartier of the University, and was plainly heard at the Louvre, where it struck terror into every breast, while at the Hôtel de Guise every heart beat with joy.

The people now charged the soldiers on all sides, and a fearful tumult arose, the troops having given up all resistance. Even the French guards implored mercy; while the Swiss, with joined hands as if in prayer, pleadingly appealed to the infuriated people, as "*Bons français;*" "*Bonne France.*"

Showers of shot, tiles, and paving-stones were rained upon them. But at last an order came from the Louvre for the troops to retreat, and Maréchals de Biron and d'Aumont endeavoured vainly to calm the people.

The former made his way with much difficulty to the Hôtel de Guise, no longer to bid the duke leave Paris, but to ask his aid in quelling the tumult, and restoring peace in the capital. Guise at first seemed but little inclined to interpose. He could have taken both the Louvre and the king had he pleased; but it appears that he did not consider the moment the most favourable one for placing himself on the throne. He therefore determined to be generous, and save the king's troops; having so deeply humiliated the king himself that he believed he could refuse no terms he chose to propose as the price of his services.

Simply attired in a white velvet doublet, black velvet hat with small white plume — no armour of any kind — and carrying in his hand a slight switch or riding-whip, Guise left his hôtel by the gate opening on the Rue du Chaume. As he proceeded to the Place de Grève, amidst the enthusiastic acclamations of the infatuated people, "*Vive Guise!*" "*À Rheims!*" "We must take monsieur to Rheims and crown him!" met him at every turn of the narrow, winding streets of the old city.

Acknowledging with gracious smiles and bows

the greetings of the ladies, and scarcely less intoxicated with the *éclat* of his triumph than the admiring populace, he yet felt compelled to feign a desire to restrain the ardour of his partisans. "Enough, my friends, enough; rather cry, ' *Vive le roi!*' " he murmured; and at the mere sound of his voice, gentle and caressing in tone, though now slightly reproachful, the adoring multitude obeyed — obeyed so far as to be less clamorous for awhile for his journey to Rheims, but not to cry "*Vive le roi!*"

Arrived at the Hôtel de Ville, he begged the populace to grant him their pardon for the poor soldiers. His request was instantly complied with. The Swiss had laid their arms at his feet. He restored them, and sent them safely escorted to the Louvre. Other regiments were also released from the perils that threatened them, and Guise was overwhelmed with the benedictions of both the Swiss and French troops.

Scarcely had Guise returned from his errand of mercy, than the queen-mother made her appearance at his hôtel, to ascertain on what terms a reconciliation might be effected between him and the king. The principal conditions he proposed were, "that the lieutenant-governorship of the kingdom should be given to him, and the appointment confirmed by the States General convoked in Paris; that the King of Navarre and the princes of the branch of Condé should be excluded from the succession to the throne; that the Duc d'Épernon and other adversaries of the League, about the king, should be deprived of their offices and banished from the court in perpetuity; that the private guard, called the Forty-five, should be disbanded; that the principal posts in the government be given to the chiefs of the League; and administrative regulations be established which the king should have no power to change."

In vain the queen-mother sought to prevail on the now arrogant and imperious duke to consent to some abatement of these hard terms. The "great negotiatrix" was compelled to submit them unchanged to the king. She shed torrents of tears when doing so, but gave him hope that on the morrow — when she would see the duke again — the elation of his triumph, she said, having then in some measure subsided, more moderate conditions might be arranged.

It was an agitated night in Paris for both people and king. The barricades, instead of being removed, as expected, were strengthened, and Guise's partisans kept the popular excitement from abating. Every house was lighted up during the few hours of darkness, and there was an impatient waiting for the dawn — the cry being now *"Au Louvre!"* This cry, so pleasant to Guise's ears, was no less so to his sister's. For the gold scissors which she kept at her girdle, as she often declared, to clip Brother Henri's tonsure before putting him into a monastery, had now, she said, a fair chance of being used.

It was proclaimed in the morning throughout the city that the king had countermanded the order for marching more troops into Paris; also, that the French guards and the Swiss, who had passed the night in the vicinity of the Louvre, were already preparing to leave. The queen-mother, too, was early on her way to the Hôtel de Guise. To open the barricades for her carriage to pass was refused; she had, therefore, to use her litter, and to overcome as best she could the many obstacles she encountered.

In the meantime information reached the king (for amongst Guise's as well as Henri's confidants there were spies and traitors) that the Louvre and Tuileries would be invested before night, and that armed bands were then preparing for it. This was doubtless an agonising moment to Henri. He had to come to rapid decision respecting the course he would take. At once he left the Louvre on foot, as he was accustomed to do, to walk in the gardens of the Tuileries — passing out of Paris by the Porte Neuve. (The Tuileries were then in the faubourg.) Leaning on a stone in the garden, he is said to have wept bitterly, and to have apostrophised the city as an ungrateful favourite on whom he had lavished many benefits, and had loved even more than his wife. Certainly, what little he had done in the way of building and embellishing had been done for Paris, which he made his habitual residence.

Again a mysterious messenger — "Guise is inflexible; but the queen is keeping him in debate on the various conditions proposed while the king determines what plan he will pursue."

By flight only, Henri decided, could he hope to save his crown. The princes, courtiers, grand dignitaries and councillors of state who had joined him, seem to have been of the same opinion. The king then mounted a horse from the Tuileries stables. Others followed his example; while those for whom no horses were left pursued him on foot, and a sort of *sauve qui peut* ensued. None seem to have expected to decamp in this fashion — all being destitute of riding-boots and cloaks, while others wore their robes of office. At the Porte de Nesle the guard saluted them with a volley from their arquebuses and many insulting epithets. The Swiss and the corps of French guards, who were preparing to leave, now served the flying party as an escort.

The hasty movements and precipitate flight of the king and his companions alarmed Guise's spies. They hastened to inform him of these suspicious circumstances. He was still in conference with the queen-mother; but hastily rising when his confidential agent had whispered the news in his ear, "Madame!" he exclaimed, "while you are striving to detain me here to listen to your suggestions, the king is plotting my destruction!" This put an end to their discussion. The queen-mother, who knew not of the king's resolve, was also anxious to ascertain what had happened.

The king, with his party of fugitives, having reached the heights of Chaillot, turned once more towards his "*bonne ville de Paris*," and thence cast his malediction on the perfidious, ungrateful, disloyal city that had received so many favours from his hands.

"Never," he swore, raising his hand towards heaven, "would he reënter it but by the breach!" — Destiny had, however, decreed that he should enter in no more.

CHAPTER XVI.

The King and His Ministers Arrive at Chartres.— The Massacre Countermanded.— Brother Ange and a Scene of the Passion Play.— Guise Appointed Commandant-General of the Armies. — The Invincible Armada. — Its Destruction. — Soissons's Letters of Abolition. — More Catholic than the Pope. — The Assembling of the States General at Blois. — The Grande Salle of the Château de Blois. — The King's Address to the Three Estates. — His Proposals Rejected or Overruled.

THE king, with the officers of the crown, courtiers, and ministers, who had followed him in his flight from Paris, arrived at Chartres on the following morning (May the 14th). The town contained many Leaguers, yet Henri and his retinue met with a favourable reception. At the same time Paris was getting rid of her barricades, and an effort was being made to restore, temporarily at least, quietude in the city and to its excited yet weary inhabitants. The Duc de Guise, now "King of Paris," remained triumphant on the field, whence he sent letters to the "good cities," urging them to unite with the Leaguers of Paris.

"The Arsenal, the Bastille, the Château-fort of Vincennes, had all surrendered to him," he told them. The coffers of the state had also passed into his hands, and he professed to have "sealed them for restoration to his majesty, when he should have become as pacific in his views as they, the Leaguers, by their prayers to God and the intercession of his holiness hoped to render him."

Henri's anger, however, had died away on his journey, and he was now "only vexed" — as he told the Pope — "that his good people should have thought so ill of him, and have compelled him to leave the city he had loved so well, and hoped again to receive into his favour and affection. He was content that his wife and his mother should remain and negotiate in his name; as the rupture with his good city seemed to him thus less complete."

At the suggestion of the queen-mother, deputations daily sought the king to crave his pardon for his "good city;" also to press on him the necessity of various reforms and many changes, as well in the *personnel* of his household as in the several departments of the government. But Henri would make no definite promises. Everything was to be left to the decision of the States General, to be convoked in September or October at Blois. Return to Paris he would not, though greatly urged to do so.

"If the suggestions of evil counsellors — friends of heretics and promoters of heresy — continue to prevail with the King of France," wrote Guise to the Spanish ambassador, "I rely on the king your master." The day of the barricades had been expected to conclude with its sanctification by a general massacre of suspected Protestants; and "Guise sent one of the chief Leaguers to offer the English ambassador a safeguard. It was refused. He could accept no safeguard, he replied, but from the king, to whom the queen, his sovereign, had accredited him. Guise, however, on second thoughts, forbade the massacre, deeming moderation at that moment more advantageous to him than sanguinary religious zeal." *

* Ardent Leaguers were, therefore, gratified only by the burning of two young women, sisters, condemned to death by the Châtelet for heresy. This pleasant spectacle was also deferred for a fortnight, for, as these heretics were young and good-looking, it was thought worth while to make pious efforts to convert or pervert them; or to offer them life — as had already been done — on terms to which they could only listen with disgust, and reject with disdain. In the same prison, also awaiting death for the same offence, was an aged man in his eightieth year — the once famous artist-potter, Bernard Palissy. The queen-mother had not concerned herself with his heretical opinions so long as she needed his services, nor indeed had any of his noble and royal Catholic patrons; but, when zealous Leaguers threw him in his old age into prison as a heretic, she took no steps to obtain his release. Henri III. visited him in his prison, to urge him to recant his errors; otherwise, though willing, he dared not release him — Guise, as he acknowledged, being more powerful than he, as he "constrained him to act, and not in this matter only, contrary to his wishes." Palissy was to have been burnt at the same stake as the heretic sisters. However, for some reason he was left in his prison. There he remained for several months longer, in misery, in chains, a mass of vermin. In 1590 death kindly put an end to his sufferings. Both his patrons and persecutors had then passed away by the assassin's knife.

But while strenuous efforts continued to be made, sanctioned by the queen-mother, to induce the king again to put himself in the power of his ambitious rival and enemy, that enemy was using every means to establish his authority and strengthen his position in Paris — his aims being greatly furthered by the pusillanimity of the wretched king. The clergy, both secular and regular, had duly made the pilgrimage to Chartres with little or no result; but on the 18th of May a procession set out from Paris, which was expected to produce an effect which no preceding deputation had accomplished.

It was composed of Capuchin and Bernardine monks, and the members of Henri's own brotherhood — the White Flagellants — who came to entreat the king, in moving terms, "to consent to a reconciliation with his *bonne ville de Paris*,' in memory of the merits of the Passion of Jesus Christ." The procession was headed by the brother of the late Duc de Joyeuse (killed at Coutras). He had joined the Capuchins, and was known as Brother Ange. On the occasion in question, "he appeared disguised as Christ ascending Mount Calvary, and seemingly bowed down by the weight of a painted pasteboard cross."

A crown of imitation thorns was on his head, and his face was bespattered with blood, in representation of "his sweat was as it were great drops of blood," etc. Wearily he seemed to drag along under his burden, while two executioners followed, pretending to urge him on by blows with their heavy thongs. The Virgin and the Magdalen were personated by two young Capuchin novices. This revival of a scene in the ancient "Mysteries" was by no means generally approved.* Most persons thought that this travesty of sacred things, but for its profanity, would have been ridiculous. Even the king, who had a taste for religious masquerading, and for whose edification this fragment of the scene of the Crucifixion had been arranged, treated it with more than indifference.† Henri suspected that it concealed some plot, as so many Leaguers arrived in the train of the monks.

He therefore betook himself to Rouen; where, apparently, the state of his kingdom troubled him so little that he passed his time in rambling from church to church, praying in one, making vows in another, and ending the day pleasantly in witnessing jousts and other games on the water. So far, however, he yielded to the commands of the League and its chief, as to dismiss the Duc d'Épernon — whose efforts to rouse him to energetic action wearied him — from the posts and commands he had lavished upon him; while, at the same time, he conferred on Guise the general

* The Mysteries were superseded in the reign of Charles VIII. (1483–1498) by satirical farces and Italian comedies.
† L'Estoile.

command of the armies. D'Épernon and his brother, Bernard de La-Valette, immediately joined the Duc de Lesdiguières, the King of Navarre's lieutenant-general.

Henri III. was now humiliated and reduced to a state of powerlessness that might well satisfy even Philip II., towards whose warlike operations all eyes were now directed. France for awhile forgot her own troubles, and, with Europe generally, anxiously awaited the result of the struggle between England and Spain. In Flanders 30,000 troops, commanded by the Prince of Parma, were waiting to pass over to England, also a numerous fleet of flat-bottomed boats destined for their conveyance. The armada was to carry 20,000 other troops. The ships were to assemble at the mouth of the Tagus, and to sail on the 29th of May. The world had never beheld a fleet so powerful as that which Philip had formed by exhausting the resources of Portugal — at that time immensely rich — with the hope of subduing England, and adding by that conquest another province to Spain.

The armada consisted of one hundred and fifty vessels; seventy of them were galleons, three and four deckers, of enormous dimensions for that period. They were armed on both sides with cannon. The galleasses were of lower build, and had artillery only at the poop and prow. The galleys were vessels with but one deck, but having

Philip II. of Spain.
Photo-etching from painting by Titian in 1549.

both sails and oars. Very eagerly the Spanish nobility joined this expedition, whose glorious aim it was to fight for God and the Church, and to destroy the " stronghold of heresy."

The Church was represented on board by a vicar-general of the Inquisition, which holy institution was to be established as soon as the vicar and his familiars — a hundred and seventy Jesuits, monks, and begging friars — could be landed. That it was possible they might never land was a fatality which none of course even dreamed of. Instruments of torture, satanically ingenious, were unsparingly provided for refractory heretics, and the Pope had a legate ready to despatch as soon as news arrived of the successful descent on England.*

The unwillingness of Sixtus V. to contribute in money towards Philip's expedition — though prodigal of benedictions and prayers — was near occasioning a rupture between his holiness and the Spanish monarch. Sixtus is said to have secretly expressed admiration of Elizabeth's political ability as a sovereign; as he rather admired than beheld with disfavour the King of Navarre's bold defiance of his Bull of excommunication — while, as heretics, he of course abhorred them both. He, however, promised Philip, after much hesitation, a million ducats as his portion of the expenses of the expedition; the King of Spain agreeing to

* The legate was Cardinal William Allen, the founder of the English Catholic Seminary of Rheims.

hold his kingdom of England, by "fealty and homage," of the Holy See.

The announcement that the mighty fleet, organised and commanded by the great captain, Santa-Cruz, was on its way to the English coast, took the usually foresighted Elizabeth, her ministers, and people, rather by surprise. Drake's ravages were, perhaps, less destructive than they were supposed to have been. But, at all events, while the Spanish fleet was refitting, Philip had entered into negotiation with Elizabeth, with the object only of diverting attention from the necessity of preparing to meet the foe, who had so long deferred making his appearance that he was no longer expected.

Time was wanting to equip a fleet capable of opposing the "invincible armada." But when many hearts were filled with fear, the winds and the waves providentially rescued the Island Queen and her people from the danger that had seemed so immediately to threaten them. A tempest dispersed the armada along the northern coast of Spain, and with difficulty the vessels reassembled in the port of Corunna. "Two or three of the galleys, manned by slaves of various nations, were driven by the force of the tempest on the coast of France. They succeeded in landing at La Teste de Buch, near Arcachon, and freedom and an asylum were conceded to them."

Towards the end of July the armada was again

ready to put to sea, under the inexperienced command of the Duke of Medina-Sidonia (Santa-Cruz had died in the interim). The delay had afforded England the opportunity of preparing for the armada's reception. The royal navy was no overwhelming force at that time; but on this emergency the whole of the mercantile marine was put into requisition to support it. As for land forces, England was ready to rise *en masse* to repulse the "Demon of the South" from her shores.

The disastrous result to Spain of this vain attempt of an invasion of England is too well known to need repetition in these pages. Philip's floating citadels were grandly imposing to look at, but, as the Spaniards found to their cost, they proved very unwieldy and inefficient in the manœuvres of naval warfare. After several calamitous engagements, the Spanish admiral decided, in order to avoid further rencounters with the English and Dutch fleets in the Channel, to steer northward, and return to Spain by sailing round Scotland. But between the Orkneys and the Isles of Fero they were assailed by a terrific tempest.

"He blew with His winds, and they were scattered," as the device on Elizabeth's commemorative medal expressed the terrible fate of the armada, and her own and the nation's signally providential deliverance from a threatened overwhelming disaster. A cry of gladness echoed through Protestant Europe. "God Himself," it was said, "had fought for the Reformers and His gospel."

But when the startling news was revealed to Philip of the defeat of his armada; of the loss of eighty of his vessels and 16,000 of his sailors and soldiers, and amongst them the flower of the Spanish nobility, "his bronzed countenance betrayed no emotion;" he merely ejaculated his "thanks to God, who had made him sufficiently powerful to repair a loss of such magnitude." This was but a groundless boast. He could not repair it. He had ruined Portugal to conquer England. He had failed, and his dream of a European monarchy, of which he would be the ruler, had vanished into nothingness; as had the similar ambitious aspirations of his father, Charles V.

Scarcely could Henri III. conceal his intense satisfaction at Philip's discomfiture and the catastrophe to his fleet. It revived his courage, as he fancied that Philip would now be intent on repairing his disaster; and that Guise, less powerfully supported by Spanish ducats, would be less haughty and less exacting in his demands. But Guise was rather glad to be freed from the control of his arbitrary protector. He resolved to pursue his plans diligently, and to lose none of the advantages he had already gained. The queen-mother, too, had determined on making an effort towards speedily realising the one idea that now absorbed her — the revocation of the Salic law.

With these different objects in view, the king and queen, the queen-mother, and the duke, with their respective suites, repaired to the Château de Blois, on the 1st of September. The Three Estates assembled for preliminary operations on the 16th, when it was evident that, owing to recent events, they were swayed by passion rather than reason, and that very stormy discussions might be looked for. Even then a strong feeling of opposition was roused by the announcement that the Vicomte de Soissons, who, with several hundred of his gentlemen, had fought at Coutras so bravely on the heretic side, and, until recently, had been amusing himself at Nérac in making love to a heretic princess, would shortly attend the sittings of the Three Estates in his quality of prince of the blood.

The viscount, it seems, had made his submission to the Pope for his heretical acts, and had received from Sixtus "Letters of abolition," which absolved him from the consequences, otherwise imminent, of his wanderings in the paths of error. But the States refused to acccept these letters, and the king's orders to the Parliament to register them were not obeyed. Less opposition was shown by the nobles than by the clergy and the Third Estate; and on their representation that to refuse the Pope's letters was to declare themselves more Catholic than his holiness himself, this view of the matter, after some discussion, was adopted, and Soissons's presence tolerated, to the great displeasure of the Duc de Guise and his brother, the cardinal.

They desired not only to expel the Condé branch of the Bourbon princes from the Assembly of the States General, but to deprive them of their eventual rights to the succession. They also hoped to obtain a decree authorising the confiscation of the King of Navarre's domains, and his expulsion from France as a heretic — unless, indeed, they could burn him, which, of course, would have been more satisfactory. Soissons's brother, the Prince de Conti, refused to seek pardon from his holiness; he, therefore, could not sit in the Assembly of the States, being guilty of contumacy, and under the ban of the Church.

On the 2nd of October, the king and the Three Orders were present at a solemn procession of the Host. On the 9th, the whole of the deputies made public profession of Catholicism, and received the sacrament — the Cardinal de Bourbon officiating. On the 16th, the royal sitting was held in the *grande salle* of the château. A large stage with three steps was placed between the third and fourth pillars of that immense apartment. On it was a daïs with three chairs of state covered with violet velvet, with *fleurs-de-lys* and fringes of gold. The centre chair was for the king; the smaller ones at the sides for the queen and queen-mother. On the right of the king sat the three Bourbons — De Soissons, De Montpensier, and the Cardinal de Vendôme. The old Cardinal de Bourbon was ill; and De Conti, of course, was absent. At the back of and around the stage stood the king's guard and two hundred gentlemen of his household, with battle-axes. Galleries were arranged for the ambassadors and ladies of the court. The walls of the *salle* were hung with tapestry, bordered with rich fringes; and the pillars of the hall were enveloped in green velvet, embroidered with *fleurs-de-lys* in gold.

The deputies of the Three Estates then present numbered upwards of four hundred. The man in whom, however, the chief interest in this meeting centred — the Duc de Guise — occupied, in his quality of Grand-Master of the King's Household, a tabouret, or stool with arms, but without a back. It was covered with violet velvet, and placed in front of the king, but on the lowest step of the stage. There, pale, and with rage in his heart, he listened to the king's eloquent address; in which he promised to forgive and forget the past, but declared that, having been prevented by the inordinate ambition of some of his subjects from making the reforms he had intended, and from exterminating the "new opinions," he should consider all who did not immediately withdraw from the League as attainted and convicted of high treason. He concluded by charging the Three Orders with the responsibility of the state's salvation, before God and man, if they did not loyally and without reservation second his "good intentions."

These were bold words for Henri III., pronounced, too, with a firmness and decision so unusual with him, that those who knew him but little might well suppose he would resolutely carry them into effect. But when, on the morrow, the printed address appeared, the reference to the "inordinately ambitious subjects" — who, it was generally understood, were the Guises — was omitted. Guise had exacted this, and the weak king, after some angry remonstrances, had yielded. The duke from this time became daily more arrogant, more haughty, and the unfortunate Henri soon discovered how utterly vain were all his concessions and the humiliations to which he had submitted to content him. To the troubles of the day were added the terrors of the morrow — the States continuing their sittings, and passing resolutions utterly regardless of the royal authority.

Guise felt that he had gone too far to stop, or even to revise his plans, which historians of the time declare were denounced to the king by his own family. It is asserted that he intended that the sword of Constable of France should be decerned to him by the States General, and the king's sanction, if not willingly given, forced from him. This would have irrevocably confirmed the lieutenant-generalship of the armies, lately conferred on him, and have made him actually Mayor of the Palace. He would then have taken the king to Paris, and have allowed him to leave it no more. Such were the plans attributed to him. Apparently they were likely to be realised; and the king no longer doubted that the duke would seek to complete at the States of Blois what he began in Paris on the day of the barricades.

A similar project crossed his own mind. Why should he not forestall him, and accomplish at Blois the deed he had wished, but had not dared to do, when Guise arrived in Paris the day before that of the barricades?

CHAPTER XVII.

The King's Patience Exhausted. — Arrest and Trial, or a Coup-de-Main? — Crillon's Reply to the King's Request that He Would Assassinate the Duc de Guise. — Guise Warned of the Plot against His Life. — He Refuses to Give any Heed to It. — Council Assembles at Break of Day. — A Desperate Struggle with the Forty-five. — The King and His Dead Enemy. — Death of the Cardinal and Queen-mother.

THE deputies of the Tiers État, who were chiefly Leaguers, had audaciously declared that sovereignty belonged to the States, not to the king. That the king was but their president, and that in them all power resided. The clergy and the noblesse, though they did not go quite so far, yet did not strenuously oppose this usurpation of authority. The feeble-minded king could, therefore, no longer endure the insolence and insult he continually met with from "his ambitious subject," the head of the League, and his partisans. Yet he was slow in making up his mind to carry into effect his longing desire effectually to disembarrass himself of an enemy so powerful. At one moment he would seem to nerve himself for the necessary effort to accomplish his purpose; the next he would fall back into his usually irresolute state of mind, influenced also by fears for his personal safety. But when Maréchal d'Aumont, on the 18th, confided to him that the Duc de Guise had very persistently sought to induce him to join the League — meaning of course to forsake the king and the royalist party — he hesitated no longer. A secret council was held — the marshal, the Marquis de Rambouillet, and the Sieur de Beauvais-Nangis — to whom Henri explained his many grievances and the perils that threatened him, and entreated their aid to save him. "One man," he said, "was the sole cause of all he had to endure, and some prompt means of relief he anxiously desired."

No decision was then come to, but they met again on the morrow; the Corsican colonel, Alfonso Ornano, and the Baron de Maintenon being also present. The marquis and the baron suggested the duke's arrest and trial. But this was declared by the others an impossible course in the then state of popular feeling. Perhaps understanding better what were the king's wishes, the colonel recommended a *coup-de-main*, as more effectual — assassination in fact. Assassination was then an affair of every-day occurrence. Therefore a proposal of that kind to most persons had nothing startling in it. Yet many specious arguments were adduced to allay any possible scruples of conscience on the part of the king, who however scarcely needed to be thus reassured. His only anxiety was the difficulty of carrying out what he had resolved on.

A fortnight had not yet elapsed since the queen-mother had succeeded, as she believed, in effecting a reconciliation between Henri and the duke. The former "had sworn at the altar that perfect friendship and confidence should henceforth subsist between them." Yet if any change had arisen in their mutual relations, it was exhibited on the part of Guise only by a more haughty and contemptuous demeanour towards his sovereign, and a more eager pursuit of his ambitious schemes; while greater irresolution and timidity were evinced by the king, when presiding at the conferences of the States General. Every proposition emanating from him was disregarded or overruled by the Leaguers. Smiles were on his face, rage within his heart; his fears, doubtless, then suggesting murderous projects to free himself from the tyranny he had not the spirit openly to oppose.

It was impossible that the intended assassination could be kept entirely secret. At every meeting there was a traitor, concealed or in its midst, and warnings that his life was in danger reached the duke from many quarters, even as the king was daily informed of Guise's projects to deprive him of his crown. But who were to be the actors in this drama? Henri made his first application to the celebrated Captain Crillon, who, if not exactly a Huguenot, must have been a very moderate

Catholic, as he had been the companion-in-arms and was then the familiar friend of Henri of Navarre.* Crillon replied to the king's request that he would assassinate the duke: "Sire, my profession is that of a soldier, not of an assassin. But if it is your majesty's pleasure that I should make a hostile appeal to the duke, and take my chance of life or death in an encounter with him, behold me ready."

Henri pressed him no further, but required strict secrecy to be observed on the subject. A more ready agent was found in the first gentleman of the chamber, M. de Loignac, who, assisted by a certain number of the Forty-five, undertook to do the deed. It was necessary to impart the secret to one or two other gentlemen of the household, to whom large rewards were promised, and to select those of the Forty-five who were to take the most active part in the plot (December 21st). Being so far prepared, the king at a private council on the 22nd informed those present, amongst whom were the Duc de Guise and his brother, the cardinal, that he proposed to pass the festival of Christmas in retirement at Notre-Dame de Cléry, therefore would hold another council very early on the following morning, for the despatch of business before his departure.

* After the battle of Arques, in the following year, Henri thus wrote to him: "*Pends toi, brave Crillon, nous avons vaincu à Arques, et tu n'y étais pas.*"

The king named this early hour under the idea that Guise would then be attended by a less numerous escort than was customary with him, and that generally waited in an anteroom of the council-chamber, well within call or hearing. But as a further precaution, Larchant, the captain of the king's guards, who was in the secret, informed the duke as he left the council that the king's guards would assemble in the morning to present a petition to him — as Grand-Master of the Household — praying for payment of the arrears due to them. There was nothing to arouse suspicion in this; he was too much accustomed to receive such petitions. He therefore left Larchant the keys of the château to admit these guards, who were on that occasion to exclude Guise's guards from their usual post.

Many warnings that his life was in danger were received by the duke in the course of the day; many entreaties also from friends to leave Blois. Concealed in his dinner-napkin was a note imploring him to be on his guard, as the king had certainly determined on his death; but after writing on it, " He dare not !" he threw it contemptuously under the table. The Marquise de Noirmoustier (Madame de Suave, the celebrated beauty who twelve years before so fascinated the Duc d'Alençon, Henri of Navarre, and the Duc de Guise, and who is said to have "received the homage of all the princes of Europe") undertook a journey to

Blois expressly to entreat her still ardent admirer not so rashly to risk his life. Henri's resentment, she had learned on good authority, was sustained by that of the Forty-five, whose dismissal Guise had urged on the king, and thus, as well as offending him, had made those men his mortal enemies. But the duke, though flattered by the interest the belle marquise evinced in his fate, declared her fears groundless.

His extreme contempt for the king, his conviction that his utter want of force of will, or power of sustained resolution, would effectually restrain him from venturing any attack upon him, however eagerly he might desire it, made him disdainfully neglect the most ordinary precautions, and smile at the solicitude with which his friends recommended prudence. The reconciliation sworn at the altar the duke had no trust in. His reliance was on the influence of the queen-mother, who considered her interests bound up with the Guises', and without whose sanction Henri, as the duke believed, dared do nothing — and least of all so bold a deed as the attempt to take his life.

His friends were less confident. The chiefs of the League urged his departure, and the Cardinal de Guise was inclined to second their advice; but the duke declared that "should he see death entering by the window, he would not go out by the door to avoid it." He appears not to have known that the queen-mother had left Blois on the 18th, the day on which the king, taking advantage of her absence, made known to Maréchal d'Aumont and others his desire for release from the duke's tyranny.

She was giving a *fête* at one of her châteaux, in celebration of the marriage of her granddaughter, the Princesse Christine de Lorraine, with the Grand Duke of Tuscany. She returned to Blois on the 22nd suffering from gout, and was confined to her bed in consequence. The king's plot was carefully concealed from her.

At four in the morning of the 23rd two priests, sent for by the king, entered the royal oratory by a private staircase, and were desired to pray for the success of an enterprise which the king had greatly at heart, securing the repose and the welfare of his kingdom. While the priests were praying, the king remained in his cabinet, restless, anxious, and half disposed, as the morning advanced, to draw back from his purpose. He would probably have done so, but two companions were with him, Loignac and another of the Forty-five, charged with calming his terrors and exciting and sustaining his ever-wavering energy.

At seven o'clock Guise was informed by his *valet de chambre* that the king was preparing for departure, and that some members of the council had already assembled. He dressed and hastily descended to the council-chamber, receiving on the grand staircase of the château the petition of the guards announced the previous evening. As they attended in large numbers, and filled the staircase and obstructed the entrance to the *salle de conseil,* where Guise's escort on his appearance was accustomed to be stationed, the latter received orders to await the duke on the terrace.

When he entered the council-chamber, the Cardinal de Guise and the Archbishop of Lyons were the only members of the council present. As he leaned against the mantelpiece conversing with them, the king's first *valet de chambre* brought him some Brignolles plums in a *drageoir* (sweetmeat-box). While he was eating them, Révol, the Counsellor of State, came to the door and said to the duke, "Monsieur, the king desires to see you; he is in the *cabinet vieux.*" Immediately he drew up his mantle on his shoulder, and, holding his *drageoir* and gloves in one hand, crossed the antechamber and passed through the small door at the end of it, which the officer in attendance instantly closed upon him.

Guise was then in the power of his murderers. He was in the *cabinet vieux,* to which he had been summoned to speak with the king, but where only assassins awaited him. It adjoined the king's bedroom, and, as he extended his hand to put aside the tapestry covering the door, Montresy, one of the Forty-five, who in concealment watched his movements, sprang upon him, seized his right arm and struck him with his poniard, exclaiming, "Ah, traitor! thou shalt die!" Others of the same band then rushed in. Des Effremets threw himself on the duke's legs to prevent any freedom of movement. Saint-Malines struck him in the throat. Loignac, first gentleman of the chamber, buried his sword in his back.

Then ensued a desperate struggle, for Guise was a man of powerful frame, and all were eager to take part in the butchery, and conscientiously to earn the price of blood. Some struck him on the head, others on the back and abdomen, while he, with his sword entangled in the folds of his mantle and his legs firmly grasped by the assassin at his feet, was unable to parry their blows. At every new wound he exclaimed, "*Ah, mes amis, mes amis!*" Loignac having struck him with his dagger in the lower part of his back, he cried in a louder voice, "*Miséricorde!*" — an appeal as vain as that which many poor dying wretches had often made to him. But at that moment, though already pierced by ten mortal wounds, he yet retained the power of will, if not actual strength of body, to endeavour to escape.

Blood was fast flowing from him, yet by one supreme effort he momentarily freed himself from the cluster of assassins clinging to him, and advanced a step or two into the king's bedchamber. His arms were extended, his hands clenched, his mouth open, exhaling his last breath. Montresy, the first of the Forty-five who attacked him, was in the room and saw him approaching. Hastily he rushed forward, and presented the scabbard of his sword to his breast. Consciousness and life had already fled, and that feeble blow stopped the almost automatic movement which yet animated his dead body. Beating the air with his hands, he sank on the carpet at the king's bedside — rigid, motionless.

The wretched, dastardly Henri III., his ear pressed close to the door of the *cabinet neuf*, was endeavouring thus to ascertain all the incidents of the struggle.* When the last confused noises of the contest ceased, and the dull, heavy sound of the body, as it fell on the floor, reached his ear, he then very cautiously opened the door, and, slipping his pale face under the tapestry, embraced in one view the whole scene of the catastrophe.

"Do you think he is really dead, Loignac?" he inquired of the chief assassin.

"I should say so, sire," he replied, lifting up his victim's head. "There is the paleness of death on his face."

Then only did the contemptible Henri of Valois venture to enter the chamber and contemplate the countenance of his dead enemy. After gazing long and fixedly on him, "Mon Dieu!" he exclaimed, "how tall he is! taller, he seems to me,

---

* The *cabinet vieux* and the *cabinet neuf* were two small chambers communicating at either end with the king's bedchamber.

than when living.*" He then pushed him with his foot, and L'Estoile asserts that he kicked him in the face — as Guise himself, sixteen years before, had in the same way insulted the massacred Admiral de Coligny.

The confusion and noise of the struggle in the king's bedchamber were heard by the members of the council. The cardinal, much alarmed, rushed to the grand staircase to call for aid, but found none to appeal to. The Archbishop of Lyons's first impulse was, if possible, to assist the duke. But Maréchal d'Aumont, drawing his sword, arrested the cardinal, and the archbishop was seized by the king's guards when attempting to enter the king's bedchamber.† Many arrests were made in the course of the day in the duke's family, and amongst the most prominent Leaguers. The king was quite elated with his victory.

The queen-mother, who was ill in bed, and whose suite of apartments was immediately under the king's, had heard the noise as of persons wrestling together, and the fall of a heavy body. She perceived terror, too, on the countenances of all who approached her. Much alarmed, she inquired what had happened; but none dared tell her. Soon, however, her son entered, radiant with smiles, to inquire after her health, and to inform

---

* The duke was six feet four.

† Narrative of the king's physician, Miron; L'Estoile; Mathieu.

her that he had that morning become once more King of France, having put to death the King of Paris.

"You have killed the Duc de Guise!" she exclaimed with consternation. "God grant that this death may not be the cause of your being king of nothing at all." To which he replied, "*Morte la bête, mort le venin!*" Seeing only dismay on the countenances of those around him, whilst they who hitherto were the most factious had suddenly become the most servile, he thought that he had filled all hearts with terror, and that faction was dead. He had provided against everything, he told his mother, and had sent to Lyons to arrest the Duc de Mayenne and others.

But what should he do with his prisoners, especially the cardinal? He summoned his new counsellors to discuss the matter with him. The cardinal, though now a captive, and, as it were, with the knife at his throat, threatened his gaolers, and behaved with much haughtiness. If he was free, it was contended he would doubtless think it right to seek to avenge his brother's death. After considerable discussion, it was resolved that he should die. But none was found to lift his hand against a prince of the Church. The Forty-five, who had been so eager to share in the assassination of the duke, shrank from the sacrilegious act of laying their murderous hands on a cardinal. The king's guards, the provost and his archers, all declined to risk their souls by engaging in such a deed; though they would gleefully have joined in a general massacre of heretics, or, as they had just now given proof, have felt no hesitation to imbrue their hands in the blood of one of their own faith, if it served their interests, or the bribe for the deed was large enough.

The cardinal, on being arrested, was conducted to an upper room of the Tour de Moulins, called "*les chambre des oubliettes.*" He was soon after visited by the queen-mother, who, contrary to the advice of her physician, left her bed to condole with the cardinal, and, probably, to promise to effect his release. But he, believing that she had counselled the king to assassinate his brother, received her with haughty disdain, and so overwhelmed her with reproaches that she retired to her chamber, apparently more distressed and humiliated than she had ever been at any previous event of her thirty years' reign.

At length a man was found, a captain of the king's guards, bold enough to dare the anathema of the Church. This brave Captain Guast, with four of his soldiers, entered the cardinal's prison early on the morrow (24th), and, suddenly falling upon him, the captain and his soldiers stabbed and beat him to death with their halberds. The bodies of the two brothers were, by the king's command, delivered to M. de Richelieu, Grand Provost of France. "After being cut in pieces, they were burnt with quicklime in the ground-floor cell of the tower." * Henri III. refused the application of the dowager duchess for the bodies of her sons. He thought it better to utterly destroy them, and prevent the possibility of the Leaguers making relics of them for distribution amongst the people.

Catherine de' Medici did not long survive the excitement of her interview with the imprisoned cardinal. The news of his death, and the manner of it, with the burning of the bodies following it so speedily, made a deep impression on her, and so greatly increased the bad symptoms of her malady (the gout), that she rose from her bed no more, and died on the 5th of January, 1589, in her seventieth year. She is said to have given Henri excellent advice on her death-bed. "Peace," she urged on him, "was an absolute necessity for France; but that the kingdom might enjoy that blessing it was essential," she told him, "that he should grant his people liberty of conscience."

These counsels, given and acted upon many years before, might have saved France much of the intestine trouble of which she had so long been the victim. Now, unhappily, they came too late to be of any avail; and, in the furious tempest of popular passion raised by the king's assassination of the Guises, the death of the remarkable woman who for thirty years had figured so promi-

* "*Relation de Miron.*"

nently in the affairs of Europe excited scarcely a passing notice.

Henri spared the life of the Archbishop of Lyons, and those of the Parisian deputies whom he at first intended to have hanged, and released most of the persons who had been arrested as partisans of the Duc de Guise. Also he wrote to the Marquis de Pisani, his ambassador at the Papal Court, desiring him to explain to his holiness the necessity he had been under of defending his crown and his life. His release from the tyranny of Guise and from the control of the queen-mother would seem to have imbued him for a time with unwonted energy. But his satisfaction in the success, as he believed, of the course he had so boldly taken, was destined to be but of brief endurance.

CHAPTER XVIII.

Startling News for the Parisians and People of Orléans. — Guise's Great Reputation Chiefly Due to the King's Extreme Weakness of Character. — The Mass of Midnight, of Dawn, of Day. — The Children's Procession. — "May God Extinguish the Race of Valois!" — Christening of the Duke's Infant Son, François-Pâris. — Henri III. Seeks the Aid of the Heretic King of Navarre. — Proposing to Assault Paris. — Jacques Clément Sent to the Royal Camp to Assassinate the King. — Death of the Last of the Race of Valois.

FUGITIVES from Blois made known to the Parisians, on the evening of the 24th, the startling fact that " M. le Duc de Guise had been treacherously murdered by order of the king." At first the fatal intelligence was doubted; but gradually the people assembled in the streets, and questioned each other with the view of eliciting a contradiction of the truth of a report which to believe filled them with anguish. As the sinister rumour spread through the city, the shops were speedily closed, and information was eagerly sought by some of the people at the Hôtel de Guise; by others, of the guards at the city gates; and of travellers who chanced to arrive from the neighbourhood of Blois or Orléans.

To the latter place, the duke's *écuyer*, who had contrived on the 23rd to leave the château unnoticed, conveyed the news of the duke's assassination and the cardinal's imprisonment, together with a warning of his intended arrest to the Duc de Mayenne, who thus escaped falling into the hands of the king's emissaries. The people of Orléans were maddened to fury on learning that their "grand Guise" had been murdered, and openly vowed vengeance on the king. At the midnight mass in Paris on Christmas Eve, the preachers with sobs and sighs and voices broken by strong emotion, less real than affected, announced to the crowded and agitated congregations the "great homicide of Blois." A long wail of distress responded to it, and to many hearts this Christmas Eve was probably one of real sorrow and woe — a night of desolation.

For Guise, with his popular manners, his handsome person, his affected graciousness, had inspired the people with a passionate attachment amounting almost to adoration. Yet he owed his great reputation chiefly to the extreme weakness, folly, and depravity of the king, and to the turbulent and fanatical spirit of the times. He was abhorred in his own family for his haughtiness and vanity. His military reputation, which it answered the purpose of the seditious Leaguers greatly to exalt, was founded only on two or three exploits of treachery and cruel butchery, such as that of Anneau — planned and executed by him, to his eternal disgrace. Retributive justice at last overtook him, and in the manner of his own death that of Coligny was partly avenged. The cardinal was of as turbulent and dangerous a character as his brother, and the king probably hated and feared him no less.

The preachers, the Jesuits especially, made the most of this opportunity of inciting the people, in the name of God, to further diabolical treatment of the Reformers. At the masses of midnight, of dawn, and of day, it was Guise, not the Saviour, who was the object of the people's adoration. With their prayers were mingled muttered curses, heavy sobs, violent weeping. The most excitable seemed with difficulty to prevent their feelings from bursting forth in maddening shrieks when the priests, their utterance feignedly choked by sobs, recommended "the soul of the late M. de Guise" (a murderer, who had drenched the soil of France with Huguenot blood) "to the earnest prayers of the faithful."

Henri meanwhile was liberating his prisoners, the Cardinal de Bourbon, Archbishop of Lyons, and two princes of Lorraine at Amboise excepted; and as the States would agree to none of his proposals, he brought their sittings to a close on the 16th of January. He then charged the deputies to endeavour, on their return to their several provinces, to calm the minds of the people.

"Certain things," he said, "had recently happened which he much regretted; but for the peace and prosperity of the kingdom he had been compelled to sanction them."

But neither in Paris nor the provinces were the minds of the people calmed. Rather agitation was increased, and "hatred of the tyrant" was intensified, when it was ascertained beyond doubt that the cardinal was not a prisoner, but that he, too, had been sacrificed. The fury of both people and priests now knew no bounds. The royal arms were torn from the entrance gates of the churches, and dragged in the gutter. Henri de Valois was declared by the Sorbonne deposed; the people freed from their allegiance to him, and authorised to take up arms against him. The Pope excommunicated him, and confirmed the declaration of the Sorbonne. Yet Sixtus V., while he condemned as a priest, approved Henri's deed as a sovereign; and according to the despotic ideas of those times, it was, in fact, far more justifiable than many of the assassinations then of so frequent occurrence. Henri was, however, generally regarded as an assassin and a perjurer, and the Parliament, at the suit of the Guise family, instituted a criminal *procès* against him as "Henri de Valois, lately King of France and Poland."

A singular procession of all the little children in Paris, carrying wax-lights, was arranged by the priests, and conducted by them from the Cimetière des Innocents to the Abbey of Sainte-Geneviève. On arriving at the porch of the abbey, the priests and children, as they entered, turned down their wax-lights and extinguished them on the ground, crying as they did so, "May God thus extinguish the race of Valois!" The whole population of Paris appears to have been in a state of delirium. The churches generally were hung with black, and there were nocturnal processions of men, women, and children, barefooted, singing the "Miserere," and often with chemise or shirt for their only clothing on those cold January nights. As with some of the king's processions with his Flagellants, gross depravity was mingled with this so-called religious and penitential enthusiasm.

The Guise family, with a numerous retinue clad in deepest mourning, passed through the city daily, weeping and wailing, the Duchesses of Nemours and Montpensier, Guise's mother and sister, sometimes addressing the people, and invoking maledictions on the head of the "tyrant and assassin, Henri de Valois." On the 31st of January a new interest was added to these public family demonstrations of sorrow, by the appearance of the Duchesse de Guise in a litter with her infant son, born in Paris on the 20th. The city was proclaimed the sponsor of this new-born babe, who was christened François-Pâris de Lorraine, and with rejoicings as exultingly and extravagantly expressed, as the passionate grief with which his father's death was bewailed.

Philip II. heard of the death of the Guises with amazement, and, like the Parisians, was at first little disposed to believe it. He declined a proposed negotiation with Henri III., and was very reserved in his communications with the League. He had, indeed, enough on his hands just then with his own affairs, for the English, elated by their recent triumph over his armada, were ravaging with a numerous fleet the coasts of Spain and Portugal. All overtures from the king were rejected by the League, whose Council of Sixteen was endeavouring to prevent any falling away of their partisans, by giving out that the League was in no manner weakened by the removal of their chief. "It did not depend on one man. Another would soon be placed at its head"—this was the Duc de Mayenne.

An unwillingness to submit to the domination of the League caused many of the noblesse to desert it, and again to rally round Henri. His army was faithful to him, but too small to attack with any hope of success the forces the League now commanded. The Grand Duke of Tuscany, who appears to have been very wealthy, secretly lent him 200,000 gold crowns, and would have advanced a much more considerable sum if Marseilles could have been placed in his hands as security—the duke's object being to take steps for freeing himself from the harassing supremacy of Spain. Venice gave Henri good advice and good wishes, but had no money to lend. Once more he made unsuccessful advances to the League, and the legate Morosini endeavoured to effect a conciliatory arrangement for him with the Duc de Mayenne — since Guise's death its recognised chief. But "no confidence," the duke replied to the legate, "could be placed in Henri de Valois."

It was very repugnant to the king to seek aid of the heretics. But on all sides the large armies of the League were triumphing over the smaller force of the royalists. The King of Navarre, combating the League on his own account, surprised several small towns, and had taken up a position at Maillé, within two leagues of Tours, which Mayenne was threatening. Henri III. was staying at Plessis-lez-Tours. He therefore proposed an interview to his cousin of Navarre, who on his part offered to present his respects to the king in the faubourg of Saint-Symphorien, on the north bank of the Loire. Henri, however, sent Maréchal d'Aumont to the King of Navarre, praying him to cross the river and bring his people with him to the château.

This proposal met with great opposition from the Protestant officers and army generally. If he went, they declared he was a dead man, and that his head would be the pledge of the king's reconciliation with the Pope and the League. He was reminded of the invitation and flattering reception given by the court to Coligny. But Coligny's son, François de Châtillon, urged him to go, as France must be saved at all hazards; and Henri, after a little reflection, determined not to refuse. But, before allowing him to run the risk of entering the château, his friends, as a precaution against any intended treachery, took possession of one of the gates and surrounded it with Huguenot troops.

When Henri arrived, his cousin of France was strolling in meditative mood in the grounds of Plessis — his thoughts solely occupied with devising measures for his own safety. He embraced and welcomed his visitor with much cordiality, and the two kings then discussed the steps to be taken to rescue France from the Leaguers. A bold plan of campaign was then proposed by the King of Navarre as the only one he was prepared to lend his assistance in carrying out. Dilatory measures would have been more acceptable to Henri III., but his more active ally assured him that a policy of watching and waiting would, in their case, lead only to ruin.

The combined armies were in movement towards the end of June. Together, they numbered from 30,000 to 35,000 combatants — a large force in those times. On their march they took Étampes and other towns; the chiefs of the League established there being put to death by order of the king. Changing their route, they besieged Pontoise, where again the inhabitants would have been cruelly destroyed, but Henri of Navarre interceded for them and the garrison, and an honourable capitulation was granted. All vehemently expressed their gratitude, Leaguers included, whose lives he was the means of sparing; and the fanatical preacher, Boucher of Saint-Benoît, declared from his pulpit that the "Béarnais," though a heretic, was deserving of more honour than the tyrant Henri de Valois. A detachment of royalists and Huguenots also achieved great successes at Senlis and at Vincennes — whence they sent their bullets even into Paris. Seven hundred gentlemen, under François de Châtillon and the young Baron de Rosny, surprised Châteaudun, and dispersed a body of Leaguers. The Parisians, in alarm, recalled Mayenne, who was besieging the Huguenot city of Alençon.

The armies of the two kings, being reinforced by 10,000 Germans and Swiss, now changed their course, and marched on Paris. Henri III. established his quarters at Saint-Cloud; Henri of Navarre at Meudon. Great alarm prevailed in the capital. Their general returned; but had with him not more than 8,000 or 9,000 men. Deep gloom, extreme dejection, succeeded the recent furious threats and frenzied acts of the people of Paris. Mayenne, though reputed a more able general and statesman than his late brother, possessed not the sympathetic power and magnetic action that enabled the duke to captivate the masses, to excite them to the highest pitch of enthusiasm, and again to calm and subdue them, at his pleasure and as it suited his schemes.

The two kings were preparing to assault Paris on the 2nd of August, and with every chance of success; for its walls were ill defended, and would not long have resisted the vigorous attack of the combined armies. The passionate appeal of "the Sixteen," even the anathemas of the priests, fell unheeded on the ears of the depressed people, who refused to mount guard in the trenches — leaving that duty to the priests. "Paris might hold out fifteen days," said the Spanish envoy, Mendoza; but the Politiques declared that within three days there would be so many Leaguers to be hanged that Paris would fail to supply wood enough for the gibbets, and that it must be brought from Vincennes.

The bare idea of a Huguenot occupation of the capital occasioned paroxysms of rage in the cloisters. Was there no one there who had a poniard, asked the Duchesse de Montpensier, and with it the courage to win a martyr's crown of glory by immolating himself for the honour of God, and the salvation of his country from the rule of the heretic of Béarn and the tyrant of Valois! The Dominican or Jacobin convent of the Rue Saint-Jacques soon produced the hero demanded, who professed to have been charged by God in a dream to free France from her tyrant. This dream had long occupied his waking thoughts; but when it arose in his mind in, as he conceived, a vision of the night, he regarded the murderous suggestion as a mission laid on him by God.

He, however, consulted his superior, who, glad to have found in this poor ignorant fanatic a willing agent to do the much-desired deed, encouraged him in his resolve to obey the heavenly command. The one scruple he entertained — whether it were not a mortal sin for a priest to slay a tyrant — was set at rest also by superior authority, who reminded him of Judith and Jehu. The Ducs de Mayenne and d'Aumale unhesitatingly accepted the heaven-sent messenger, Jacques Clément, who came by divine authority to preserve Paris for the Leaguers.

The Duchesse de Montpensier was especially desirous of seeing this devoted youth, who for some days had been preparing himself for his heroic deed by prayer and fasting. He was sent to her on the 30th of July, when she incited and encouraged him with a view to supporting his firmness, and compelled him to swear that he would unfailingly realise his purpose.

Henri III. had informed the duchess that "he would burn her at the stake when he entered Paris." She replied "she would do her best to prevent him from ever entering it, and that burning was for such as he, not for her." Their mutual hatred was most intense.

Very heartily she bade the young monk God-speed, when, provided with the necessary credentials and passport (obtained, by misrepresentations, from the Comte de Brienne and the Président Harley, prisoners in the Bastille), Clément set out for the royal camp. If he escaped with life, the duchess promised him a cardinal's hat. But the infatuated young man (he was but twenty-two) rather desired that he might die. The worldly honours which he expected would be thrust upon him, he much feared, might occasion the loss to him of the crown of glory prepared for him in heaven. He therefore went on his way rejoicing in the hope of meeting death.

He arrived at Saint-Cloud towards the evening of the 31st, having been arrested at the outposts; but his papers, and satisfactory replies when questioned, obtained his release, and permission to proceed to the camp. Again he was detained and questioned, and his credentials examined by M. de La Guesle, the king's advocate-general. The king could not be seen until the following morning. Clément, therefore, was allowed to remain with the advocate's servants. He ate a hearty supper, was in a very gay humour, and afterwards slept so late and so soundly that he had to be rather roughly awakened.

The king being informed in the morning that a

monk desired to speak with him, having important letters to deliver, Brother Jacques was immediately allowed to enter. On handing his letters to the king, he mentioned that he had also a private verbal message for him. Henri made a sign to the gentlemen who were with him to withdraw. Suspicion seems to have crossed their minds at that moment, and M. de La Guesle and one or two others withdrew only a few paces. The monk then advanced towards the king, and, leaning forward as though to prevent his communication being heard except by the king, drew a long knife from under his sleeve and stabbed him in the stomach. The king exclaimed, "*Ah! malheureux moine, tu m'as tué!*" at the same time, rising from his chair, he drew the knife from the wound and struck the assassin in the face.

La Guesle, by a blow with his sword, threw him on the ground, and several of the Forty-five, hearing the king's cry of pain, rushed in, massacred the assassin on the spot, and threw his mangled remains out of window. The king's wound was not at first expected to prove a fatal one. The queen, princes, and others were informed of the "accident, which, thanks to God," they were told "was likely to have no serious results." Henri of Navarre hastened from Meudon to the king's quarters at Saint-Cloud. He was affectionately received, and declared by the king the legitimate heir to his crown. He exhorted him to return to the true Church, as well for his salvation in the next world as for his advantage in this.

All who were present, at his request, made oath to acknowledge, after his death, Henri de Bourbon as his rightful successor. Henri then left, at the king's desire, to inspect the posts and reassure the army. But in the night a messenger summoned him in all haste to repair to Saint-Cloud. He arrived too late; the king had already breathed his last. He expired early in the morning of the 2nd of August, the day on which the siege of Paris was to have begun. He received absolution and communion from his confessor, on promising, if he survived, to obey the Pope's commands with reference to the murder of the cardinal.

With Henri III. ended the Valois dynasty, which had given thirteen kings to France in two hundred and sixty-one years — the last perhaps its worst, and the most deeply stained with crime.

Henri III.
Photo-etching from an old print.

CHAPTER XIX.

News of the Death of Henri of Valois Received with Shouts of Joy. — The Saviour of Paris; the Liberator of the Church. — The Assassin's Deed Eulogised by the Pope in Full Consistory. — Henri IV. Required to Abjure. — He Demands Time for Reflection and Instruction. — The Battle of Arques. — Surprising the Faubourgs. — Sainte-Geneviève Implored to Save Her Good City. — Compliments from the Sultan. — Soissons's Escape from Nantes in a Basket. — Battle of Ivry. — La Belle Antoinette Supplanted.

HE populace of Paris — expecting no mercy from "Henri of Valois" should he return a conqueror to the "good city" he left as a fugitive; believing, too, that even greater atrocities threatened them at the hands of his heretic allies — passed at once from deepest despondency to delirious joy when, on the morning of the 2nd of August, the tyrant's death was announced. At first there was an unwillingness to believe that Heaven had so opportunely come to their relief — for the mission of the monk, lest it should fail, had been kept secret as far as possible. But all doubt was banished when the carriages of Mesdames de Nemours and de Montpensier issued from the Hôtel de Guise, and those heroines of the League drove through Paris,

stopping at all the public places and open spaces of the city, proclaiming "*les bonnes nouvelles!*" "Rejoice, my friends!" they cried, "rejoice! There is good news! the tyrant is dead!" and, as the people gathered around them, green scarfs were distributed (green representing hope and gladness) to replace the mourning ones generally worn since Guise's death.

Songs of joy now resounded through the streets so lately filled with mourners, and soon the churches were crowded with strangely demented congregations — all mirth and hilarity, and apparently more disposed to dance and sing than to express their thankfulness for their deliverance in prayer. The Duchesse de Nemours, in the exultation of gratified vengeance, actually ascended the steps of the high altar in the Church of the Cordeliers, and thence harangued the people; making known to them the mode of Henri's death, and that a new saint was added to the calendar.

Their devotions ended, the people, to show the unanimity of their joy, brought tables into the streets, spread with various viands, wines, and sweetmeats, and held a sort of open-air public banquet, of which every one was welcome to partake. In the evening, as on public festivities, dark, dreary old Paris was lighted up by numerous bonfires, around which danced frantic mobs, singing the praises of the regicide, whom they named the "Saviour of Paris and Liberator of the Church."

Small prints and wooden and plaster images of the poor fanatic were in great request, and were abundantly distributed by the League.*

The ladies of the Guise family were far more demonstrative than their sons and brothers. The Duchesse de Montpensier, violent and impetuous beyond the rest, almost insisted on the Duc de Mayenne boldly placing the crown of France on his own brow. The Leaguers were willing that he should do so, and, as the duchess forcibly urged on him, such an opportunity as the present moment afforded him might possibly never again occur. Mayenne would not have objected to wear the royal diadem; but he had not the audacity of his late brother, who at once would have taken it, or his ability when taken to keep it. His ambition, too, being less ardent, he was able to see the many obstacles to his adopting the course recommended. But, reserving the question for further discussion, it was decided, after long consultation with "the Sixteen," the chiefs of the League, the Spanish envoy Mendoza, the agents of the dukes of Lorraine and Savoy — all representing pretenders to the crown — to proclaim the old Cardinal de Bourbon king, as Charles X. (he being then ill and in captivity at the Château de Chinon), Mayenne remaining lieutenant-general during his absence.†

---

* L'Estoile — "*Journal de Henri IV.*"

† The cardinal was transferred by Henri IV. to Fontenay-le-Comte for greater safety.

When the news of Henri's assassination reached the Vatican, Sixtus V. — who was highly incensed against the late king for refusing to repair to Rome at his bidding, to make confession and do penance for the crime of putting a cardinal to death — in full consistory, eulogised the deed of the fanatical young monk. "He compared it in its 'miraculousness' to the incarnation and the resurrection of the Saviour, and raised the memory of the poor demented regicide above that of Eleazar Maccabee." His wounded pride as pontiff induced him to act thus contrary to the monarchical principles it was his habit to uphold. For in the case of the assassination of the Guises, his holiness would have remained entirely neutral had Henri revenged himself on the duke only, as a rebellious subject; but the cardinal's death he, as supreme head of the Church, was compelled to notice.

The unexpected death of the last contemptible prince with whom ended the line of Valois, though it made Henri of Navarre King of France, yet occurring at so critical a juncture was really a misfortune for the kingdom; for it prevented the deliverance of Paris from the rule of the fanatical and seditious faction of the League. Never surely did a king ascend a throne under greater difficulties. "The crown was his, but he had to fight for it before he could wear it, and to conquer or ransom almost every province of his kingdom." His religion served as a pretext to half at least of the chiefs of the army to abandon him, and to the League and the Sorbonne, of course, to refuse to recognise him. The several pretenders to his crown were all more or less formidable. The Huguenot army, on which alone he could rely, was small, his pecuniary resources next to nothing.

The Pope vigorously opposed the succession of a heretic. Even those of the nobility who fought under his banner as "Politiques," withdrew from his standard now that he claimed to be their king. "His closest adherents, hitherto amongst moderate Catholics, suddenly became less cordial; and his family, possessing neither influence nor wealth, was powerless to aid him — with the exception, to a certain extent, of the old Cardinal de Bourbon, now put forth by the League to oppose him."

Amongst the Catholic nobility who had sworn to Henri III. to acknowledge "his brother of Navarre" as his successor, many now declared that it was only on condition that he abjured his errors and returned to the fold of the faithful. This, he declared, could not be done without due reflection. He was, however, willing to submit to be instructed by a free and legitimate general or national council, and to give them meanwhile every assurance that he would allow the exercise of no other religion but the Catholic, except in those cities where the reformed worship was already established. Also he readily guaranteed that no change should be made in the offices or dignities of the princes, officers of the crown, or other faithful subjects of the late king.

By large promises of lucrative posts, etc., privately made, Henri IV. induced the avaricious, but very able general and politician, Maréchal de Biron, to espouse his cause. The marshal professed himself satisfied, and on Henri's proposed conditions willing to recognise him as king; *en attendant* the convocation of a general assembly of the princes and nobles, faithful servants of Henri III., to deliberate on the affairs of the kingdom. Biron's adhesion to this arrangement secured that of many others. The pact was signed on the 4th of August. It did not quite please Henri's Huguenot adherents. His promise to seek instruction in the Catholic religion was the occasion of many desertions.

On the 8th he decamped, taking with him the body of the late king, and, accompanied by Maréchal de Biron, about 20,000 troops (the Swiss having consented to remain with him), and the Princes De Conti and De Montpensier. The Parisians were still fêting their "glorious martyr Saint-Jacques Clément, of ever-blessed memory." They had sought out his poor old mother, who was now among them, and were parading her about the city as a sort of wonder. All eagerly desired to see this "marvellous woman" who had given birth to their saint, "the Liberator of the Church of God." Presents innumerable, of all sorts, and from all quarters, poured in upon her, and from the richest to the poorest. Naturally these extraordinary demonstrations of approval of her son's crime, instead of gratifying the poor simple old woman, puzzled and alarmed her, and, it is asserted, rendered her imbecile.*

Henri and his army crossed the Seine at Meulan, of which town he took possession; then ascended the Oise, and securing the small places, or villages, on that river, proceeded to the Abbey of Saint-Corneille de Compiègne, there to deposit the body of his predecessor, until the state of his kingdom gave him an opportunity to transfer it to Saint-Denis, as he had promised the queen. Dividing his army into three corps, he marched with his own division rapidly towards Normandy, desiring to approach the sea to receive the assistance, both in troops and money, promised by Elizabeth to him and the late king. The possession of a good northern seaport was then of great importance to Henri. Unexpectedly the Governor of Dieppe declared in his favour and gave up that important place to him, unconditionally and unreservedly.

Henri acknowledged that he owed to that brave officer, Aimar de Chastes, his own and the state's safety. Caen followed his example, the governor rallying to the royalist cause. The commandant of Boulogne also sent his submission to the king, but all prayed for his conversion. News, however,

* Palma-Cayet; L'Estoile.

reached him that the Duc de Mayenne had been considerably reinforced by Spanish, Walloon, and other foreign troops; who, united, expected by one great effort effectually to crush the "pretender." The duke had begun his march with 30,000 men, announcing to the Parisians that he was going to capture the "Béarnais," and would lead him on his return through the Rue Saint-Antoine to the Bastille.

To enjoy the amusing spectacle promised them, "many simpletons secured at a high rate the windows of the houses along the line of march by which the victor was to return with his chained captive" (L'Estoile). But Henri was not so readily captured. He did not allow Mayenne to shut him up in Dieppe, and compel him either to surrender or escape to England, as the duke had too hastily promised Spain and the Vatican that he would do — was, in fact, certain of doing. Henri established his camp on the hill of Arques, a very strong position, distant a league and a half from Dieppe, between three small rivers, woods, ravines, and marshes; the Faubourg of Pollet was also strongly fortified.

The first attack (23rd of September) was vigorously repulsed, and although the Catholic German troops treacherously obtained entrance as Huguenots to the intrenchment, and fell savagely on the Protestants, whom they pretended to join, yet Biron's able generalship and the reckless valour with which Henri fought and inspired his troops, resulted in the discomfiture of Mayenne and his allies, and their humiliating retreat before an army less than half their number. Some few days after 5,000 or 6,000 Scottish and English troops landed at Dieppe, and the two detachments of his own army joined him from Picardy and Champagne.

The victory of Arques caused a great sensation throughout France and the German States, and the " Béarnais," as the Leaguers persisted in calling him, rose greatly in the people's estimation. While Mayenne was retiring towards the Somme to seek fresh aid from the Duke of Parma, Henri, after giving some days of repose to his troops and reassembling his army, now upwards of 20,000 strong, marched direct to Paris.

"On All Saints' Day, 1st of November, under cover of a fog which, as if by miracle, suddenly rose, after prayer in the Pré-aux-Clercs, the king, at about six in the morning, surprised the faubourgs of the left bank of the river, and in less than an hour all were carried. The Comte de Châtillon cried as he entered, 'Saint-Barthélemy!' (L'Estoile) which had the effect of exciting his troops and causing bloodshed that Henri would have prevented. About a thousand of the poorer inhabitants were slain and thirteen pieces of cannon taken. Between seven and eight the king entered the Faubourg Saint-Jacques and went to the Petit Bourbon, a house then belonging to one of the late king's secretaries. A bed of fresh straw was made up for him at the foot of a table in the *salon*, and there for about three hours he slept very soundly.

"On that same day, being desirous of getting a general uninterrupted view of his good city of Paris, he went to the top of the belfry of the Church of Saint-Germain des Prés, conducted by a monk, with whom he remained alone. On descending, he said to Maréchal de Biron that 'finding himself alone with this priest, a sort of apprehension came over him, and Brother Clément's knife presented itself to his mind.' He declared that he would never again allow a monk to accompany him anywhere until he had been thoroughly searched, and that he had no knife concealed about him was clearly ascertained."

"The Sixteen," in all haste, despatched messengers to their lieutenant-general, who was then at Amiens. He arrived the next day, which revived the courage of the alarmed inhabitants; for the king having attached a pétard to the Porte Saint-Germain, to effect there, if possible, an entry into Paris, the people believed that the city was threatened with utter destruction. But these recently invented explosive machines were of very uncertain action. The one in question refused to explode, which, together with the mishap that occurred to the brave Huguenot captain, La Noue — who was nearly drowned while attempting to effect an entry by fording the Seine at its slightly shallower part, opposite the Tour de Nesle — was attributed to the good offices of Sainte-Geneviève, who had been entreated to save her good city and her faithful people from the accursed heretic. She was probably pleased with the substantial bribes offered her, as she so signally granted the prayer of the suppliants.

The next morning the "Béarnais" withdrew his troops, and left the city free, having vainly endeavoured to draw Mayenne into giving battle. The soldiers, however, before their departure, searched all the houses of the faubourgs for copper and iron pots, and other such utensils, for conversion into bullets for their artillery.

In spite of the Pope's remonstrances, and the Bull of excommunication launched against Henri IV., the State of Venice — the first Catholic Power that acknowledged him — ordered the ambassador accredited to Henri III. to continue to perform the same functions to his successor. Philip II. also joined Rome in wrathfully menacing the Senate, but without effect.* Other Italian states, who

---

* Venice, constrained by similar threats, had unwillingly sent three or four of her vessels to follow in the wake of the invincible armada, and had lost them in the tempest. In their vexation at this, to them very considerable loss (for the greatness of Venice had then begun to decline), the Senate recognised the rights of the heretic king, thus expressing their displeasure at Philip's attempt unduly to control them, and their defiance of him.

dared not, like Venice, openly brave the anger of the Pope and the Spaniard, privately assured him, through their agents, of their friendship and goodwill. The Sultan, Mourhad III., also recognised Henri IV. as King of France, and wrote him a letter, wishing him all prosperity, because of his clemency, abhorrence of image-worship, and because he was left without parents at so early an age. He offered to aid him with 200 vessels that he might successfully attack Spain.

It had, however, become necessary that Henri should give some brief attention to the affairs of Navarre; that he should promote his lieutenant-general to the post of regent, assisted by carefully chosen advisers; and Catherine, whose whole life was a continual attestation of her devotion to her brother, was proud of this proof of his affection, and of his confidence in her ability to preserve for him the people, the nobility, and the country they both loved so well. She had, indeed, for some time taken an active part in the government of the little kingdom. A rigid Calvinist herself, she yet was tolerant towards the Catholics, though sometimes unjustly represented as otherwise.

Catherine still remained faithful to her promise to the Comte de Soissons. She regularly corresponded with him, and it was believed they sometimes contrived to meet through the agency of the Comtesse de Grammont, whose regard for

Catherine had not abated, though the faithless Henri had carried his vows of love elsewhere, and was sighing in vain at the feet of the Dame de La Roche-Guyon. La belle Corisande resented this desertion by aiding more faithful lovers whom he had separated, to soothe at least, by frequent tender missives, the pain of absence. Soissons, after returning to the Court of France, was appointed by Henri III. to the command of a small detachment of troops destined to suppress the spread of the power of the League in Brittany. On arriving at his destination he was surprised by a larger force, was taken prisoner by the Leaguers, and confined in the Château-fort of Nantes. His own servants were allowed to attend on him, and to pass in and out, supplying him with all he needed.

His needs appear to have been rather numerous, as a basket so large and so heavy that two or three men were required to carry it, passed in and out through the *corps de garde* daily. This went on for the space of six months. Now and then the basket was examined; but nothing ever was found but what an extravagant gentleman of *recherché* tastes and habits of the count's position might be supposed to require. One fine morning, however, neither basket nor bearers appeared at the château. The day wore on; still they came not. The governor was informed of the unusual circumstance, and the count's apartment — by no means a cell — was visited. Behold! the bird had flown, or rather had been flown away with, on the previous evening in the basket. When the search was made he was safe in his own château. It was suspected that both governor and guard had been napping — perhaps a little gold-dust had been thrown into their eyes and made their eyelids heavy.

Of the three Bourbon brothers, the Prince de Conti, the eldest, was with Henri; the second, the Cardinal de Vendôme, a young man of exceedingly narrow capacity, had made some attempts — influenced, it was suspected, by Soissons, the most active, able, and intelligent, but intriguing of the three — to gain partisans to put him forward as a candidate for the throne in opposition to his cousin, and as the rightful heir and successor of his uncle, the old Cardinal de Bourbon — Charles X. by the grace of the League. But Soissons, of whose valour there was no question, was then in command of a royalist *corps d'armée*. The estrangement, therefore, between him and his cousin must have been considerably lessened. But Henri's consent to the marriage, which Catherine and Soissons still looked forward to, appears to have been then less likely to be given than when it was refused two years before.

The moment was, indeed, scarcely favourable for marrying and giving in marriage, for there was war in every province, even in every canton.

France from one end to the other was the theatre of an incessant struggle, of which it is impossible to follow the innumerable changes and turns of fortune. Again Henri must don the cuirass, for Mayenne is again about to take the field (6th of January, 1590), burning to retrieve his military reputation, greatly compromised by the affair of Arques. He now undertook to deliver the environs of Paris of the royalist garrisons. After some successes, the capitulation of Vincennes, and some determined resistances, the armies on the 21st of February were face to face on the two banks of the Seine.

News of the taking and retaking of the old Château of Rouen then reached both commanders, who at once turned their forces in that direction. But Mayenne being greatly reinforced *en route* by Spaniards and Walloons, though he would have preferred more Spanish dollars and fewer of Philip's men, was compelled to accept battle at a disadvantage, as regarded position, but with a force greatly exceeding that of his opponent. His new allies were more eager even than he to begin the attack on the heretic, who again, alive or dead, was a promised trophy of victory to the Parisians.

On the morning of the 14th of March the two armies were drawn up in line of battle in the plain between Nonancourt and Ivry. Before giving the signal for attack — for Mayenne remained immovable — Henri invoked the protection of the

God of justice. Then, as he put on his helmet, adorned with a lofty plume of the feathers of the white peacock — the head of his charger being similarly decorated — he called to his soldiers: "Comrades, God is for us! There are His enemies and ours! Here is your king! Now, at them! If you should lose your standards, rally to my white plume; you will find it in the road to victory and honour!"

The result of the battle of Ivry was another signal triumph over Mayenne and the army of the League. All, except the Swiss, who deserted to the king, were pursued by the royalists as far as Mantes. There was, of course, much bloodshed. "Save the Frenchmen!" Henri cried to the pursuers; "but spare not the foreigners!" "It was really an astonishing victory, not only over superior numbers, but over an army well provided with artillery and every requisite for the needs of so considerable a force. But in spite of these advantages — wanting to the royalists — the cannon, the baggage, the colours of the enemy, all fell into the hands of the conquerors; and three-fourths of the army of the League were either killed, drowned while fording the Eure, or taken prisoners." *

Great was the dismay of the people when news of the destruction of the army of the League reached Paris. Had Henri, turning his victory to account, marched immediately on the capital,

* F. Servan — " *Guerres des Français.*"

which was very scantily provided with artillery, ammunition, or provisions, it was believed that the city would have capitulated. The future of France might then have been very different, it was supposed, could the king have entered his capital without being himself compelled to capitulate with the religion of the state and embrace Catholicism. But Henri remained for upwards of a fortnight at Mantes with his army.

The troops needed repose, and heavy rains rendered the roads almost impassable. Money, too, was wanting to pay the murmuring Swiss and Germans; the booty and the pillage of the towns and villages they passed through, which Henri was compelled to tolerate, was frequently all these thousands of ragged, wretched mercenaries received for their services.

But another reason interfered, as at Coutras, with the following up of the advantages his victory of Ivry had given him. The ugliest, but the bravest and most gallant gentleman in France, could not tear himself from the neighbourhood of Mantes, where dwelt the beautiful Châtelaine la Dame de La Roche-Guyon, who, for the time being, was mistress of his heart, or part of it, without duly laying the trophies of his victory — the colours taken in the battle — at her feet.

The reign of la belle Antoinette of Roche-Guyon was, however, but of short duration. Henri, who played by turns the part of general and that of skirmisher, varied at times by some expedition of knight errantry, in the course of one of those frequent episodes of the war, had heard of the beauty of the fair Gabrielle, daughter of the Sieur d'Estrées, Baron de Cœuvres. Secretly leaving his army one evening in disguise, he proceeded to the château where dwelt this miracle of beauty, and, as in some accounts asserted, representing himself as a poor pilgrim, was by Gabrielle's direction supplied with wine, and fruits, and bread. Her beauty surpassed his expectations, prepared though he was to gaze on a vision of loveliness.

Of course he fell desperately in love with her, and did not, or perhaps he could not — having a heart so readily inflammable — conceal his admiration. At all events he told her, after expressing his gratitude for her kindness in supplying his wants, that "she would soon hear of what love for her had inspired him to do." Keen eyes, however, are said to have at once detected the heretic King of France under the disguise of this weather-beaten, wayworn pilgrim.

The lady of La Roche-Guyon, to whom Henri had given a promise of marriage, signed with his blood (not the first, or indeed the last), to be fulfilled as soon as he had obtained a divorce from Marguerite — but which did not induce "La Dame" to consent to be his mistress — was, very shortly after the battle of Ivry, forsaken for the younger and more beautiful Gabrielle d'Estrées.

CHAPTER XX.

The Blockade of Paris. — Death of the Cardinal-King of the League. — Famine; Suffering and Revolting Horrors of the Siege. — An Appeal to Notre-Dame de Lorette. — Famine-worn Fugitives from Paris. — The Starving People Await Death in the Churches. — Great Joy. — The Besieging Army Decamps. — Death of Sixtus V. — Aid for the Huguenot King from Elizabeth and Protestant Princes. — Death of La Noue and Châtillon.

HAVING taken a last and tender farewell of the belle Dame de La Roche-Guyon — for whom he always retained the highest respect, though the flame of love now burnt less brightly — Henri left Mantes on the 28th of March at the head of his half-naked, shoeless army, and marched towards Paris, levying contributions of provisions on all the villages they passed through. The Parisians, now partly recovered from their first stupor on learning the loss of Mayenne's army, were preparing for the defence of the capital.

But Henri had renounced the idea of penetrating into Paris by force of arms. "He thought that France could never pardon her king the sack of that city. He feared, too, the fury of his army, and the despair of the people." His present design then was not to assault, but to blockade Paris, believing that the Parisians, fond of good cheer and accustomed to be abundantly supplied with not only the necessaries but all the luxuries of the table, would capitulate at the very first pangs of hunger that assailed them, and, by occupying the Upper Seine and its affluents, he would be able to intercept all supplies of provisions for the capital.

The king, however, was compelled by the penury of his exchequer to thwart, for a time at least, his own designs, by closing his eyes to a partial revictualling of the city. For a considerable bribe, one of his officers permitted large supplies for Paris to pass the bridge of Chamois. It was not a treasonable act, but one of dire necessity. Money for both officers and troops, and even for the king himself, was imperatively needed and must be obtained, no matter by what means, or at what risks.

Corbeil, Montereau, and Lagny, called the keys of Paris, either surrendered to the king, or were taken; and the posts on the Lower Seine were already occupied. The first detachment of the royalist army, passing close to the city on the morning of the 29th or 30th, gave the *réveil* as they drew near, with drums, trumpets, clarions, and hautbois. This caused a terrible panic; the people rose from their beds in great haste, fancying that the Huguenots had taken the city by surprise.

Henri, when informed of the terror the *réveil* had occasioned, laughed heartily. "His mistress," he said — thus he was accustomed to call Paris — "was very cruel to him, being displeased when he bade her 'good morning,' or sent soft music to enliven her."

The Parisians endured the pangs of hunger much longer than Henri had supposed possible. Many doubtless would gladly have capitulated; but the fanatical Jesuit and other priests, who had secretly stored their convents with salted provisions, vegetables, fruits, hay and forage, with biscuit in abundance — faring well while others starved — raved imprecations from their pulpits on all who ventured even to speak of or allude to negotiation with the accursed heretic. "Rather a thousand deaths," they exclaimed, "than such treason towards God!" The walls of Paris were repaired and strengthened by terraces. Sixty pieces of cannon were put into order and mounted, and the river was barred by chains protected by armed boats.

On the 8th of May the captive king of the League, "Charles X.," died at the Château de Fontenay-le-Comte. His death was an event of no interest to the suffering people; but greatly concerned Mayenne, who reigned in his name in Paris, expecting eventually to reign there in his own. The question was now, who should be elected to succeed the "cardinal king?" The Sorbonne in consequence assembled to renew their determination to reject Henri de Bourbon, even should he be absolved by the Holy See. The same evening Henri appeared before Paris at the head of 15,000 men. He took Charenton by assault, but was repulsed at Saint-Denis (afterwards taken), and at Saint-Martin.

A few days after his attack on the faubourgs, a new militia was organised to assist the *bourgeoisie* in their labours. It consisted of 1,300 priests, monks, and scholars of the university. This strange force was reviewed by the legate on the quays and the bridges. At the head of these monks marched the Bishop of Senlis, in helmet and cuirass, an arquebuse on his shoulder, and following a crucifix for an ensign, with a large banner having the image of the Virgin embroidered on it.

But famine, gaunt famine, was fast depopulating Paris. Every kind of nauseating food had been resorted to. Horses, cats, dogs, rats, and mice, had all been devoured; even the children — who suffered greatly, and were smitten down in large numbers — sometimes furnished a horrible repast which afterwards ended in death or madness, from feelings of self-disgust, horror, and remorse on the part of those who had eaten of this revolting feast; some of them with avidity. The convents were searched, and the Jesuits ordered to supply the people from their ample stores for a fortnight.

Many' of the famishing inhabitants lay dead, unheeded, in the streets just as they had fallen.

An appeal was made to the miracle-working image of Notre-Dame de Lorette, and a silver lamp and bowl, with other valuable offerings, promised for the benefit of her prayers, as soon as the city was delivered from the horrors of famine. An immense concourse of people of all ranks attended to supplicate this image. Some of them, too weak to support the pressure of the crowd, paid the penalty of death for their miserable superstition. Daily the state of things became worse, and the mortality increased. The horrible suggestion of taking the dead from their graves was made — it was reported, by the Spanish envoy — to the League. He proposed that these human bones should be reduced to powder, and what he called bread made from them. Madame de Montpensier praised this as a happy idea. The experiment was tried, and all whose desperate condition led them to partake of this horrible bread are said to have died. How Madame de Montpensier herself fared is not very clearly stated, for she would neither taste nor touch the bread she recommended to others (Henri, it seems, gallantly sent provisions now and then to the "princesses of the League"); but 2,000 crowns' worth of jewellery was offered for her dog, "to make broth of its brains for a sick person"— certainly a very brainless offer. Madame de Montpensier, however, cruelly refused to part with her dog, even for so benevolent a purpose; "she kept it," she said, "as a last dainty morsel for herself."

But, notwithstanding the menaces and imprecations of the priests — nearly all of whom were sold to the Spaniard — some attempts were secretly made to negotiate with the king. The piteous tales that reached him of the sufferings of the people moved him deeply; but policy struggled in his breast with pity.

One evening, however, there arrived at his camp several men of gaunt and starved appearance, who had escaped from Paris by throwing themselves from the walls into the moats. They came to implore him on their knees for bread, and to pray him to permit a certain number of the most wretched of the poor inhabitants to leave the city. Affected by the tears of these famine-worn suppliants, Henri gave permission for three thousand of the people to leave the besieged city. More than four thousand succeeded in passing out, and thousands behind were pressing forward to follow them, when the advanced posts of the royal army barred the passage to this crowd of despairing men and women.

Henri had been nearly three months before his "good city." He thought the time had arrived to strike a decisive blow and compel surrender. While besieged Paris had been growing weak, the royalist army, now numbering 25,000 excellent troops, had increased in strength and improved in its organisation. Divided into ten detachments, they attacked, on the night of the 24th of July, the whole of the faubourgs on both sides of the Seine, the evening being starlight but moonless. Henri witnessed this nocturnal combat from the top of the Abbey of Montmartre, whence Paris seemed enveloped in a circle of fire, while the light from the volleys of musketry illumined the whole of that intricate network of crooked streets, blind alleys, and narrow lanes forming the centre of Paris. In less than two hours the whole of the faubourgs were in the possession of the besiegers; a lengthened resistance being impossible to a people exhausted by misery and famine.

The principal citizens now entreated the governor (the young Duc de Nemours) to capitulate. But on the same day — 1st of August — a messenger from the Prince of Parma contrived to enter the city to announce that the prince in about fifteen days hoped to effect a junction with the army of the Duc de Mayenne, and with him to march to the relief of Paris. Mayenne was then at Meaux. He had not shared in the privations of the siege, and the people declared that he was either a coward or indifferent to their sufferings. But when told that fifteen days must yet elapse before relief could reach them, a wild cry of despair rang through the city. "All would then be dead!" they exclaimed, and many, resigning themselves to their fate, fled to the churches, to await in the sanctuary the death which, in numerous instances, there fell upon them.

Some attempt at negotiation followed; but without result. Henri's demands were moderate; but to gain time was the only object of the League. The fifteen days passed slowly away, another fifteen followed, and still neither Mayenne nor Parma appeared. Thousands had died in the interval; it was more wonderful that so many thousands survived.* However, on the morning of the 30th, the joyous cries from the sentinels caused starving Paris to hasten to the ramparts. What words shall express their joy! The royalist *corps de garde* are empty. The siege is raised!

Information that Parma had entered France and joined the lieutenant-general and his Leaguers at Meaux had reached the king by one of his scouts. He determined to immediately assemble his troops and march out to meet the enemy. Taking up a position at Chelles on the Marne, Henri, resolved to vanquish or die, offered battle. The prince declined the combat, and, in the course of the night, his soldiers surrounded his camp with earthworks. Another useless effort to enter Paris was made on the night of the 9th. The hopes of those who had looked forward to the pillage of Paris being thus dispelled, discord began to show itself in the

* L'Estoile mentions 30,000 as the number of deaths from famine during the siege.

royalist camp. The Protestants and Catholics disagreed; the foreign auxiliaries demanded money; the nobility, harassed and worn by the length of siege that had ended so unsatisfactorily, required their *congé*.

Henri, therefore, abandoned the campaign to his enemies, and retired with a small force to Beauvaisis — his victories again proving fruitless.

Sixtus V. died on the 27th of August, an event that Henri regarded as unfavourable to him, notwithstanding the Bull of excommunication. Sixtus was a zealous persecutor of heresy, and a no less zealous enemy of Philip II., whose righteous wrath he incurred for declaring his willingness to recognise Henri's right to the throne of France, if he would renounce his heresy and return to the bosom of the Church. In the space of about fourteen months, three Popes succeeded and died. A younger man was then selected, Hippolito Aldobrandino, who took the name of Clement VIII. Immediately he sent a legate to assist at the assembly of the States of Paris, about to meet to elect a successor to the cardinal-king of the League.

The dangers threatening the Spaniards in Belgium compelled the Prince of Parma to return to his government. Leaving a few troops with Mayenne, he began his retreat, followed by the royalists, who harassed him even to the frontier. Henri then turned towards the Somme, and was welcomed with enthusiasm at Saint-Quentin, where he received the news of the taking of Corbie. Bordeaux, which, with its parliament, had hitherto remained neutral, now sent a deputation, which awaited him at Senlis, to recognise him as king, and at the same time to exhort him to become a Catholic. To this exhortation he, as usual, replied that "as soon as the cessation of war gave him leisure he would seek instruction."

Henri was desirous of securing the support of the royalist Catholics; but to conciliate them and also to satisfy the Reformers was a difficult undertaking. He had, indeed, enough on his hands with his diplomacy, his wars, and his affairs of gallantry — always with him, unfortunately, affairs of importance. The Vicomte de Turenne, meanwhile, was travelling through England, Holland, and Germany, negotiating in Henri's name and seeking aid in troops and money for the support of the cause of the Huguenot King of France.

Elizabeth suggested the restitution of Calais as the price of her services. But Turenne convinced the queen that such an arrangement would not advance but ruin Henri's cause. She, however, sent him money; not in very considerable sums, yet frequently renewed. The German princes, who hitherto had done but little for him, now promised a powerful reinforcement, — Elizabeth guaranteeing, in part, the payment of these troops. Henri's prospects thus appeared more promising.

The famous Dauphinais captain, Lesdiguières, one of the most active and successful of the Huguenot leaders, drove the League almost entirely out of Dauphiny, and compelled Grenoble to open its gates and acknowledge Henri IV. Many of the nobility who had abandoned the king now returned to his camp, alleging the exhaustion of their means as the cause of their desertion; and this appears to have been really true. The king being destitute of the necessary resources, his wars had brought many of his followers to penury. Their reward was to come when he should be established on his throne, and they appear to have expected that the kingdom should be divided amongst them.

Paris being surrounded by royalist garrisons, hostilities were carried on through the winter. But no cavalry had been left to prevent the people from leaving the city, or supplies from entering it; yet provisions were scarce and dear in the capital, and want and disease prevalent. The Chevalier d'Aumale, who aimed at ruling Paris as "the Seventeenth" at the head of "the Sixteen" proposed an attack on Saint-Denis on the *fête* night (2nd of January) of the patron saint of Paris, Sainte-Geneviève — the enterprise being placed under her patronage. But so little interest did the saint condescend to take in the success of the scheme that she allowed the assaulting party to be vigorously repulsed, and the Duc d'Aumale to be killed. It was reported that she had deserted the cause of the Church and espoused that of the Politiques — thus seriously jeopardising her popularity in her "good" city."

She was supposed, however, to have made the *amende honorable* for her infidelity, when, about three weeks after, the royalists attempted to surprise Paris, entering, it was proposed, by the Porte Saint-Honoré by means of a party of troops disguised as millers, and having with them several carts filled with sacks, representing sacks of flour, but really concealing armed men. The millers arrived at four in the morning, but found that an earthwork had been thrown up in the night to oppose their entry. Another proof, too, was given them that their scheme was betrayed, and that the besieged were on the alert, in the sudden vociferous clanging of the tocsin.

An attack by force of arms was not the besiegers' intention; a retreat was therefore promptly ordered. The Parisians regarded this defeat of the "Béarnais'" project as a revenge granted them by their saintly patroness for their discomfiture at Saint-Denis and the loss of an ardent Leaguer. They chanted a "Te Deum" as though for a victorious battle, yet not a shot was fired. The shrine of Sainte-Geneviève, with the scaling-ladders as trophies of victory, which the besiegers had left behind them, was carried in procession; and the League, in memory of the threatened attack that resulted in a fiasco, instituted an annual *fête*, to be called "the day or *fête* of the flour-sacks."

But a more important and unfavourable result of this attempt to surprise the capital was the opportunity it gave both Spain and the League for urging the necessity of garrisoning Paris with Spaniards. The Parisians had long been vehemently opposed to the admission of a foreign garrison, but on the present occasion they gave way; the more effectually, as they imagined, to thwart the designs of the thrice-excommunicated heretic. For Landriano, the nuncio, had just arrived from Rome, laden with furious Bulls, anathemas, briefs, and admonitory letters from Gregory XIV. against Henri and "all and every, whether clerical or lay, who should not within the space of fifteen days from the receipt of the said documents have quitted the country under the rule of the 'King of Navarre.'"

Those cities that had recognised Henri as King of France resented this violent conduct on the part of the Pope. The Parliaments of Tours and Châlons-sur-Marne took the offensive, and on the 10th of June " declared the Bulls abusive, scandalous, seditious, null, full of deceit, and contrary to the holy decrees, rights, and liberties of the Gallican Church." The said Bulls, it was therefore ordained, were to be burnt in the public square of the city by the executioner of justice. Henri also defended himself, and with moderation and dignity protested against the blind and unseemly violence which Gregory XIV. displayed towards him. Gregory, however, survived only long enough to waste the treasure amassed by Sixtus V. for the embellishment of Rome, on grants of money to the League, and in equipping and paying an army to aid in defending Paris, which he termed the "bulwark of the true faith."

But Henri thought that the best response to all opposition was to continue his conquests. After a resistance of two months he took the city of Chartres, the capital of Beauce, called from its great fertility, and especially the excellence and abundance of its wheat and other grain, the granary of France. As this conquest interfered with the regularity with which the monasteries received their supplies from this province, the pulpits of Paris resounded with explosions of rage against the victorious "Béarnais," and predictions were freely hazarded of the wrath of heaven about to descend on him. Mayenne also received his due share of malediction for leaving Chartres unprotected. But, says L'Estoile, "the common people wished both Mayenne and the war at the devil, and openly declared that they cared not which party triumphed, so that they might once more have a little rest and quiet."

Again Henri triumphed at Noyon (17th of August), which capitulated almost under the eyes of the duke. But the satisfaction he derived from the success of his arms was greatly abated by news, which arrived at the same time, of the death of the valiant François La Noue, from a wound received at the siege of Lamballe.*

This loss was very soon followed by another, which the Protestants lamented as irreparable — that of Comte François de Châtillon, the worthy son of the admiral. He was but thirty years of age, but the privations and hardships of incessant warfare told on a constitution said to have been far from robust. His wife was one of the Protestant heroines of that time. With her household she had defended, with arms in her hand, the Château de Châtillon from an attack of the Leaguers, during the count's absence, and had taken their leader prisoner. Châtillon's Protestantism was of a far more sedate cast than Henri's, and much of the latter's success was owing to the bravery, zeal, and fidelity of Coligny's son. Yet he was neglected by the king while living, but greatly bemoaned when death brought home to him how trustworthy and zealous a friend and partisan he had lost.

Another notable event of this month of August was the escape, by means of a rope attached to the window of his prison, of the young Duc Charles de Guise, who had been a prisoner in the Château-fort of Tours ever since the assassination of his

* "*Homme sans peur et sans reproche* — the Bayard of the Huguenots" (L'Estoile).

father, and the arrest of several members of the Guise family by Henri III. His escape was made on the 15th, the *fête* of Notre-Dame. It was attributed to the protection of the Virgin Mary, and to the prayers of the Jesuits of Lorette, who asserted that they had daily with that object in view addressed prayers to the Virgin and celebrated mass, by order of their general.

The courage and intelligence displayed in his escape — though he had but slipped down a rope placed for the purpose at his window, and passed through gates that were opened for him — were lauded as most remarkable. Then there was the romance of the interference of the Virgin on his behalf, plainly pointing out that he was favoured by heaven. At Orléans and Paris this heaven-sent youth was received with the wildest enthusiasm. The Parisians seemed to believe that in him another "grand Guise" was about to arise and rule over them. The Duc de Mayenne viewed the escape of his nephew with less satisfaction than the League generally. He was desirous of consolidating his power and suppressing the Council of Sixteen, which, encouraged by the Pope, and at variance with the Parliament, was authorising many atrocities, having even had the audacity to send the Président Brisson and two of the counsellors to prison, and to hang them at night on gibbets in the Place de Grève.

The appearance of the young duke added another to the already numerous pretenders to the Crown of France. The long-deferred assembling of the States at Paris to decide on their respective claims was shortly to take place. Henri IV., whose aim was to prevent the election of any one of these claimants as leading to further troubles in France, though vexed at the loss of his illustrious hostage, consoled himself with the knowledge that the young duke would be but a new element of discord in the League, and the rival of his uncle.

CHAPTER XXI.

Henri's Latest Conquest. — Soissons Visits Pau in Disguise. — Soissons a Prisoner. — Catherine Ordered to Repair to Henri's Court at Saumur. — A New Suitor. — Plessis-Mornay's Sympathy with Catherine. — The Siege of Rouen. — Maréchal de Biron and His Son. — Exploits of the Great Huguenot Hero Lesdiguières. — The States General. — Mayenne's Mishap. — Philip Urges His Daughter's Claims. — Henri Meditates Abjuration. — Gabrielle's Influence. — The Promise of Marriage. — Henri Abjures.

WHILE Henri was lamenting the loss of his friends, congratulating himself on his victories, thwarting the young Cardinal de Bourbon's treacherous designs on his crown, and especially rejoicing in his latest conquest — that of securing the most beautiful woman in France for his mistress — his domestic peace was again troubled by his cousin, the Comte de Soissons. Henri had partly promised his sister to the young Prince de Dombes, son of the Duc de Montpensier, who had been very faithful and loyal to him. An indirect sort of proposal was also made to the Prince of Anhalt, when Henri went to Sedan * to receive the German reinforcements

---

* Henri, while at Sedan, rewarded the viscount's services on his behalf by obtaining for him the hand of the young Duchesse Charlotte de La Marck, sovereign princess of Sedan.

that Turenne's visits to the Protestant princes had secured for him.

Soissons, hearing of these matrimonial suggestions, secretly left the army, and under various disguises reached Pau, where, at the residence of the Comtesse de Grammont — the forsaken and resentful once belle Corisande — he and the Princesse Catherine solemnly renewed their promise of marriage. Soissons, however, required that the ceremony should immediately follow the promise, and Palma-Cayet, Catherine's reader, was requested to give the nuptial benediction. But he declined, having no authority, he said, from the king. Soissons, in a rage, threatened to kill him. To which he replied, "he would rather die unjustly by the hand of a prince, than merit death from that of the executioner."

Tidings of what was passing at Pau soon reached the royal camp, and Henri, in alarm, wrote to M. de Rovignac, whom he had appointed the princess-regent's chief adviser:

"MONSIEUR,
"I have heard with extreme displeasure of the object with which the journey of my cousin, the Comte de Soissons, to Pau has been taken. I will only observe to you that if anything has passed to which, contrary to my orders, you have consented, or at which you have assisted, your head shall answer for it. "HENRI.
"*Saumur, January, 1592.*"

The Baron de Pengeas was also sent to Pau to arrest the prince and declare him a prisoner. The council hastily assembled in the presence of their princess, and M. de Rovignac formally accused her of desiring to marry the Comte de Soissons against the wish of the king, and of having consented to be abducted by him. Catherine, highly indignant at the charges brought against her, replied, with proud disdain, that "to the king alone was she accountable for her actions, and that she did not comprehend what the council required of her." Rovignac replied, but with many excuses and in evident sympathy with the princess, that he had orders to consider her a prisoner, and to guard her closely as long as the count remained either in the château or the town.

Soissons in his despair vainly sought to brave the will of the then (in Navarre at least) all-powerful Henri. His resistance filled the château with trouble, and the town with confusion, before he could be brought to give up his sword to the baron and allow himself to be escorted to prison. The people assembled and menaced the prince who "had come to carry off their princess. By those magical means and infernal arts employed by the Medici and the courtesans of the Louvre, he had charmed madame," they said, "and her reason had left her." They vowed that she should be avenged and delivered from her enemy.

But Catherine wrote a touching letter to the king, entreating pardon for her lover. It was granted; but Henri required her to leave Pau and immediately to repair to Saumur, where he then held his court. Soissons had already returned, not by any means in a penitential mood, but with a bearing both defiant and audacious. So much so, that, meeting with the Baron de Pengeas, whom he had threatened to kick downstairs, he literally carried out his threat — giving, of course, great offence to Henri, and annoying the poor baron not a little.

It was a great sorrow to the Princesse Catherine to leave the country she loved so well, and where she was so generally beloved. A large concourse of the people assembled to see her depart, and bade her Godspeed with many tears, and prayers for her safety. A hundred cavaliers also escorted her. The retinue sent by Henri was a truly royal one, and the same honours were paid her *en route* as had been customary when the late queen-mother was taking a journey. Parties of Leaguers hovered around the princess's *cortège*, hoping to surprise and arrest her.* She, however, reached

* The Leaguers, and especially their Spanish allies, were exceedingly wroth against Catherine for allowing Antonio Perez to take refuge in Béarn in 1591, after his escape from Spain. Perez wrote a supplicatory letter to the princess, praying her to grant him protection, and permission to reside at Béarn. She replied that he might come boldly and would be welcome; that he would find in Navarre full freedom of action, coming, going, or remaining, at his pleasure, with entire liberty of religious worship. With her reply she sent him horses and an escort to protect him.

Saumur in safety, and was received there by Mesdames de Rohan and Plessis-Mornay.

The king being about to lay siege to Rouen, presented the Prince de Dombes to his sister, leaving to Plessis-Mornay's diplomacy the destruction, as he said, of Soissons's ambitious hopes, by inducing Catherine to bestow her hand on this new aspirant for that favour. The serious, placid Mornay was far more sympathetic than the gay gallant to whose service he had devoted himself. The Prince de Dombes had recently, by his father's death, become Duc de Montpensier. He appeared to admire Catherine, who, if not really beautiful, was exceedingly attractive — slight and elegant in figure, and of a very gay temper like her brother, but more refined, by the reserve imposed by her religion. As were so many princesses of that period, she was also highly educated.

The new suitor strove to make himself very agreeable to the princess, and laid many valuable presents at her feet. Her repugnance to receiving them she explained to Mornay, who, perceiving that this marriage which the king very greatly desired could never take place, urged him on his return from Rouen not to press it on her. But Henri had not returned from his expedition in quite so gay a mood as he set out. Rouen had been valiantly defended by the governor, Admiral Villars, and Henri, followed by the Prince of Parma, compelled to retire. Yet the royal army, notwithstanding the check it had received, might, it was asserted, having been reinforced, have put an end to the war. But Maréchal de Biron's manœuvres aimed at preventing a complete defeat of the enemy. It was not his first act of disloyalty towards the prince whose interests he professed to serve. Both Paris and Rouen were believed to have been lost to Henri through Biron's treacherous counsels.

During the campaign in question, the army of the League under Mayenne at one period of the attack seemed to be giving way, when Charles de Biron, the marshal's son, demanded of his father 500 cavalry, with which he declared he would put the whole of the enemy to the rout. The marshal turned angrily on his son with a positive refusal. "What!" he exclaimed, "would you send us to plant cabbages at Biron?" On which the son is reported to have replied: "Were I the king, your head should instantly fall."* Henri was wounded in the back in that engagement, and would have been completely overpowered and slain, had not his officers rallied around their reckless chief, and to save his life risked their own. The Prince of

---

* This, possibly, is one of the numerous doubtful anecdotes of which it may be said, "*Se non e vero e bene trovato.*" If intended to place the son in a more honourable light than his father, his future conduct did not justify it. He fully inherited the late marshal's vices, but only in an inferior degree his general ability and military genius. For his connivance in a plot against Henri IV., he was beheaded in 1602 (L'Estoile).

Parma then effected in the face of the royal army his famous retreat, regarded as a *chef-d'œuvre* of the art of war. Some few months later Maréchal Armand de Biron was killed by a ball from a "falconet"—a small cannon of the period—at the siege of Épernay.*

The war languished for a time after the disasters of Rouen, and Henri was compelled, from want of means, to disband the greater part of his army; to send the English and Scotch to their homes, and to prevail on the Germans to stay with him.

The loss of one great captain was, however, amply supplied by the exploits of another. The military genius of the Duc de Lesdiguières impressed the events of the war with a grander character in the southeast of France. The Duke of Savoy, who had invaded France, had very formidable enemies in this great Dauphiny captain and his second in command, Bernard de La-Valette. "The latter was killed after defeating 'the Savoyard' at the siege of a small town in Provence." But Lesdiguières, whose activity was remarkable, immediately passed into Provence and prevented the enemy from profiting by the death of that

* The marshal, according to L'Estoile, "as well versed in *les belles-lettres* as in the art of war," left memoirs whose loss is much to be regretted, as he was a good captain and great warrior, "though always preferring his own private profit to the welfare of the people." Charles de Biron, his son, was appointed by Henri Admiral of France.

brave officer, by driving back the Duke of Savoy from place to place as far as Nice.

But while making war outside his own province, the Leaguers reëntered it. With the rapidity of the eagle, Lesdiguières returned and swooped down on the Leaguers, while Charles Emanuel reappeared in Provence. Lesdiguières then, at the head of a handful of picked troops, boldly descended from the Alpine heights into the plains of Piedmont. At the approach of the famous Huguenot chief, the Vaudois of the valleys revolted, hoisted the banner of France, and with the utmost enthusiasm dragged the French hero's cannon from rock to rock. La Perouse and Cavour were taken, and Brigueras fortified in the very face of the duke, who hastened with a superior force to the relief of those towns. But the Savoyards were completely driven out of Provence and Dauphiny—the French avenging Charles Emanuel's attack on Saluzzo by again invading Piedmont (October—December, 1592).

While the great Huguenot captain and his army were triumphing in the South, the question of Henri's abjuration of his heresy was occupying the minds of many of his adherents in the North. They called upon him to perform the promise which had led them conditionally to embrace his cause, and to name the council to whose instruction in Catholicism he would be willing to submit, with a view to his renunciation of heretical opinions and return to the true faith. Three years had elapsed, and the promise which was to be realised within six months remained still unfulfilled. It was continually impressed on him that unless a compromise could be effected the present struggle must inevitably result in the ruin of France.

The Estates of the kingdom had named the month of January for the assembling of the deputies in Paris for the purpose of electing a Catholic king. The Duc de Mayenne therefore sent a formal document to the Parliament for registration (22nd of December), declaring that "just and necessary reasons compelled him to continue to make war on the 'King of Navarre,' who was unworthy, and, as a *hérétique relaps*, incapable of wearing the crown of France." He then exhorted all good Catholics to withdraw from their allegiance to this heretic prince, and unite with him (the duke) for the preservation of the religion of the state — otherwise, for France and Frenchmen he foresaw only misery and ruin. On the 4th of January, Mayenne and the young Duc de Guise left Paris, to fall by surprise, as they hoped, on Henri of Navarre at La Roche-Guyon. Secretly informed of their project, Henri jestingly said : " My cousin of Mayenne is a great captain, but I am an earlier riser than he."

Failing in his enterprise, Mayenne, rather crestfallen, returned to Paris, "where Vitri, in command of the garrison, entertained him at dinner

Duc de Mayenne.
Photo-etching from an old print.

very magnificently, and in full Spanish costume." On his return home from this grand repast, the duke — whose habit it was to drink freely when the wine was good — fell from his horse. He had become of late very corpulent, and being also fully armed, twelve of his servants with difficulty raised him up. As they could not put him on his horse again, a carriage was provided. Had the enemy been apprised of this mishap, very easily, his servants said, the chief of the League might have been made prisoner.

Good news, however, awaited him on recovering his sober senses — the death of the Prince of Parma on the 2nd of December. This opportune event released Mayenne from the prince's control, which he had borne so impatiently. The League, and Spanish influence that gave it prestige, were both weakened by the demise of the cold, calculating and cruel agent of the fanatical despot of Spain; while to Philip himself the prince's death was a calamity no less disastrous than the defeat and loss of his armada. All parties, in fact, regarded it as a great political event.*

The several factions then existing in France had been anxiously looking forward, from various

* M. Michelet says of Alexander Farnese, Prince of Parma, "This great tactician, this strong and cool-headed genius, by mingling victory with crime, mildness with cruelty, reconquered for Spain the whole of the Catholic Netherlands." To which M. Martin, who gives the quotation, adds: "A great man, if greatness can exist where morality and humanity do not."

motives, to the expected arrival of the prince and his troops in Paris. No precise date for the assembling of the States had been named, it being doubtful whether the prince would allow them to assemble at all. For Philip was not desirous that any one of the seven or eight claimants of the throne should be elected sovereign of France, however zealous a Catholic he might be. It was a queen, in the person of his daughter, the Infanta Clara Eugenia, for whose claims he sought recognition; and to share the throne with her he had determined on the Cardinal Archduke Albert of Austria, who, when released from his vows, was to marry the infanta — France to be ruled by them under his suzerainty.

It was suggested that the young Duc de Guise would be more acceptable to France than the archduke. But there was still the difficulty of the Salic law. It was contended that the Parliament of Paris was competent to annul it by an edict to that effect. The president and counsellors, however, declared the Salic law to be the fundamental law of the kingdom, which neither they nor any other judicial body in the state had power to abolish. On the 26th of February the States General — or a small part of them, the royalists refusing to send deputies — assembled in the *grande salle* of the Louvre, to consider the great question, who should govern France.

The Duc de Feria was deputed by Philip II.

to enforce his daughter's claims. The Duc de Mayenne and this haughty grandee were unable to act in concert — the former seeking the crown for himself — but not to break with the ruler of Spain, whose doubloons, though scarcer than formerly, were still thankfully received, Mayenne solemnly swore in the presence of Feria never to make peace, on any terms, with the heretic Henri of Navarre, or to acknowledge him as king, even should he renounce his heresy and return to the true Church.

On the other hand, a protest addressed to the States in the name of Henri IV., by the grace of God, King of France and Navarre, pronounced the States illegally assembled, and all their decrees and decisions null and of no effect. Feria — his *amour propre* already deeply wounded by the refusal of the Tiers État to rise and uncover when he, a grandee of Spain, entered the hall, to be present, by their permission, at their discussions — proposed that the protest of the heretic pretender should be rejected, and destroyed as of no account. The clergy seconded his proposal; but there were many "Politiques" amongst the deputies of the noblesse and Tiers État who would not consent to an act contrary to the rules of the assembly, which required the registration of all documents addressed to them; and further, allowed no foreigners to take part in their debates.

This shadow of an assembly of the States dragged on month after month, disputing, menacing, the clergy being especially violent, yet coming to no decision whatever. Meanwhile, Henri of Navarre was endeavouring to reconcile his conscience, by specious arguments, to the step he had determined on taking. "Should he sacrifice France and the throne which Providence had prepared for him to some obscure points of theology? It would be resisting Providence, who had called him to that throne, and destined him to bring the sanguinary era of fanaticism to a close, and to inaugurate a reign of tolerance of which he had often dreamed, and which a Catholic king alone could render acceptable to France."

As regarded the "instruction" the king was to receive, even Plessis-Mornay, one of the pillars of Reform, did not refuse to arrange the "preliminaries," which he probably expected would be both the beginning and end of the matter. But in Rosny the king found an adviser who, stern as he was, set many scruples at rest, and who allowed himself considerable latitude in his acceptance of the doctrines of Calvin. Gabrielle's wishes, also, are supposed to have influenced the king greatly. He passed much of his time with her, and seemed to become daily more devoted and passionately attached to his *belle maîtresse*. She was credited even then with cherishing the ambitious hope of being Queen of France should Henri embrace

Catholicism, and thus be able to obtain from the Pope a divorce from Marguerite of Valois.

Notwithstanding Henri's affection for the Princesse Catherine, he was probably, in this question of his so-called conversion, in no manner swayed by her wishes or entreaties. She remained true both to her religion and her lover. Her steadfastness astonished him. It annoyed him also, as the suitors he still anxiously proposed to her all met with rejection. Scenes, sometimes violent, at others tearful and saddening, occurred between them. Hesitating and timid when he employed tenderness, she was proud and passionate as himself when he displayed anger; but for all Soissons's reckless and audacious acts, Catherine, at her brother's feet, would sue for pardon.

Latterly, Henri had confided to Rosny his wish to obtain the promise of marriage signed by his sister and Soissons, and charged him to obtain the document for him. Rosny liked not the office, and sought to evade undertaking it. But Henri insisted; and remember, he said, "ruse, if it must be — force, if necessary." And ruse probably was employed; for the marriage promise signed by both was given up, but under, it would seem, the impression that marriage was to be the reward of this act of submission. Henri, however, had no such intention. Soissons was violent, and, to annoy Henri, encouraged his brother in pressing on the assembled States his pretensions to the throne.

Catherine resigned herself to her fate, sorrowing in silence; while Henri, satisfied with what Rosny had accomplished for him, repaired to Mantes to calm the minds of the disappointed Reformers, who heard with sorrow and alarm of the possibility of his "renunciation of God for idols."

But a month before he had assured the Calvinist ministers, with many protestations, that he had no thought of "returning to the mass." Without listening to their reproaches, he now told them, that "*if* he determined on the change, there was no occasion for vexation or alarm on their part. *If* he should enter 'the house,' it would not be to dwell there, but to purify it. He would promise them that, and for themselves personally, they might rest assured that he should treat them no worse than he had always done up to the present time." Then, with a faltering voice, for he was much affected, he said: "Now, pray to God for me, my friends, and I shall love you for it."

He had, however, fully resolved on the change; yet, before taking leave of the assembled ministers, he attended for the last time the Calvinist service. From Mantes he returned to Saint-Denis, where the Catholic theologians and prelates were assembled, ostensibly to convince him of his errors and to instruct him in Catholicism. He had, as he said, made up his mind to be convinced; but he could not refrain from contesting several points of doctrine with his instructors, and that so ably as to show how easily he could have refuted them had he been so minded.

The royal catechumen was leniently dealt with. No doubts of his thorough conviction were expressed, and the 30th of July was appointed for the public abjuration. A simplified form was prepared for him, in accordance with the extent he was willing to go in assenting to the Catholic doctrines. "To-morrow," he wrote to Gabrielle on the 29th, "I take the perilous leap."

At eight o'clock on the morning of the 30th, the king, escorted by several princes, his grand officers, French, Scotch, and Swiss guards, went in procession — twelve trumpeters preceding — to the Abbey of Saint-Denis. The gates of the ancient edifice were closed. On knocking at the grand portail, it was opened by the Archbishop of Bourges, who, when Henri was about to enter, inquired what he wanted and whence he came. He replied, he was King of France, and desired to be received into the bosom of the Catholic, Apostolic, and Roman Church.

He then knelt, read his profession of faith, and delivered it, signed, to the archbishop, whose ring was presented to him to kiss, and absolution and benediction given. Conducted to the grand altar, he there, on his knees, repeated his oath; and was afterwards heard in confession by the archbishop. Meanwhile, through the long-drawn aisles and fretted vaults of the old basilica, resounded the

"Te Deum," chanted in full choir. High mass was then celebrated in the presence of the court, the people, and the royalist magistrates, who arrived in a body from Tours.

On Henri's return, he found the streets strewed with flowers, and filled with enthusiastic people, amongst whom the Parisians, in spite of the legate and the lieutenant-general's prohibition, were there in crowds, and cried "Long live the king!" with greater energy than the rest.

CHAPTER XXII.

Henri's Conversion Rejoices the People.— The Truce for Three Months.— Refusal to Prolong It.— Coronation of Henri IV. at Chartres.— The New Crown.— The Sainte-Ampoule and the Holy Oil of Saint-Martin.— Mayenne Appoints a New Governor of Paris.— He Opens the Gates to the King.— The Entry into Paris.— The Foreign Garrison Marches Out.— The King Sends "Le Bon Jour" to Madame de Montpensier. — The King Much Elated; Dines at the Louvre.— Rendering to Cæsar the Things that are Cæsar's.

THOSE who have judged Henri of Navarre most leniently, both Catholics and Protestants, with reference to his abjuration, have found it impossible to approve either his act or his example. "He suppressed," they say, "present troubles only at the expense of the future." Yet mere ambition was not his only motive, but a sincere desire also to put an end to the cruel strife which had then for thirty-four years desolated France, and still seemed destined to continue. The people, however, of the Catholic provinces, who regarded not the dim future, but looked only for present relief, rejoiced exceedingly when they heard of the "heretic Henri's conversion." Nor could the chiefs of the League control the enthusiasm displayed in Paris, or even in those provincial towns where the Leaguers predominated. A general three months' truce was signed on the day following the abjuration — the preliminary, it was hoped, to a permanent peace.

The plague was raging — then so often the case in the pestiferous purlieus of old Paris; and a great scarcity of food, threatening famine, caused the populace to clamour for "*la paix ou le pain*," peace having the preference, as bringing in its train all other blessings. Even to the suffering and dying the prospect of a settled peace, after years of the ever-recurring miseries of war, brought a momentary feeling of repose and a gleam of joy. But Mayenne, to whom a permanent peace meant the cessation of power, exerted himself to prevent the realisation of the hopes of those who anxiously desired it, by obtaining from the States at their last sittings, notwithstanding strong opposition, the reception of the decrees of the Council of Trent. For years past they had been resolutely rejected by the Kings of France, the Parliament, and the States General, as incompatible with civil authority and national independence. Thus he placed an obstacle to a reconciliation between the League and the king.

It was a gratifying act to Clement VIII., who declared that he "would never believe in the conversion of the 'Béarnais' unless an angel was sent from heaven to assure him of it." His refusal, however, to receive the Duc de Nevers, Henri's ambassador, had an effect directly contrary to that he intended, the greater part of the French Catholics at once acknowledging Henri without waiting for the intervention of Rome. But every provincial governor who recognised the new ruler stipulated for the retention of his governorship, a good round sum in cash and a substantial pension, with any other trifling favour of which his "patriotism" might be decreed worthy. The ancient privileges of the cities were also to be confirmed, and past rebellious acts consigned to oblivion.

The truce had been already prolonged when Mayenne applied to Henri for further delay. He refused, and summoned the Leaguers (27th of December) to submit within a month to his authority. The Governor of Meaux and his parliament had recognised the king on the 24th; Provence yielded on the 7th of January; Lyons on the 7th of February, after having burnt the arms of Spain and destroyed the allegorical figures representing the League. But all these provinces and minor towns gave in their adhesion only on similar conditions to those granted to the towns that had voluntarily preceded them. Not a foot of ground was yielded that was not fully paid for, or payment promised and guaranteed; for Henri had not cash at command for his own needs, much less to satisfy the greed of all those harpies.

However, white scarfs and white plumes became the order of the day in those cities of the League that had declared for the king, and the green scarfs and banners with the effigy of the League, in the form of a sorcerer, were thrown on the bonfires in the public squares, the people dancing gleefully around them.

The Baron de Rosny — who appears to have filled Plessis-Mornay's office as Henri's negotiator until the slight estrangement occasioned between him and the king, by the latter's abjuration, was overcome — was vigorously forwarding an arrangement with Admiral de Villars, Governor of Rouen and Havre, for the recognition of Henri of Navarre as King of France. Mayenne had been informed that the admiral intended to treat with the king if the Spaniard's pretentions were not rejected. Signatures were secretly exchanged early in March, and Henri then determined to delay no longer the ceremony of his coronation, for until that had taken place, he was not in the eyes of the people really king.

Again the legate and those of the clergy who were opposed to the royalist party raved against the excommunicated heretic and his "simulated conversion," threatening with the pontiff's anathema "all, both clergy and laity, who should take part in, or be present at, this unholy and unauthorised act." Nevertheless the ceremony took place (27th of February, 1594) — not at Rheims, the "city of the sacre," which the Leaguers then held with a strong garrison, and which Henri determined not to lay siege to — but elsewhere, of which the annals of France afforded several instances. In the present one, the Abbey of Notre-Dame de Chartres was selected — the bishop, Nicolas de Thou, representing the Archbishop of Rheims. Instead of the miraculous Sainte-Ampoule of Saint-Remy, the Bishop of Chartres employed for the king's anointing an equally miraculous phial of holy oil, sent from heaven to Saint-Martin, the Apostle of the Gauls, and preserved in the Abbey of Monmoutier. The old Carlovingian crown, together with the ornaments of the royal treasure of Saint-Denis, had been taken by the Leaguers and melted down to make coin. A new crown and the rest of the regalia had therefore to be made for the occasion, and probably on a promise of payment when the League was suppressed and the king really seated on his throne.

Henri was desperately poor at that time, and while in all parts of his kingdom governors of provinces and marshals of France were making arrangements with his agents for the princely fortunes to be secured to them for their recognition of his rights, he, as he afterwards wrote to Rosny, was greatly embarrassed by the low state of his finances.

"I am very near the enemy," he says, "and have scarcely a charger fit to carry me into battle, or a complete set of harness to put on his back. My shirts are all in rags, and my doublets in holes at the elbows. My saucepans are often empty, and for some days past I have dined and supped first with one officer, then another—my purveyors telling me that they no longer have the means of supplying my table, having been six months without receiving any money. Do I deserve to be thus treated, and ought I longer to allow the financiers and treasurers to starve me to death, while their tables are well served and abundantly supplied with dainties, and that indigence and need should dwell in my house, and in theirs opulence and riches?"*

The financial question was at this time his chief embarrassment. Temporary aid, however, came from England, and from some of the German states. Elizabeth had been greatly irritated on being informed of Henri's "apostasy;" but when he assured her, as he already had the German princes, that his change of religion would make no change in his policy, she relented, and assisted him with money and 2,000 troops.

On the morning after his coronation, Henri received from the Bishop of Chartres the collar of the Order of the Saint-Esprit, and declared himself Grand-Master of the Order. Nevertheless, the capital of his kingdom was held by a foreign garrison, and seemingly as firmly closed against him as when he attempted, five years before, to reduce it to obedience by famine. But extreme agitation prevailed therein. The people

---

* " Henri IV. à M. de Rosny "—" *Mémoires de Sully.*"

would gladly have opened their gates and welcomed their king — for "they had heard that he was a prince of great clemency." The League, however, was not willing to admit him, and Mayenne, suspecting that the Comte de Bélin, Governor of Paris, was in communication with Henri, deprived him of his post, and gave it to Maréchal de Brissac.

The Parliament opposed this arbitrary act; but resistance seeming likely to lead to further strife and to bloodshed, they consented to the change, and registered the new appointment. Mayenne then left for his government of Burgundy, taking his wife and family with him. Brissac, to whom the lieutenant-general confided Paris in his absence, had thoughts of attempting to establish there a republic, after the manner of that of ancient Rome. Finding that scheme impracticable, he resolved, after consulting the president, Le Maître, the provost of the merchants, L'Huillier, and the échevin, L'Anglois, to open the gates of Paris to Henri IV. The course adopted by the Parliament had allayed the disquietude of the Leaguers. Yet there existed amongst the Spaniards vague suspicions of some plot on foot, and two or three of their officers made the rounds of the ramparts with Brissac during the night of the 21st and 22nd of March, ready to stab him at the slightest sign of treason.

The king, who arrived at Saint-Denis on the

previous evening with four or five thousand soldiers, should have reached the Porte Neuve by three in the morning. But the weather was rainy and tempestuous, and retarded their march a full hour — a very anxious hour it proved to those whom Brissac had gained over to assist in this plot, and who waited in fear and trembling the king's arrival, their lives being forfeited if detected. At last he and his officers and troops presented themselves. The gates were opened, and four detachments of soldiers, successively introduced, took up the positions assigned them. Under the walls of Paris Brissac and L'Huillier waited to receive the king, who saluted the former as marshal of France, and threw over his shoulders his own white scarf. From the former he received the keys of the city. Henri entered by the same gate by which the last of the Valois fled from it, before the same Brissac who now opened it for the entry of the first of the Bourbons.

The city was reduced to obedience without sack or bloodshed, beyond the death of a few of the German infantry who, as L'Estoile says, "would unnecessarily mix themselves up in the matter" (they refused, in fact, to lay down their arms), also two or three *bourgeois* of the Rue Saint-Denis. These, the king afterwards said, he would have gladly ransomed for 50,000 gold crowns, had he been able, in order to leave to posterity a testimony that he had taken Paris without occasioning loss of life to any one individual.

As though dreading the possibility of some snare, Henri hesitated when about to enter that labyrinth of winding streets and lanes forming the centre of what was then called "*La belle et bonne ville de Paris.*" Turning to Maréchal de Matignon, he inquired if he had given strict orders to his troops at the Porte Saint-Honoré to be well on their guard against a surprise. But fears and anxiety were soon dispelled, and as the morning wore on, and the Parisians on awakening became aware that their city was held by royalist troops, and that the king was amongst his people, all hastened from their houses to gaze on the royal *cortège*, and to swell the chorus of "*Vive le roi!*" which, taken up from street to street, echoed and reëchoed at every turn, rose in the air a mighty shout, at times overpowering the grand and joyous volleys of the church bells.

Having arrived at the bridge of Notre-Dame, and hearing the people cry so joyously "*Vive le roi!*" "I plainly perceive," he said, "that these poor people have been tyrannised over." On alighting at the grand portail of the cathedral, where the clergy were waiting with the cross to receive the king, the people pressed about him so closely that the officers of his guard began to disperse them. But he forbade it, saying "he would rather suffer a little inconvenience than prevent them from gazing on him at their ease, as they evidently were ravenously hungry for the sight of a king." He then entered the church preceded by the clergy, chanting the "Te Deum." The nave and the galleries were filled, as on a grand *fête* day. Crowds had already assembled on the quays, the bridges, and on the open spaces in front of the cathedral.

In accordance with his arrangement with Brissac, the king sent M. de Saint-Pol to the Spanish general, the Duc de Feria, to inform him that, "although he had now in his hands the lives and the property of his officers and troops, yet he would take neither the one nor the other, but make them a present of both, on condition of their evacuating the city without loss of time, delay, or excuse." The duke, who was in consultation with his officers as to the course they should pursue in the present unexpected state of affairs, very readily promised what his majesty demanded. He had been far from expecting such easy terms. After musing for awhile on the matter, he seemed to be struck by their generosity, and exclaimed, "A great king! a great king!"

A general amnesty was also proclaimed, including even the Council of the League — "the Sixteen." To the heroines of the League, Mesdames de Nemours and de Montpensier, Henri gallantly sent *le bon jour*, and an assurance that, as he had taken them under his protection and safeguard, neither to their property, to their persons, nor to their hôtel would any harm be done. They humbly thanked his majesty, yet were a little disquieted; for Madame de Montpensier, on being informed early in the morning that "the 'Béarnais' was in Paris," was so much enraged that she behaved like a madwoman, and cried with passionate vehemence, "Is there no one in Paris who has a poniard, and will stab him to the heart?" When afterwards she recovered her senses a little, she turned her anger against M. de Brissac, "who she had long known, she said, was a coward, but that he was also a traitor she had learned only that day" (L'Estoile).

About four in the afternoon the Spaniards left Paris by the Porte Saint-Denis, marching out with the honours of war — drums beating, colours flying. The king went up to the window over the gate to see them leave. As they passed it, Feria saluted the king in Spanish fashion. Henri returned the courtesy, but called to him: "Recommend me to your master; but come not hither again." Similar compliments were exchanged, when the Italians about an hour later followed the Spaniards, and Paris was freed from her foreign garrison, to the satisfaction, not only of the king, but also of his "good people."

The king then went to dine at the Louvre. "It seemed to him," he is reported to have said, "that he was in a dream when he triumphantly entered the gates and crossed the courtyard to take up his abode in the palace of the French kings, and amidst the loud acclamations of the people who had so long and so implacably made war against him. He was in a very gay mood, and, while at dinner, for amusement sent for the secretary Nicolas, who was, or had been, an ardent Leaguer. After some few questions relative to the duties of his office, Henri inquired of what party he had been a follower during the recent troubles.

"Of a truth, sire," he replied, "I left the sun to follow the moon."

"But what do you say now, seeing me installed in my good city of Paris?"

"I say, sire," replied Nicolas, "that there is rendered unto Cæsar the things that are Cæsar's, as there must be rendered unto God the things that are God's."

"*Ventre Saint-Gris!*" exclaimed the king, "I have not been treated as Cæsar, for nothing has been rendered, but everything sold to me." ("*On ne m'a rien rendu, mais tout vendu.*")

This he said in the presence of Brissac, the provost, and others, who had been the means, each for a valuable consideration, of opening the gates of Paris to him. Brissac proposed, and Henri, glad to be received in his capital on any terms, without debating the matter, agreed, that a sum of 200,000 gold crowns once paid should be handed to him, with the grant of a pension of 20,000 crowns, and the marshal's bâton, given by Mayenne, confirmed to him by the king. The rest stipulated for no less liberal rewards for their services, which were of course complied with.

CONCLUSION.

WITH the entry of Henri IV. into Paris the limits of this work are reached. The king was in possession of his capital, but not in possession of his kingdom, and still was far from being the generally recognised Ruler of France. The League was but partially suppressed; Charles Emanuel of Savoy, the Duc de Mayenne, and several governors of provinces, were still in arms against him. The papal absolution was also withheld, and Henri was recognised by Clement VIII. merely as Prince of Béarn. Consequently, his throne was yet but a tottering one, and his power, even in Paris, by no means firmly established. Four years were yet to elapse before he felt himself sufficiently secure to brave the jealous displeasure of the Catholic nobility, the violent fanaticism of the priesthood, and the superstitious ignorance of the people, to do justice to the fidelity and loyalty of his Huguenot subjects, by issuing in their favour the famous Edict of Nantes (1598) — an "Edict revoked in spirit," as has been observed, "before it was granted," by Henri's coronation oath, from which political necessity forbade him to omit the words that bound him "to exterminate from the earth, to the full extent of his power, the heresies denounced by the Church." This formula he repeated with his lips, while swearing in his heart never to fulfil it; nor was he ever required to do so. But the formula being retained was fulfilled by his degenerate grandson — the so-called Grand Monarque — who by his revocation of his ancestor's Edict brought misfortune on his kingdom, and inflicted misery, sorrow, and sufferings incalculable on his unhappy Protestant subjects.

The events, political, domestic, and social, of the reign of Henri IV., and those which concern the arts and *les belles-lettres* of that period, being both numerous and interesting, are reserved for narration on some future occasion.

THE END.

INDEX

Agenais, war of, II., 174.
Alva, Duke of, cruelties of, I., 249, during Inquisition, 264, tortures imposed by, 311.
Amboise, Château de, attack upon, I., 66, tortures of Huguenots at, 70.
Anet, Château of, I., 12.
Anneau, battle of, II., 245.
Antoine de Bourbon, characterisation of, I., 21, intimidation of, 28, lack of energy of, 59, timidity of, 108, treacherous plots of, 112, concessions to Catherine of, 117, at States General at Orléans, 127, made lieutenant-general, 128, project of, 150, fear of Philip II., 152, falls victim to Catherine's projects, 156, at Saint-Germain, 161, religious views of, 168, temptation of, 170, treachery of, 175, upholds Duc de Guise, 179, at Fontainebleau, 184, negotiations of, 193, death of, 195.
Armada, description of, II., 278, defeat of, 281.
Arnay-le-Duc, battle of, II., 245.
Arques, battle of, II., 325.
Bathory, Étienne, made King of Poland, II., 68.
Bayonne, visit of French Court at, I., 236.
Beaugency, Protestant camp at, I., 193.
Bézé, Théodore de, doctrine promulgated by, I., 164, famous reply of, 180.
Biron, Maréchal de, attacks Nérac, II., 140, sentiments toward Henri of Navarre, 322, treachery of, 357, death of, 358.
Blois, Château de, meeting at the, II., 284.
Boesme, death of, II., 67.
Bourbon, Cardinal de, appointment of, I., 183; arrest of, II., 298.
Brissac, terms made with Henri IV., II., 381.
Brouage, capitulation of, II., 89.
Caen, devastation of, I., 190, submission of, 202.

Cahors, taking of, II., 138.
Calendar of Gregory XIII., adoption of the, II., 158.
Calvin, doctrines of, I., 54, condemns Condé, 213, death of, 240.
Carcistes, origin of name, II., 68.
Casimer, Jean, command of troops, I., 261; moneys paid to, II., 80.
Castelnau, Baron de, compliance of, I., 68; execution of, 75.
Catherine de' Medici, hatred of Diane, I., 7, superstition of, 44, plans of, 67, influence of De l'Hôpital upon, 83, anecdote concerning, 87, distrust of Guises toward, 102, interview with King Antoine, 117, at States General at Orléans, 128, influence over Charles IX., 130, policy of, 136, heretical letter of, 157, at Saint-Germain, 161, flight to Monceaux, 172, perplexity of, 182, court intrigues of, 185, negotiations of, 193, visit upon King Antoine, 195, after death of Duc de Guise, 209, gives *fête* at Chenonceaux, 215, at Troyes, 231, plans for marriage of her daughter, 236, at Moulins, 238, influence over Charles IX., 250, projects of, 251, at Meaux, 253, love for Henri III., 259, builds new hôtel, 266, policy of, 272, intrigues with Philip II. and the Pope, 279, proposition to Elizabeth, 324, plan for D'Alençon, 325, assembles council at the Louvre, 353, at massacre of Saint-Bartholomew, 362; policy toward Sancerre, II., 20, murderous design of, 23, made Regent, 38, pacific measures of, 40, projects of war, 51, *fête* at Chenonceaux, 93, diplomacy of, 127, claims throne of Portugal, 150, machinations of, 199, desire for repeal of Salic Law, 222, designs against Henri of Guise, 258, death of, 301.
Catherine of Navarre, education of, I., 201, at Blois, 319; at Nérac, II., 103, suitors of, 105, intolerance of, 130, matrimonial propositions to, 141, 169, engagement of, 240, goes to Saumur, 355.
Caylus, death of, II., 108.
Cellini, declines offer of Catherine de Medici, I., 93.
Chambord, Château de, court at, I., 87.
Champagne, march of Huguenots through, I., 261.
Chantilly, palace at, I., 18.
Charles IX., youthful character of, I., 32, personal appearance of, 124, impression made by Mary Stuart upon, 145, at the

Louvre, 185, treachery of, 227, hatred toward Huguenots, 238, return to Paris, 246, influenced by Catherine, 250, treatment of German Envoys, *ib.*, fondness for the chase, 260, jealousy of, 285, advice of, 293, seeks matrimonial alliance, 305, consents to massacre, 356, at the massacre of Saint-Bartholomew, 362; illness of, II., 26, death of, 38.

Chartres, siege of, I., 262; capture of, II., 348.

Châteauneuf, Madame de, at Chenonceaux, II., 97.

Châtillons, suspicions toward the, I., 77.

Chaumont, Château de, description of, I., 12.

Chenonceaux, Château de, I., 11, description of, 93.

Claude, Princesse, marriage of, I., 31.

Clément, Jacques, interview of, II., 313, assassination of Henri III. by, 315.

Cléry, devastation of, I., 190.

Coligny, Admiral de, resignation of, I., 19, at Fontainebleau, 95, characterised, 185, besieges Paris, 202, in Normandy, 212, plans of, 252, attempted poisoning of, 287, wounded, 290, projects of, 296, ambitious plans of, 314, attempted assassination of, 349, death of, 361.

Condé, Louis de, characterisation of, I., 21, suspicions against, 77, plot against Guises, 101, arrest of, 110, sentence of death, 115, pardon, 120, return to court, 150, proceeds to Meaux, 183, besieges Paris, 202, imprisonment of, 212, proposition of, 215, offers made to, 228, escape from Noyers, 269, death of, 283.

Condé, Henri de, abjuration of, II., 6, death of, 250.

Condé, Prince de, at Angers, II., 212.

Conspiracy of Amboise, cause of the, I., 55, failure of the, 61, effect of, 79.

Council of Moulins, I., 245.

Council of Trent, decrees of, I., 227.

Court, manners of the, I., 295.

Court of Parliament, menace of power of, I., 133.

Coutras, battle of, II., 235.

D'Albret, Jeanne, reply to Antoine de Bourbon, I., 174, leaves court, 175, plans for son's education, 197, appeal to Charles IX. and Catherine, 200, at Bayonne, 236, return to Béarn, 246, leaves Nérac, 271, zeal of, 285, at Blois, 319, death, 328.

D'Alençon, plan of, II., Catherine's hatred of, 30, projects of, 31, plans to escape, 33, demands on Catherine, 71, at Touraine, 72, becomes Duc d'Anjou, 80, designs of, 113, escape from Louvre, 117, victories of, 120, visit to England, 122, made sovereign of Netherlanders, 143, enters Cambray, 146, again visits England, 148, defeat of, 160, death of, 175, burial of, 178.

D'Amboise, Bussy, escape of, II., 117.

D'Andelot at La Rochelle, I., 270, death of, 286.

D'Anjou (see D'Alençon).

De Bellegarde, retreat of, II., 58.

De Châtillon, death of, II., 349, wife of, *ib.*

De L'Hôpital, Michel, characterisation of, I., 82, policy of, 83, at States General at Orléans, 127, influence of, 131, moderation of, 156, influence over Catherine, 181, amnesty proposed by, 194, memorial of, 267, retirement of, 273.

D'Épernon, Duc, negotiations for marriage of, II., 225, attitude toward League, 227, victories of, 248, dismissal of, 277.

Diane of Poitiers, retirement of, I., 8.

Dieppe, submission of, I., 202.

Don Carlos, death of, I., 274, character of, 275.

Don John, projects of, II., 113, death of, *ib.*

Drake, Sir Francis, victories of, II., 219.

Dreux, battle of, I., 203.

Dubourg, Counsellor Anne, execution of, I., 51.

Du Plessis-Mornay, influence at court of, II., 176, power of, 196.

Écouen, palace at, I., 18.

Edict against Huguenots, I., 279.

Edict of peace, at Longjumeau, I., 264.

Edict promulgated by Catherine, I., 226.

Edict promulgated by Guises, II., 211.

Edict of Romorantin, decree of, I., 84.

Edict of Tolerance, decree of, I., 165.

Elisabeth, Princesse, marriage of, I., 31, impressions of Spanish court, 41, meets Catherine at Fontarabia, 234, death of, 273.

Elizabeth of England, policy of, I., 59, irritation against Mary Stuart, 140, offers of help to Condé, 192, offer accepted,

194, gives money to Jeanne d' Albret, 281, matrimonial projects of, 325; visited by D'Anjou, II., 122, second interview with D' Anjou, 149, measures adopted by, 183, presents Order of Garter to Henri III., 192, plots against, 216, condemns Mary Stuart, 218, sends money to Henri IV., 344.

Embassy, sent by German princes, I., 250.

Epinay, marriage of, II., 116.

Étampes, capture of, II., 310.

Ferrara, Cardinal, in Paris, I., 161, policy of, 167.

Fontainebleau, assembly at, I., 95.

François II., accession to throne of France, I., 9, coronation of, 25, mysterious illness of, 42, influence of Guises upon, 67, at Amboise persecutions, 72, suspicions of, 85, banquets of, 90, interview with Prince de Condé, 113, death of, 119, burial of, 122.

Gabrielle d'Estrées, Henri's first meeting with, II., 334.

Gaillon, Château de, description of the, II., 186.

Gregory XIII. after massacre, I., 368; indulgences sent by, II., 190, death of, *ib.*

Gregory XIV. promulgates Bulls against Henri IV., II., 347.

Guises, the, ambition of, I., 5, persecutions instigated by, 48, arrogance of, 53, pamphlets against, 57, treachery of, 78, at Fontainebleau, 95, concessions made by, 98, advice to Mary Stuart, 144, intrigues of, 198, at massacre of Saint-Bartholomew, 361.

Guise, Cardinal de Lorraine, at Saint-Germain, I., 164, suggestions to Antoine de Bourbon, 169, anecdote of, 241, jealousy of, 286; death of, II., 55.

Guise, Cardinal, at Rheims, I., 134, intrigues of, 194, arrest of, 299, death of, 300.

Guise, Charles, Duc de, escape of, II., 349, pretensions of, 351.

Guise, Charles, head of League, II., 337.

Guise, Duc de, made lieutenant-general, I., 67, despatch from Antoine, 172, at Vassy, 177, assassination of, 208.

Guise, Henri de, ambitious projects of, II., 84, plots against, 259, victory of, 267, at Château de Blois, 284, assassination of, 297.

Havre, siege of, I., 224.

Henri II., death of, I., 7.

Henri III., made lieutenant-general, I., 260, triumph of, 291, matrimonial projects of, 309, at the Massacre of Saint-Bartholomew, 362; proclaimed King of Poland, II., 19, departs for Poland, 26, return to Paris, 40, visits Emperor Maximilian, 45, at Venice, 47, overtures to, 50, professions of piety, 54, journey to Rheims, 57, coronation and marriage, 59, unpopularity of, 66, demands of Polish subjects, 68, concessions of, 80, attitude toward League, 87, court of, 99, creates new order of Knights, 110, measures adopted by, 188, receives Order of Garter, 192, negotiations with League, 197, weak policy of, 200, submission to League, 221, wars against Huguenots, 230, triumphal entry into Paris, 247, demands made upon him, 253, plots against the Duc de Guise, 260, flight from Paris, 272, interviewed by White Flagellants, 276, at Château de Blois, 286, plans for assassination of Guise, 290, deposed by the Sorbonne, 306, interview with Henri of Navarre, 310, battles waged by, 311, assassination of, 315, rejoicings at the death of, 317.

Henri of Navarre, at La Rochelle, I., 271, made chief of the Huguenot Army, 285, at Arnay-le-Duc, 297, betrothal of, 336; abjuration of, II., 6, projected escape of, 33, flight from Paris, 77, warfare of, 88, signs treaty of peace at Bergerac, 101, at Court of Nérac, 131, opens campaign, 137, arbitrary acts of, 152, declared heir to throne of France, 179, attempted assassination of, 183, applies to Elizabeth for money, 201, reply to Papal Bull, 208, at Poitou and Dauphiny, 212, losses of, 214, wars waged by, 233, interview with Henri III., 310, battles of, 311, declared king by Henri III., 316, difficulty in claiming his throne, 321, at Dieppe, 323, at Arques, 325, recognition of claims by European powers, 328, at Ivry, 332, meets Gabrielle d'Éstrées, 334, carries on siege of Paris, 345, takes Chartres, 348, at Noyon, *ib.*, letter to Soissons, 353, at Rouen, 356, policy adopted by, 363, influence of Gabrielle upon, 364, abjuration of Protestantism, 367, power recognised by various governors, 371, coronation of, 373, receives Order of Saint-Esprit, 374, triumphal entry into Paris, 377, position in Paris, 382.

Henri IV., see Henri of Navarre.

Heretics, persecutions of the, I., 26.

Huguenots, origin of name, I., 54, persecutions of the, 70, exasperation of the, 133, desecrations committed by the, 189, uprising against edicts, 279; gathering of the, II., 28.
Inquisition, comments on the, I., 264.
Issoire, siege of, II., 100.
Ivry, battle of, II., 331.
James Stuart, interview with Mary Stuart, I., 143.
Jarnac, battle of, I., 282.
Jesuits, power of the, I., 247.
Joyeuse, Duc de, elevation of, II., 153; victories of, 227.
La Charité-sur-Loire, siege of, II., 90.
Lainez, Iago, at Saint-Germain, I., 161.
La Noue, at Fontenoy, I., 297; at La Rochelle, II., 18, death of, 349.
La Renaudie, Barry de, plans of, I., 56, death of, 65.
La Roche-Guyon, Madame de, fascination of, II., 333.
La Rochelle, Huguenots at, I., 263; negotiations at, II., 13, siege of, 16.
La Valette, elevation of, II., 153.
League, papers signed of the, II., 84, reorganisation of the, 180, plots of the, 184, manifesto issued by the, 197, power of the, 202, declarations of the, 308.
Lesdiguières, military genius of, II., 358.
Limeuil, Isabelle de, intimacy with Condé, I., 216, marriage of, 219.
Louise, Queen, her love for Henri III., II., 166.
Lyons, depredations at, I., 190.
Marguerite de Valois, betrothal of, I., 336; at Naumur, II., 112, conducted to Henri of Navarre, 125, in Béarn, 130, at Nérac, 135, ordered to leave France, 170, quarrels with Henri, 173, arrest of, 174.
Marriage Festivals, description of, II., 155.
Mary of Guise, thwarted by Elizabeth, I., 59, death of, 86.
Mary Stuart, effect of marriage of, I., 5, Catherine's hatred of, 102, beauty of, 103, treatment by Catherine of, 138, retires to Rheims, 142, at Nancy, 143, interview with James Stuart, 143, leaves France, 146, reception at Scotland, 148; death of, II., 219.
Massacre of Saint-Bartholomew, description of, I., 362.

Maurice of Nassau, election of, II., 182.
Maurignon, death of, II., 108.
Maximilian II., attitude toward Lutherans, I., 151.
Mayenne, Duc de, as a commander, II., 89, victories of, 100.
Mazères, Chevalier de, execution of, I., 75.
Méré, Poltrot de, assassinates Duc de Guise, I., 207, tortures and death of, 210.
Minard, President, assassination of, I., 50.
Moncontour, battle of, I., 289.
Mons, taking of, I., 332.
Montbrun, aggressive act of, II., 53, condemnation of, 67.
Montgomery, surrender of, II., 41, death of, 42.
Montluc, Blaise de, cruelty of, I., 191, advice of, II., 51.
Montluc, Jean de, Bishop of Valence, proposition of, I., 96.
Montmorency, Anne de, duties of, I., 13, resignation of, 19, at Fontainebleau, 94, at Orléans, 121, joins the Triumvirate, 155, taken prisoner at Dreux, 203, new appointment of, 222, death of, 257.
Montmorency, Damville, his interest in Mary Stuart, I., 146; compact of, II., 49, victories of, 55, declaration of, 202.
Montmorency, François de, appointment of, I., 19.
Montpensier, Duc de, cruelty of, I., 191.
Montpensier, Duchesse de, plot of, II., 313, during siege of Paris, 339, anger against Henri IV., 379.
Moulins, Château de, *fêtes* at the, I., 239.
Nemours, Duc de, mission of the, I., 64, assurance of good faith of, 68.
Noyon, taking of, II., 348.
Orange, Prince of, assassination of, II., 181.
Ordinance of Orléans, I., 131.
Order of the Saint-Esprit, II., 107.
Orléans, massacre of, I., 205.
Orsini, his visit to Paris, II., 4.
Paris, besieged by Protestants, I., 202, attack of, 255; barricades in, II., 267, famine in, 338.
Parma, Prince of, movements of, II., 343, death of, 361.
Peace at La Rochelle, II., 19.
Peace, between England and France, at Troyes, I., 252.
Peace of Fleix, II., 140.

INDEX 393

Peace of July, II., 198.
Peace of the King, II., 102.
Peace of Monsieur, II., 81 ; concessions made by, 85.
Peace of Saint-Germain, I., 298.
Philip II., marriage of, I., 35, reception of Princesse Elisabeth, 39, attitude toward Guises of, 60, plan to invade Navarre, 102, offers of aid to Catholics, 192, intrigues of, 198, cruelties of, 247, dark deeds of, 274; aid given to League, II., 84, aspires to hand of Catherine of Navarre, 141, deposition by Netherlanders, 144, obtains throne of Portugal, 151, proposition to Henri of Navarre, 167, in wars of Armada, 278.
Piedmont, restoration of, II., 48, battles in, 359.
Plessis-lez-Tours, *fêtes* at, II., 94.
Poissy, conference of, I., 163.
Poitou, Huguenots at, II., 34.
Polish Embassy at Paris, II., 21, plots of, 183, projects of, 362.
Poncet, characterisation of, II., 163.
Pontoise, attack of, II., 311.
Pope Pius V. instigates war in France, I., 267, bloody counsels of, 288, projects of, 300, death of, 324.
Raunay, execution of, I., 75.
Rosny, Baron de, victories of, II., 311, counsels of, 364, activity of, 372.
Rouen, depredations at, I., 190, camp besieged at, 194, fall of, 202 ; Henri IV. at, II., 336.
Ruggieri, phantoms evoked by, I., 47.
Saint-Jean-d'Angeley, siege of, I., 293.
Saintonge, Huguenots at, II., 34.
Sancerre, siege of, II., 13.
Senlis, meeting at, II., 191, attack of, 311.
Sens, massacre of, I., 188.
Sixteen, The, formation of, II., 190, policy of, 220, plots of, 263.
Sixtus V., Bull promulgated by, II., 204, characterisation of, 205, attitude toward Philip II., 279, sentiments on death of Henri III., 320, death of, 343.
Soissons, Comte de, joins Huguenots, II., 230, aspirations of, *ib.*, characterisation of, 239, rupture with Henri of Navarre,

241, policy of, 283, imprisonment of, 329, affairs of, 330, at Pau, 353.

Sorbonnists, Henri's anger against the, II., 249, decree of, *ib.*, death of head of, 337.

States General, convened at Orléans, I., 129, section of at Saint-Germain, 159.

Strozzi, Maréchal, accompanies royal family, I., 231; death of, II., 150.

Tavannes, Maréchal, cruelty of, I., 191, treachery of, 268; death of, II., 15.

Throckmorton, Sir Nicholas, plot of, I., 58, his letter to Queen Elizabeth, 118, his letter to Elizabeth, 138, his influence over Elizabeth, 187, taken prisoner, 204.

Tournelles, Palais des, destruction of, I., 92.

Tours, festivities at, II., 94.

Treaty of Amboise, I., 212.

Treaty of Câteau-Cambrésis, I., 35.

Treaty of the League at Joinville, II., 189.

Tuileries, plans first submitted, I., 91, laying of first stone of, 230.

Turenne, Vicomte de, his intimacy with Marguerite, II., 136.

Valenciennes, taking of, I., 332.

Vasari, his painting of Massacre of Huguenots, I., 369.

Vassy, Huguenots at, I., 177.

Villemongis, Sieur de, execution of, I., 75.

Vimori, attack of, II., 245.

Vincennes, attack of, II., 311.

White Flagellants, procession of the, II., 163, interview with Henri III., 276.

www.ingramcontent.com/pod-product-compliance
Lightning Source LLC
Chambersburg PA
CBHW030213170426
43201CB00006B/69